Library of
Davidson College

Joyce the Creator

Sheldon Brivic

Joyce the Creator

The University of Wisconsin Press

Published 1985

The University of Wisconsin Press
114 North Murray Street
Madison, Wisconsin 53715

The University of Wisconsin Press, Ltd.
1 Gower Street
London WC1E 6HA, England

Copyright © 1985
The Board of Regents of the University of Wisconsin System
All rights reserved

First printing

Printed in the United States of America

For LC CIP information see the colophon

ISBN 0-299-10080-4

For mom and dad,
who get better and better.

"like his own rare thoughts, a chemistry of stars"
—*Ulysses*

Contents

Acknowledgments xi

Bibliographical Abbreviations xiii

1 **Introduction: Acting Totality** 3

　The Multimind 3
　God and His Theater 6
　Problematic Presence 12
　A Critical Progress 17
　Opposition and Procession 21
　Injoyce 24

2 **Augustine Joyce** 28

　"Apostate's creed" 28
　Creation as Devotion 33
　Primal Matter 38

3 **The Metaphysics of Creation** 44

　Aristotle and Bruno 44
　Causality 47
　Polyphonic Discourse 50
　Authorial Action 55

4 Consubstantiality 59

"A being again in becomings again" 59
Artefice Interno 63
Life in Print 66
The Wounded God 71
Reconstruction 73
Imposition 77

5 The Sea of Joyce 84

The Sea's Voice 84
What the Waves Are Saying 88
Two Views of the Sea 90
Submerging 96

6 The Mind as Family 103

The Ancient Giant 103
The Mind Factory 107
The Family Unfolds 113
Cerebral Conversions 120
The Structure of the Letter 126

7 Conclusion: The Population of Absence 131

Internal Theater 131
Automysticism 135
Intrapersonal Fiction 139

Appendix 1: Synchronicities in *Ulysses* 145

Appendix 2: "What Are the Wild Waves Saying?" 154

Notes 156

Index 171

Acknowledgments

Writing this book was a great pleasure because it brought me into contact with two entertaining groups that correspond to each other: Joyceans critics and Joycean ideas. After hearing John Paul Riquelme, who is multilingual, chatting recently about Joyce's multilingual intelligence, I was reminded of an observation by Dick Beckman, a Temple colleague whose *Finnegans Wake* group I attended: everyone brings his particular knowledge and abilities to the understanding of Joyce, and this is why the *Wake* is best read by a group. As the various members make their contributions, each vision becomes a part of the Joycean totality, which is constituted by the interaction between them.

I have been finding Joyce's grace in people ever since I was converted by the sensitiveness of Marvin Magalaner in 1964. For this book, Joyce was manifested miraculously by two men, Father Robert Richard Boyle, S.J., and Elliott B. Gose, Jr. Fr. Boyle has expanded my imagination not only by his intellect, but by his generosity and tolerance, which I have tested thoroughly. Elliott met me after I had been a Joycean for fifteen years, yet his joyful wisdom effectively transformed my conceptions both of the profession and of myself.

Elliott read my manuscript and provided many helpful suggestions. A. Nicholas Fargnoli, who is a former student of Fr. Boyle's, a theologian, and a Joycean, also read the manuscript, and provided astute comments that directed me to some of my main ideas. In addition, the manuscript was read by David Bloom, who has been studying Joyce with me informally for four years.

This book has drawn on the contributions of students since its inception, for the impulse to conceive it came from ideas about Stephen

Dedalus as an extension of Joyce in a paper Stephane Duckett wrote for me in 1977. Another student who contributed formative ideas was Joanne Stearns, and some detailed observations of imagery came from Debra Kaminsky.

I organized a panel, "Joyce: The Artist as Deity," at the 1981 MLA convention, and another, "Joyce's Consubstantiality," at the Eighth International Joyce Symposium in Dublin in 1982. Participants in these groups included Father Boyle, Robert Adams Day, Marilyn French, Arnold Goldman, Elliott Gose, Margot Norris, and Darcy O'Brien. They were all helpful, even when they disagreed with my thesis. More recently, Michael Patrick Gillespie of Marquette University volunteered useful information.

Much of *Joyce the Creator* was written on a study leave given me by Temple University in the spring of 1982. Portions of the book have appeared in different form in *James Joyce Quarterly* and in *The Crane Bag*, and I thank the editors of these journals for permission to reprint this material.

One of the most curious sources for this book was Andrei Tarkovsky's film *Solaris*, based on a novel by Stanislaw Lem. In this film, space explorers landing on the planet Solaris encounter strange phenomena, ranging from monsters to departed loved ones. It turns out that the entire planet is an immense ocean of mind, so that whatever its inhabitants want materializes for them. In more than one sense, it could be said that I landed on Solaris around the time I became interested in Joyce over twenty years ago, and this brings me to my final acknowledgment.

The person who helped me most was my wife, Barbara. For four years she and our children, Elisabeth, Jeremy, and Gregory, have managed things so well that I have had very little to do but teach and write. February 2, 1984, was our twentieth anniversary.

Bibliographical Abbreviations

CW   *The Critical Writings of James Joyce,* ed. Ellsworth Mason and Richard Ellmann. New York: Viking Press, 1959.
FW   *Finnegans Wake.* New York: Viking Press, 1939, 1958. I identify passages in the *Wake* by page and line numbers.
JJ   Ellmann, Richard. *James Joyce.* 2nd ed. New York: Oxford Univ. Press, 1982.
Letters *Letters of James Joyce.* Vol. 1, ed. Stuart Gilbert. New York: Viking Press, 1957; reissued with corrections, 1966. Vols. 2 and 3, ed. Richard Ellmann. New York: Viking Press, 1966.
P   *"A Portrait of the Artist as a Young Man": Text, Criticism, and Notes,* ed. Chester G. Anderson. New York: Viking Press, 1968.
SH   *Stephen Hero,* ed. John J. Slocum and Herbert Cahoon. New York: New Directions, 1944, 1963.
SL   *Selected Letters of James Joyce,* ed. Richard Ellmann. New York: Viking Press, 1975.
U   *Ulysses.* New York: Random House, 1934 ed., reset and corrected, 1961.

Joyce the Creator

1   Introduction: Acting Totality

The Multimind

The canon of James Joyce enacts a continuous development of his concept of mind, which is based on Aristotle's definition of it as the primary organization of knowledge and motivation in a living thing (*De anima*, 412). Joyce's concept of mind grows more powerful and complex from one work to the next and within each work as his means of representing the mind grow more sophisticated. Such progress goes along with a steady shift in the focus of the works from an external world to an internal one, a world enclosed by mind. The emphasis finally shifts from the minds of the characters to the psychic superstructure that includes them, the mind of the work. Joyce expands this mind into elaborate involutions in an effort to make it alive through its interactions, because the only kind of model that can resemble the mind is a living one.

Joyce employed a number of theories of the mind that work together within the entire mental structure he built, but the central position in this structure is occupied by the double-aspect theory. This theory is associated with Spinoza, but Joyce learned it from Giordano Bruno. It sees mental and physical entities as aspects of the same substance. Joyce uses this concept to see himself as a mental presence in his words, and it also serves him as a mental conduit connecting the more external concerns of the earlier fiction with the internal ones of the later work. Because it posits the union of matter and spirit, the double-aspect theory is a nexus between Joyce's naturalism and his mythology.

Daniel A. Dervin wrote to me after reading my previous book, *Joyce between Freud and Jung*, and asked, speaking freely of the Freudian and Jungian concepts of the mind, how I could possibly hold that the mind was both a hydraulic engine and a haunted house. I realized then that the mind could include both of these things and a good deal more. Joyce's works aim steadily at expanding the maximum range of possibilities of what the mind can be.

All concepts of the mind are metaphorical and are exceedingly difficult to relate to physical reality. Julian Jaynes argues that consciousness is made up of a group of metaphors we learn, a theory with some affinity to Jacques Lacan's idea that the structure of the unconscious is the structure of language.[1] If metaphor is the substance of mind, then it is notable that a metaphor has two aspects, usually a concrete one and an abstract one. Whether or not the mind is made of metaphors, it can be described only by them, for no physical image actually embodies mental substance.

The point at which a metaphor for the mind goes wrong is generally the point at which it is taken literally, thus reducing the complexity of the mind by taking a part for the whole. The creative writer, however, because he deals in metaphors as such, and because he tends to be obliged to assume various points of view, is relatively free from the danger of assuming that his figures for the mind are physically real. Joyce elaborated his metaphorical construct to make it harder to understand or reduce as he gave it more scope, and he surrounded it with ironies and doubts as he committed himself to it increasingly.

In *Finnegans Wake,* which deals with eternal principles, the perimeters of this construct pass outside the realm of mortality; but by this time the construct is removed from earthly knowing because its multiplicity exceeds the cognition of a single person. As the Joycean mind grows through the canon to include more parts and levels of personality, this developing conception comes to unite a group of minds in one multimind without a single center.

The value of this conception rests on the fact that such an elaborate, populous model of the mind had never been imagined in action before, with one multitudinous exception—the mind of God. Yet through all of this expansion, the construct remained a projection of Joyce's own personal identity. For just as every mind is alive, so each has an identity. The multimind of Joyce's work continued to express his mind even while it included those of his characters, narrators, and readers.

In Joyce's first work, *Chamber Music,* a collection of poems, the expression of his mind is contained by conventions of poetic tradition. In *Dubliners,* his first book of fiction, the mind is controlled by social conventions that restrict both the author and the characters into either subordination or opposition. The Dubliners in these stories are incomplete and unable to connect with each other because they do not possess their own existences. Only in the last story, "The Dead," are the possibilities of freedom and being suggested. *A Portrait of the Artist* shows a young man growing aware of the controls of society and using his knowledge to develop an individual mind. At the end of the novel, however, that mind is in need of another mind to complete it.

After *Portrait,* Joyce wrote *Exiles,* his first work to present a deep connection between people. In this play, Richard Rowan and his common-law wife, Bertha, find themselves bound to a system of reciprocal needs. Moreover, the two protagonists are attached to two secondary figures, Robert Hand and Beatrice Justice, who embody their weaknesses. The presentation of active relationships is accompanied by the doubling of the characters—a pattern prefigured in "A Painful Case" and "The Dead," where emotional connections cause internal conflicts.

In *Ulysses,* two people, Stephen Dedalus and Leopold Bloom, come into contact with a mind that unites them, an extraindividual or multipersonal mind. The life of the book is oriented toward their union, for Bloomsday is meaningful insofar as it aims at that union, and their world gains much of its depth by being seen from their two perspectives. This union, working psychologically under the surface, is the central enactment in Joyce's work of the double-aspect theory, for it indicates that the physical (Bloom) and the mental (Stephen) can share the same substance. The dual mind of *Ulysses* adds a kind of Holy Ghost to its Father and Son when Molly Bloom reveals herself at the end as the spirit underlying and proceeding from their relationship.[2]

The mind that seems to come to include the characters in *Ulysses* may be said to incorporate them utterly in *Finnegans Wake.* As a dream, the *Wake* takes place within the mind, a mind which apparently includes the whole world and all of history. The shifting characters of the *Wake* world are mental impulses, and their recurring roles make them functions of a psychic organization. The *Wake* expands this organization from a trinity to a quaternity to a quincunx.[3] The five archetypal figures of the eternal family in the *Wake* embody the interacting parts of a universal mind, a mind that could not be as complete as it is without the interaction of five beings.

In the course of Joyce's career, the central configuration of mind in his work enlarges itself from a naturalistic nullity to a striving for unity to a compound mentality made up of two, three, four, and then five minds. This steady unfolding of mental faculties is accompanied by a progressive increase in levels of reference and in narrative personae. As these sources of being multiply, they grow more firmly bound to each other. Only occasional undertones suggest that the four figures in *Exiles* are not merely individuals caught in an emotional entanglement, but parts of a symbolic system. In *Ulysses,* however, such suggestions are parts of a massive emphasis on the breakdown of boundaries between individuals. In the *Wake,* these boundaries become so permeable that they are often hard to locate. Figures in the *Wake* generate each other, interchange, and merge in ways that reveal them as parts of a larger personality.

God and His Theater

From early in his life, before he encountered Freud, Joyce seems to have been inclined to regard the mind as a group structure. *Psychology,* by Michael Maher, S.J., a volume in the Catholic Manuals of Philosophy series, seems to have been his college textbook. At one point in this vigorously Aristotelian tome, Maher writes, ". . . . *essence* points to the *reality of which the being is constituted* . . ." Joyce drew a line from the word *reality* to the margin, where he wrote, "acting totality."[4] The mind is seen here as a group of entities working together. Joyce's phrase may also suggest that the reality of being consists of behaving as if one encompasses everything.

Joyce may have picked up the idea that the mind contains other minds partly from the symbolists and decadents of the end of the nineteenth century. Stéphane Mallarmé tends to see the drama as a group of minds that function as parts of a total mind. "Whoever hovers around an exceptional character such as Hamlet," says Mallarmé, "is merely Hamlet himself"; and he speaks of Ophelia as a "virgin child in the mind of the" prince. In a passage on *Hamlet* that is quoted from in *Ulysses* (*U* 187), Mallarmé says that the play "lies halfway between the old multiple-action method and the Monologue, the drama of the Self, which belongs to the future. The hero is alone—all others are secondary—and simply walks, reading in the book of Himself."[5] This description applies to *Portrait,* where the other characters are significant mainly because they reflect aspects of Stephen's mind.

The idea that every mind harbors concealed personalities is expressed by Oscar Wilde in "The Critic as Artist" (1890) in a passage that prefigures the effect of Bartell D'Arcy's singing in "The Dead":

> Music always. . . . creates for one a past of which one has been ignorant, and fills one with a sense of sorrows that have been hidden

from one's tears. I can fancy a man who had led a perfectly commonplace life, hearing by chance some curious piece of music, and suddenly discovering that his soul, without his being conscious of it, had passed through terrible experiences, and known fearful joys, or wild romantic loves, or great renunciations.[6]

This passage conveys the symbolist idea that the individual has the potential to uncover a great range of psychic experience, of possible beings, that his ordinary behavior keeps him from recognizing. All that is needed is a symbolic catalyst to draw out what is hidden within.

In 1908 Joyce commented on psychology to his brother Stanislaus: "What can a man know but what passes inside his own head?" (*JJ* 265). This corresponds to Stephen's statement about Shakespeare in *Ulysses* that, for a genius, "his own image . . . is the standard of all experience" (*U* 195). Such statements imply that insofar as Joyce understood the minds of any of his characters, if was because he shared their mentality, because they were extensions of Joyce. He unfolded the only mind he knew into transpersonal structures in an effort to produce the greatest possible expansion of the mind's potential for being.

While the symbolists probably contributed to this fertile division of personal psychology, it flowed into forms that were primarily religious in origin. Joyce grew up worshiping the image of a mind that contained other minds and motivated the universe, and he remained attached to this vision after he left the church. In a 1907 letter in which he told Stanislaus he was fed up with the world, he referred to it as "God and his theater" (*Letters*, 2: 217). After all, Mallarmé's image of the play as a mind is ultimately based on the idea that men act out God's will.

The image of God remained Joyce's major model of the most the mind could be, and its vitality and complexity gave it advantages over mechanical alternatives. The mind was originally conceived of as coming from God, and no matter how its features have been analyzed, no other theory has served as satisfactorily to explain the origin of its life. Science tends to claim that the mind developed by the accretion of a large number of physical reactions, but there is an enormous gap between the sum of these reactions and the subjective experience of the mind. Joyce, moreover, preferred the theological explanation.

The idea that the mind comes from God, which Joyce was familiar with in religious terms, has recently been restated in psychohistorical terms by Jaynes in *The Origin of Consciousness in the Breakdown of the Bicameral Mind*. Jaynes argues that ancient man heard voices that he perceived as coming from gods, but that actually came from his right cerebral hemisphere, which was a repository of authority, of the voices of tribal father figures. The sense of individual self was built up slowly through cultural development, as metaphors of personal space within the mind came to fill the sphere of decision-making formerly occupied by the gods. To support his argument about voices from the right lobe, Jaynes surveys scientific evidence for the existence of partial multiple selves within the brain. He focuses primarily on the distinction between the lobes of the brain, which he refers to as "almost two individuals." Experiments with patients whose lobes were partly separated have shown that one half of the brain can see, feel, smell, and understand things the other half is unaware of, and one lobe can react with irritation when the other half fails to perceive something. Jaynes also mentions specialized areas in the brain that seem to contain information repeated elsewhere in what he calls the brain's "redundant representation of psychological capacities."[7]

Here, as it often is, the idea of multiple personality is connected with that of God. Whether or not one accepts the historical thesis of Jaynes, it is generally true that areas of human motivation now occupied by psychological forces were once in charge of supernatural ones. As a separated extension or liberated colony of God, the mind approaches maximum development by imitating His independence, intelligence, permanence, and mysterious ability to unite complexity. Joyce's conception of the mind expanded these powers as he united more minds to each other more firmly in his last works. The concepts of God and multiple personality are therefore integral to a proper attempt to define Joycean psychology and metaphysics, his construction of the mind and its world.

Joyce continually played the role of a god in the world he created. Though he played the role comically as often as seriously, his presentation of himself as a parody of the Deity was partly a reaction to his sense of the awful responsibility involved in the position he filled. Ironic as he might be, he was locked into this role by a need to create that was deeper than his need to criticize. His early study of theology allowed him to give a new dispensation to the novel through the image of the artist that he found most inspiring and useful. No artist has represented himself through images of godhood more systematically or intrusively.

Joyce's use of religious concepts, like his psychology, has often been described with the emphasis on trying to match his ideas to external systems. He has been classified as a Christian, an anti-Christian, and a heretic.[8] More important than the question of exactly which doctrines he favored is that of how these doctrines are situated in relation to his work. Father Boyle, in his *James Joyce's Pauline Vision*, presents the key statement of this situation when he says that the Joycean artist, like God, produces history from his own ego and infuses his soul into the ink of his work, where it remains operative. Boyle also says that Joyce applies his theological ideas to his own being.[9] I intend to pursue Joyce's personal enactment of the principles of godhead, and to show how these principles are enriched by his skepticism, how they inform his psychology, and how they define the essential nature of his work.

Joyce had difficulty accepting one consequence of Stephen's view of the artist as deity—that Joyce's characters lived in a world in which God exists. He was amply skeptical and diffident about his divinity; but he realized that he had to assume this power insofar as he wanted to give his world life and coherence. So he came to understand his godhead and to fulfill it with quite a bit of the glory, wonder, and terror appropriate to the role.

The process by which Joyce designed himself into his work as a transcendent function that contains and informs his created universe is the subject of this book. Because Joyce knew and developed this function so thoroughly, my delineation of the activity of Joyce's personality in his cosmos will articulate potencies that many other writers have had access to and have utilized. I will show how Joyce unfolded his creation toward infinite complexity by building up his projection of the mind through a process of self-division. The theory will be explained by which he understood that the manifestations of himself in his world were essential to the vitality and depth of that world, and that he could not effectively create reality without injecting himself into it as a plural being.

The seed of the idea of describing Joyce as a self-conscious god was planted in my mind (without my knowing it) at a lecture by Jacques Lacan in a large auditorium of the Sorbonne during the Fifth International Joyce Symposium in 1975. At the end of an enumeration of Joyce's achievements, Lacan exclaimed, "*L'orbe est sur Joyce*" ("the world is about Joyce").[10] He recognized here the dominant or godlike personality Joyce projects. "My art is not a mirror held up to nature," Joyce once remarked, "Nature mirrors my art"; and he responded to Yeats's study of peasant culture by saying that his own mind was much closer to God than folklore was (*JJ* 677, 102). These are extreme statements, but they represent a major element in his thought: what he referred to in a 1909 letter to his wife as "those boundless ambitions which are really the leading forces of my life" (*Letters*, 2: 256).

Understanding of Joyce's creation has sometimes been hampered by a critical tradition alien to it: that an author should be absent from his work. This view has led many to see Stephen as saying in *Portrait* that an author disappears from his work rather than into it. But in Stephen's epic stage, "the personality of the artist passes into the narration itself, flowing round and round the persons and the action like a vital sea" (*P* 215). I will show that the sea is one of the major images of the author as god in all of Joyce's novels. In Stephen's dramatic stage, that authorial vitality "fills" the characters with their own ("proper") life, and the personality of the artist "finally refines itself out of existence" as the "mystery" of "creation is accomplished." But the creator does not disappear: "The artist, like the God of the creation, remains within or behind or beyond or above his handiwork. . . . ."

It is true that he is "indifferent, paring his fingernails," but in view of the statements that his personality and vitality have passed into the characters, he must be indifferent in the sense that he has invested himself *in* a number of *different* figures by achieving the state of drama. Distributed on both sides of a series of conflicts, he no longer appears in the work as a unified self. To avoid distorting essential reality, he must balance crucial issues not by subtracting sympathy, but by multiplying it. He remains present (as God generally does in Joyce's work after *Dubliners*), even if he is present only as a problem. In *Ulysses* and the *Wake*, he appears as a totality, a relation among parts that is each book's entelechy, Aristotle's term for the formal principle that gives something completeness. Though this form is not physically united, it is unique and unified in that every part of the work is defined and connected with every other part through Joyce's personality.

The division of the artist from lyric to epic to dramatic proceeds not through his shifting of attention outside himself, but through his observing himself. The epic emerges from the lyric "when the artist prolongs and broods upon himself as the centre of an epical event and this form progresses till the centre of emotional gravity is equidistant from the artist himself and from others. The narrative is no longer purely personal" (*P* 214–215). The artist gets outside of himself by looking at himself in order to extend or prolong himself so that he can see more of life. Because the mind must be divided in two to perceive itself, the artist begets himself upon himself by self-contemplation in order to generate the fullness of his world.

God and His Theater

Christian tradition suggests that God had to divide Himself to enter the world through His Son. Because dualities that are in conflict on earth—such as spirit and matter, self and other, and time and eternity—are transcended by God, He has been described most vividly by metaphysical poets who present him in paradoxical, self-contradictory images. Perhaps the most powerful images of God are images of multiple being, the Trinity and the Eucharist. If the Persons of the Trinity may be considered as aspects of God, then He projects himself in a series of forms that seem to represent parts of his mind.

Aquinas is speaking of beauty as a quality possessed by the Son as the Word of the Father when he says that it consists of three qualities: *integritas, consonantia,* and *claritas.*[11] This is the source of Stephen's theory of wholeness, harmony, and radiance; and if the qualities of art are the qualities of the Son, then art is conceived of as a projection with three aspects of the mind of its creator into his world. The aspects of this mental projection correspond to features of the mind that created it, for the Son is consubstantial with the Father. Likewise, Stephen's stages of esthetic perception pertain to both the artist and his object.

Joyce's conception of himself as a god was hardly orthodox, but he was subject to some of the traditional conditions of God in the way he entered his work. The more he divided himself into his creation as his career progressed, the more spiritual life he gave to his fictional worlds. Joyce presents self-division as essential to love. One gives life to one's beloved by being of two minds about her, thus allowing her to exceed any prior formulation. This pattern appears in the wound of doubt that Richard says he bears for Bertha at the end of *Exiles.*

Joyce's major development of the notion of love as self-division is Bloom's love for Molly, which suspends him in a state of doubt all day long. The mechanism is defined with neat economy in a description of Bloom's attitude toward his daughter, Milly. The catechism of "Ithaca" asks if Bloom has been afflicted by the thought of losing Milly, and answers, "Less than he had imagined, more than he had hoped" (*U* 693). The distance between his worst imagining and his best hope is a measure of his love for Milly, and the distance is greater with regard to Molly. Bloom's mind tends to oscillate between two perspectives when he thinks seriously of either mother or daughter: "O well: she knows how to mind herself. But if not? No, nothing has happened. Of course it might" (*U* 66). To love someone, then, is to divide oneself into two different positions over her, and these opposing points of view may be represented effectively as two characters.

The statement that God so loved the world that He sacrificed His only Son for us is one that has to imply ambivalence in order to define love. A variation on it appears when Stephen says that Shakespeare's son Hamnet had to die in order that *Hamlet* might live (*U* 188). The artist gives up his earthly son for his spiritual Word when he converts the worldly being of his beauty and life into forms that can be dispensed perpetually, both to the world he creates and to the one we live in.

Joyce had to arrive at this sacrifice of self into imaginary life by stages. He maintained a superior attitude toward everything outside himself for the most part in *Dubliners* and *Portrait*, but in writing *Portrait* he began to immerse himself in the otherness of his work by seeing himself from outside himself. He entered his world substantially when he divided himself between Stephen and Bloom in *Ulysses*. After this, his mind was no longer oriented outside the work, but between its components. The interplay of active forces in his last two novels gave them psychic life, generating possibilities of hope and grace, because it constituted love.

Problematic Presence

A number of widely accepted principles, both long established and recent, have made it difficult to perceive Joyce's active, divided presence in his work. A long-prevalent literary tradition tends to conceive of the novelist's art as craft rather than creation and to focus on the manufacture of "finished" inanimate objects. This view, asserted most prominently in the influential *The Craft of Fiction,* by Percy Lubbock (1921), is parallel to and ultimately derived from the Enlightenment theory that God is present in the world only as a mechanism. Arguments about the presence of God are analogous if not equivalent to arguments about the presence of mind. The deist machine-God may be said to have survived the Age of Reason in the form of empiricism, a belief that the world is run by mechanical principles. Most of us tend frequently to forget spiritual factors and to see existence as a chain of physical causality. Joyce satirizes this position through Bloom, who is continually weaving physical explanations that do not explain. Bloom believes that he alleviates the problems of his life by showing that each is "only a natural phenomenon" (*U* 304; see also *U* 395, 529, 733). His faith in science is presented as a religion that fills a psychological need. The difficulties of living without faith are so great that no one could undertake such a project without a high degree of faith in his ability to find the truth.

Toward many of the skeptical claims of modern philosophy Joyce had an ambivalent attitude. He recognized, developed, and anticipated them, but he did not affirm them any more than other ideas. He remained aware that they were only possible ways, minimal ways, of looking at life. One such claim is Ludwig Wittgenstein's argument that value cannot be expressed because the meaning of the world can be defined only from outside the world.[12] Related to this is the existential assumption that existence precedes essence. Both of these ideas are forcefully represented, for example, in the bare, disconnected style of the "Ithaca" episode of *Ulysses*. Joyce, however, was aware also of the force of alternatives to these assumptions.

He realized that it would be artificial of him to pretend that he could not go outside his fictional world to instill it with meaning—and that it would be presumptuous of him to believe that he could ever depict anything except the world as he saw it, a product of his values. Similarly, he realized that in a work of art essence precedes existence because virtually every element in that work must be an idea in the mind of its author before it can be an object. While he struggled to free his creation from his metaphysical control, he realized that this effort to deconstruct his own authority was dependent on his creative or constructive impulse for its expression.

Such understanding was ingrained in him because he came from a theistic culture in which God was seen as an active Being, and his thinking remained theistic. Stephen not only prays to God to protect him early in *Portrait,* but he repeats the gesture on the last page with the godlike figure of Daedalus, and he addresses the Deity throughout *Ulysses,* usually with defiance. As Hugh Kenner points out, "Joyce never doubted the existence of God . . ."[13] Kenner observes, however, that Joyce came to look on God as a threatening figure; and I am arguing that a major factor in Joyce's relation to God was competition. There is in fact a satanic side to Joyce's emulation of God, as Margot Norris has observed,[14] but I believe that it was subordinated in the later works to the urge to create. In *Stephen Hero* Stephen says that Satan is "the romantic youth of Jesus" (*SH* 222). I am less interested in the rebellion involved in Joyce's deity than in how that power operates productively. Because Joyce did not see God as lifeless, he saw the writer in his work not as inert, but as a living sea surrounding the characters. For him art was a sacrament, an action of spirit.

Joyce as a god tends to appear in his work as an infinite regress, an unattainable being who can be manifested only indirectly, through his creations. This accords with the traditional role of God in the world, but it also anticipates the theology of Jacques Derrida: "Is not that which is called God, that which imprints every human course and recourse with its secondarity, the passageway of deferred reciprocity between reading and writing?"[15] The relation of reading to writing, for Derrida, resembles that of man to God by striving toward a communion that will never be grasped, that will always exceed any formulation. This is why every voice in Joyce's fiction is secondary to Joyce.

The passageway Derrida describes requires a construction to contain it and a goal to motivate its deferral. Writers who claim to eliminate metaphysics tend to be obsessed with it; for the attempt to eliminate God, carried to its conclusion, ends by setting up a more arduous model to fulfill the functions of the Deity. In Derrida's case, the rigors of devotion are replaced by those of reformulation. In any case, the very act of denying what people assume to be true always has to refer to a higher truth.

Joyce administered to himself both the rigors of self-devotion and those of self-reformulation in his effort to express as many sides of God as possible. The image of the artist as God preoccupied him because only through creation can a man attain the priority of deity with regard to the secondariness of his creatures. A prime motivation for his writing may be detected in an early passage of *Portrait* that predicts the cosmic perspective of the *Wake:* "It was very big to think about everything and everywhere. Only God could do that" (*P* 16). Joyce, moreover, had the idea of reconstituting God as early as the 1904 essay "A Portrait of the Artist," which announces, in the course of listing the artist's ambitions, that "divine knowledge was to be re-established" (*P* 261).

Late in *Portrait* Stephen recalls that in his adolescence he achieved some success in an effort "to unite my will with the will of God instant by instant" (*P* 240). In *Ulysses,* Stephen quotes Goethe: "Beware of what you wish for in youth because you will get it in middle life" (*U* 196). This suggests that Joyce never gave up his desire to unite with God, but such union need not follow orthodox channels. In 1903 Joyce praised the heretic Bruno for passing "from heroic enthusiasm to enthusiasm to unite himself with God" (*CW* 134). This union with God was consummated when Bruno died for his beliefs in an auto-da-fé.

Stephen's passionate desire to create "a living thing" (*P* 170) claims a power reserved for God by Judeo-Christian tradition. In Ovid, when people see Daedalus and Icarus flying in the air, they exclaim, "They must be gods!" For the power of "changing the laws of nature,"[16] as Ovid says Daedalus does by making men fly, is likewise reserved for deity. Joyce indulged in this power increasingly and flamboyantly in his later work: the later techniques of *Ulysses* transform the principles of existence in Bloomsday Dublin, and the *Wake,* through the profuse invention of its experiments, may be said to change the laws of its nature every few words. The godlike ability to abrogate basic rules is essential to the vitality of Joyce's work, and the giving of life is felt therein as the primary power of art. In *Ulysses,* when Stephen composes a story, he says, "Let there be life" (*U* 145), and later he calls himself "lord and giver of . . . life" (*U* 415).

The other main artist in Joyce's work, Shem the Penman, creates his work as a Eucharist made from his own body in a mock liturgical passage (*FW* 185).[17] His creation is also godlike in that it unfolds "all marryvoising moodmoulded cyclewheeling history" (*FW* 186.1), and in this respect he resembles Joyce, with whom he is identified through scores of biographical details. He creates by transforming "his own individual person . . . into a dividual chaos" (*FW* 186.3-5). And his brother Shaun accuses him of "adding to the malice of your transgression" by "changing its nature" (*FW* 189.2).

Of course Joyce was aware that, as a human imitator, he could not execute God's functions in their multitude and perfection. But he knew that the better he imitated divinity, the more reality his world would have, so he sought to develop his abilities beyond human limits. If he was limited to words, he strove toward the conclusion that " . . . I can do anything with language I want" (*JJ* 702). Unable to create a large variety of characters (which would have been an imitation not only of God, but of Shakespeare), he concentrated on making those he produced live more fully than other human creations by expanding them into new levels of complexity. His ultimate aim was to reproduce the vast completeness of God's mind by uniting an entire population in a living psychic structure every point of which would express his being. If history, as Mr. Deasy says (*U* 34), leads to the manifestation of God, then Joyce's works lead to the increasing manifestation of his unique mind.

Traditionally, the chief theoretical obstacle to seeing the mind of an author in his work is the idea of the intentional fallacy. This notion has value as a warning against applying an author's statement to his work where it does not fit. It is misused, however, to separate an author's thoughts from his work absolutely—as if the fact that the hand does not always do what the mind wants were proof that the mind does not control the hand. W. K. Wimsatt and Monroe C. Beardsley are aware, in "The Intentional Fallacy," that the separation of author from work is only one way of looking at literature, a classicist one. They refer also to a two-thousand-year-old romantic tradition, including Longinus, Goethe, and Croce, that makes the author central to his work. Joyce admired Goethe and Croce,[18] and as for Longinus, his notion of the sublime is powerful in all of Joyce's novels. Stephen Dedalus says in *Stephen Hero* that the perfection of art is "a veritably sublime process of one's nature" (*SH* 171).

In *On the Sublime* (chapter 33), Longinus holds that a literary work reflects the soul of its author. The new critical theory of narratology, in fact, as developed by Gérard Genette, emphasizes the voice of the teller, thus helping us toward seeing the image of the author in his work. The leading narratologist of Joyce, John Paul Riquelme, suggests that Stephen Dedalus is the author of *Dubliners, Portrait,* and *Ulysses.*[19] This is a useful step toward perceiving Joyce himself behind his work, a process that is necessary because the mind of Joyce was unlike any other mind that ever existed.

While it is true that a writer who injects himself into his work is likely to be at fault for sending signals that are not detached, it is also true that there is need for a theory to explain the values an author's personality conveys into his work insofar as he succeeds in playing the role of a god. Joyce admired a series of personalities who played productive roles in their writings, such as Rabelais, Bruno, Swift, Sterne, Blake, Byron, and Yeats. Though he never embodied himself in fiction as a narrator, Joyce was increasingly present in his work because he projected himself in parts that added up to a complex Joycean entity. His personality unfolded itself into his work as his canon grew more intimate, internal, and self-indulgent, from social criticism to autobiography to personal depth to dream.

Patrick Cruttwell says that the separation of the author from the man has been prominent only since late in the eighteenth century—that is, since after the Age of Reason. In earlier periods, poets tended to affirm that what they created was the truth that came from their hearts. They were in contact with the tradition of creation as an infusion of spirit.[20] Joyce aligned himself with this view because he was in contact with the tradition. During the twenties, he said, " . . . one of the most interesting things about Ireland is that we are still fundamentally a mediaeval people . . ."[21]

The separation of author from fiction is useful insofar as the work is realistic, but it blocks perception of the mythological level, which works in opposition to realism by referring to systems external to the physical world of the fiction. The author of a myth is supposed to inspire it with life from a source that passes through him. In Joyce's case, the myth is largely self-generated and centered around his own personality. Frank Kermode distinguishes the "realistic" function of the Gospels that works to make Christ's story seem factual, mainly by effects of randomness, from the mythic function that sees Christ fitting prefigurations in the Old Testament. Kermode adds that insofar as Christ followed the predictions about the messiah, for example by being sacrificed on Passover, he actually seemed more real to his early followers. We have here two kinds of realism. Material realism depends on details that seem not to fit a preconceived system. Such details enhance Christ's reality as a man in a world of accidents. Spiritual realism, on the other hand, appears when Christ fulfills a predestined pattern, influenced by forces from outside his naturalistic world, such as the star under which he was born. This involves the Scholastic reality, which means closeness to the First Cause or God. Joyce cultivated both kinds of reality, and, in doing so, he was being realistic in the largest sense. For all books include both kinds of realism: the most naturalistic or absurd author can't help putting an order into his work. Kermode says that codices may have replaced scrolls because of a desire to refer scriptures to each other: "The [bound] book, then, is a permanent image of occult design and coherence."[22]

In the novels of Joyce, and most obviously in *Ulysses,* the concentration on cross-reference and external allusion indicates a presiding intelligence above the action. It is necessary to define this intelligence in order to describe how Joyce's narrative methods operate. In fact, for twenty years, Joyce critics have been contributing toward the delineation of the active, shaping presence of the author. Of course, there has also been skeptical opposition to Joyce's author-ity, and many of those involved in the critic's progress toward the heavenly Joyce have not been aware of whither their steps were tending; but the position I am presenting here is a logical extension of many current developments.

A Critical Progress

The first attempt to define Joyce's invisible presence in his work was David Hayman's concept of "the arranger" who organized techniques in *Ulysses.* Hayman says that the arranger should be separated from both the narrator of *Ulysses* and Joyce in order to see his function clearly.

Yet I believe that this function expresses Joyce's personality. Hayman anticipates my argument by describing the arranger in terms that refer both to Joyce and God: " . . . the artist-God as cosmic joker, the other side of Stephen's 'hangman god.' . . . a creature of many faces but a single impulse, a larger version of his characters with a larger field of vision and many more perceptions to control . . ."[23]

Hugh Kenner, in *Joyce's Voices,* divides the narrators of *Ulysses* into a trinity. He distinguishes a realistic one who dominates the first episodes from an imaginative one who likes to puncture realism by technical tricks, and he sees the main voice of the last two episodes as the muse.[24] In his next book, *Ulysses,* however, Kenner says, "Joyce . . . is always present in *Ulysses,* and no talk of that dyad of technicians, the self-effacing narrator and the mischievous Arranger, should permit us wholly to forget that fact."[25] By saying that the three persons are one, Kenner is recognizing that technical functions are not people. *Ulysses* is narrated by a large number of speakers, organized into three categories, who are both different and unified, parts of a single being who projects multiple personalities.

Karen Lawrence, in *The Odyssey of Style in Ulysses,* says that as the experiments with style grow more obtrusive from episode to episode in *Ulysses,* our attention shifts from the story to how it is told, from the meaning of language as description to its origin as writing. She sees that the first radical intrusions of style in the story, the headlines in the "Aeolus" episode, "announce the presence of a power outside" the story. But she feels that the voices the book adds to its naturalistic reality must be separated from Joyce because they are public and do not express an individual mind. She does not consider that Joyce may take it upon himself to express his personal vision through the voice of public culture or to speak in voices beyond personal mentality.

Through the multiplicity of styles in *Ulysses,* Lawrence sees "infinite" possibilities coming from the mind of the book, and she speaks of "a larger enterprise of the book, which is to expand its borders to include what is outside of it."[26] She does not explain what kind of mind the book has or how it gets the volition to change or to aspire to infinity. I agree with Kenner that it is necessary to see a mind in the text; but no mind has ever existed without an identity, and I believe that this mind should be given human particularity. In *The Mind of the Novel,* Bruce F. Kawin says that while some books are systematically self-conscious because they refer back to themselves, *Ulysses* is an example of books that are "authorially self-conscious, continually referring back to their authors' attitudes. . . ."[27]

Not all critics who emphasize the role of the writer in *Ulysses* are inclined to support Joyce's authority. Brook Thomas insists that the author cannot be incarnate in his text because language can present him only as an object, not as a subject.[28] Thomas's theories are sophisticated, but I believe that the claim that language cannot express subjectivity leaves out an important aspect of Joyce. The idea that subjectivity cannot be found in language is parallel not only to the idea that God or truth cannot be found in the world, but to the idea that the mind cannot be distinguished from the body. It is true that subjectivity, truth, and the mind cannot clearly be expressed with certainty, but they remain powerful factors in Joyce, who focuses on uncertainty.

A more balanced account is given by John Paul Riquelme. Riquelme sees the writer as a transcendent presence who fuses with his world and his readers through the writing process. One pattern Riquelme emphasizes is narrated monologue (*erlebte Rede*), a technique that Joyce uses often throughout his fiction.[29] An example is this account of how Stephen feels after the sermons in *Portrait:* "So he had sunk to the state of a beast that licks his chaps after meat . . ." (*P* 111). The narrator is speaking here, but he is expressing Stephen's thoughts in the third person. A subtle variant of this technique appears in this description of Bloom: "A soft qualm, regret, flowed down his backbone, increasing."[30]

The narrator here uses words, and punctuation, that express Bloom's inner feelings. In both cases, both the narrator and the character are speaking; and Riquelme argues that much of Joyce's language oscillates between two or more perspectives, embodying interactions of character, narrator, and reader.

The sharing of substance between narrator and character in Joyce's fiction, a widespread and characteristic tendency, parallels the double-aspect theory of Spinoza that mind and body have the same substance in common. I will return to ways in which Joyce's ambiguous techniques bring out the intrusion of his spirit on the matter of the text. In Spinoza, the theory concerns the inherence of God in the world;[31] and Joyce, in searching out the innermost feelings of his characters, resembles God by exercising a unique degree of omniscience.

Arnold Goldman suggested in 1966 that because so much information appears in the Nighttown "hallucinations" of *Ulysses* that is not available to the characters, "Circe" must be regarded as "a fantasy of their creator about them"; and he saw a similar "noumenal" level involved in "Oxen of the Sun" and other episodes.[32] In fact, the representation of the development of a foetus in terms of parodies of fifteen hundred years of prose styles in "Oxen" not only goes beyond what the characters know—it clearly goes beyond what any human intelligence could know.

Goldman's suggestion was carried on by Marilyn French, who says that *Ulysses* is built on the Scholastic analogies of the artist as God and the world as God's book; but she adds that Joyce related to his work as a human being as well as a god.[33] After this, Boyle came out with his *James Joyce's Pauline Vision,* which includes the precise definition of Joyce's assumption of divine powers that I cited earlier as one of the bases of this book.

An important contribution to understanding the theory of how Joyce's deity functions and how it relates to his humanity appears in *The Transformation Process in Joyce's Ulysses,* by Elliott B. Gose. Using the ideas of Joyce's hero Bruno, Gose demonstrates that Joyce's imagery portrays God as present inside his world, an extra aspect within people and material objects, a Being divided into multiplicity and passing through mutability.[34] Gose recognizes that this Brunonian fragmented God within all things must be identified with Joyce, and his theory of Joyce's immanence explains how the author is able to speak with the voices of inanimate objects, and with those impersonal voices that Lawrence noticed.

Another step in the direction of recognizing Joyce's authority, or authordoxy, was taken by John Gordon, who argues that Joyce's works refer to the facts of his life so extensively that they are really about him. Gordon says that "Ulysses consistently reflects one recognizable intelligence variously incarnated in Stephen, Bloom, and the other characters . . ."[35] But Gordon does not pursue the definition of this intelligence.

Jackson I. Cope approaches Joyce's use of deity through the influence of Gabriele D'Annunzio, in whose life and work the striving for godhead recurred quite explicitly. Other favorites of Joyce include Blake's *The Marriage of Heaven and Hell* and Nietzsche's *Thus Spake Zarathustra* both of which insist that gods come from humanity and that men should free themselves from subservience by assuming the powers they have delegated to divinity. Cope recognizes that Joyce sometimes strove to emulate God, but he associates this drive with Stephen's hubris and says that Joyce subordinated it to irony.[36] Joyce, however, did not recant his desire to be a god: in his last phases, he concentrated more and more intensely on representing infinity and eternity in personal terms. His irony and his pride strengthened each other, each making it possible for the other to advance.

A more accurate formula for controlling the uncanny implications of Joyce's assumption of divinity is the idea that it is a joke. Riquelme presents a strong statement of this position: " . . . in *Finnegans Wake, homo ludens* as *homo faber* mimes, in comic Promethean fashion, the status traditionally associated with the godhead."[37] It is true that Joyce is often funny in the role of prime mover, but this fact should not obscure the great psychological and organizational power that the role exerts in Joyce's universe. Joyce may laugh at himself as an author, but he is also serious, and his irony allows him to extend his vision. It is true that he sees more factors by taking each one less seriously, but the all-embracing totality entangles him more completely than any single vision could.

Opposition and Procession

Sharp irony and "boundless ambition" are often found together in life, and Joyce's explanation of this combination would probably center on Bruno's doctrine of coinciding contraries: " . . . every power in nature must evolve an opposite in order to realize itself . . ." (*Letters,* 1: 226). Joyce derived from this doctrine the idea, which he later found confirmed in Freud, that the mind is made up of interacting opposites. In fact, such opposition is already implicit in Aristotle's definition of the mind as the primary organization of a living thing, because this definition combines the opposing requirements of unity and life. Life, in terms of growth or motion, cannot be visualized except as an interaction of bodily parts. So its multiplicity can be reconciled to unity only by the concept of coinciding contraries, a concept which is parallel to the double-aspect theory.

Though the double-aspect theory was given its key statement by Spinoza in the seventeenth century and anticipated by Bruno in the sixteenth, it was a subject of current controversy during Joyce's youth. The debate is taken up in Maher's *Psychology,* a chapter of which, "Recent Theories concerning the Soul," is devoted to versions of this theory, which Maher condemns as a materialistic view linked to evolution. His major objection to the theory is that he cannot imagine a substance that would combine the spiritual with the physical. Joyce could, however, and I will show that he frequently refers to such a substance, which he usually calls "primal matter."

Joyce's Brunonian double-aspect theory differs from the scientific ones Maher attacks in that Joyce sees the spiritual and material sides as interacting with each other as part of his tendency to give the forces in his system active, independent natures. In fact, Joyce uses the theory primarily to refer to the substance that unites an author and his work. This substance may be identified with language, which has an actual form when it is used, but also contains a spiritual principle in that it expresses something beyond itself that can never be captured, something outside material existence.

As a mental structure made of language, the text combines the multiplicity of its details with the unity of its conception by the author — just as the Gospels described by Kermode included two kinds of reality, naturalistic and mythic. Umberto Eco speaks of Joyce's work as a continuous dialectic "between Chaos and Cosmos."[38] Insofar as Joyce brought these two extremes into lively intercourse with each other through his ability to divide himself, he was able to span with his mind a prodigious spectrum of being.

If this being is alive and unified, it is a mind. Because parts of the mind change each other qualitatively, no mechanical system can approach the complexity of the operation of the mind. In this perspective, a computer exemplifies unity without life because its parts can interact only quantitatively. On the other hand, the deconstructive model of mental activity, as described by Colin MacCabe, takes the form of a series of interferences with language.[39] This is life without unity insofar as the organization of these interferences, seen best through the personality of the author, is barred from consideration. Though both construction and deconstruction are powerful forces in Joyce, his conception of life is not encompassed by either one any more than breathing is encompassed by either inhaling or exhaling.

The metabolism of the mind of the text in Joyce's mature work combines construction and deconstruction as it combines unity with multiplicity. It may be said to exhale the creatures of the text insofar as these individuals are given the freedom of their own natures and to inhale them in that at moments of inspiration they are subject to intimations of unity and fusion that "renulite" "their disunited" (*FW* 395.33). There is no simple central intelligence in *Ulysses* or the *Wake,* but there is in each a group of natures that create each other by interaction as parts of a psychic structure. And this psychic structure should be identified as the mind of Joyce because no other mind resembles Joyce's and only it generates virtually all elements in the work and shapes their relation to each other.

Essential to Joyce's concept of the mind is the principle of transmission or procession. He first learned that the mind was dynamic from the church, which inculcated in him a sense that intelligence was generated by the first cause as a gift:

> *O Lord, open our lips*
> *And our mouth shall announce Thy praise.* (*P* 17)
>
> God loves with a divine love every human soul and every human soul lives in that love. . . . Every breath that we draw, every thought of our brain, every instant of life proceed from God's inexhaustible goodness. (*P* 128)

Aquinas says that God preserves things in existence only by perpetually giving being to them, and that He is active in everything.[40] One of my objectives will be to trace the Scholastic theory whereby Joyce understood that a mind cannot be fully represented unless it is seen in relation to a larger mind from which it proceeds. This religious version of the unconscious is one of many ideas I will concentrate on partly because they were planted in Joyce very early. However he may have sophisticated his later ideas, I feel that these early ideas remained at the root of his thinking, forming a substratum to which he was called back by emotional reactions. This substratum operated like Freud's "uncanny."[41]

The principle of procession, which generates the spiritual side of the double-aspect pattern, helps to clarify the relation between Joyce's two concepts of his divinity, the exalted "God of the creation" and the debased forger or sham who must imitate a prior creator. A crucial distinction between the debased Joyce god and the exalted one is located at the interface between the man and his work, the point of writing at which Joyce sacrifices his actual life to create his imaginary world.

Outside his work, Joyce was fallible and uncertain, but as apprehended from within his work he has absolute authority: he is the primary origin and goal of virtually every detail in the fiction. Every being in his work is derived from him, and they frequently refer to facts of Joyce's biography as if they gained validation by contact with the source they all share. But none can catch more than a distorted glimpse of the Joycean mental world "within or behind or above" their universe. Dante, in the *Paradiso*, describes man's relation to God as follows:

> . . . The One who wheeled
>   the compass round the limits of the world
> and spread there what is hidden and what revealed,
>
> could not so stamp his power and quality
>   into his work but what the creating word
> would still exceed the creation infinitely.
>   (XIX. ll. 40–45)[42]

This passage suggests that the idea of the impossibility of knowing the author's mind, which is emphasized by poststructuralist critics, is really a pattern Joyce derived from religious sources. Hermeneutics, after all, was originally the science of knowing God, and I will be focusing on a number of examples of how Joyce derived new ideas from old authors.

The sacred power that the author wields from beyond the work cannot be sustained when he is hypostatized within it, for the artist as a character is not situated in the beyond. Thus, artistic vocation is charged with great potential before it is possessed in *Dubliners* and *Portrait*. Once the artist as character assumes control over his world, however, he soon becomes insufferable, as Stephen is in *Ulysses*. Settled into his role, he is as ridiculous as Shem, who often resembles a type of clown called the Vice. The Vice originates as Satan, who claims God's power and gets knocked down in the mystery plays. In Renaissance drama, the Vice is a jester, such as Feste in *Twelfth Night,* who amuses by his pretensions, including a tendency to try to control his own little world. The artist as character tends to become a clown not because art is weak, but because the power of art has to extend beyond any actualized individual. The full creative power of the artist speaks as more than one person.

Injoyce

As "the first entelechy, the structural rhythm" (*U* 432), Joyce's mind is present within every active word of his work as a kind of inscape, a structure of meanings in the form of a series of voices. Riquelme's work is valuable because he indicates the presence of more than one voice in Joyce's writing, but he places too much emphasis on the idea of oscillation and the image of the reader's mind going back and forth between two alternative readings. I believe that a more comprehensive term for many of Joyce's most characteristic techniques is polyphony, the simultaneous presence of a series of voices. This technique is most obvious in the *Wake*, but it is already involved in crucial words in the earlier fiction.

In the *Wake*, for example, one of the answers given to Shem's first riddle—". . . . when is a man not a man?" (*FW* 170.5)—is, in part, when he is "a gnawstick." Four of the meanings of this answer can readily be listed: when he is a Gnostic; incapable of belief (agnostic); impotent (in need of oral sex); and a corpse in the late stages of being eaten by scavengers. Each of these meanings carries its own set of implications.

For example, the term "Gnostic" characterizes Shem as an intellectual, for the Gnostics believed in salvation through knowledge. Moreover, because the Gnostics did not believe that Christ was fully present at his crucifixion,[43] "a gnawstick" tends to imply that Shem is not all there. It is Joyce's mind, the creator of this verbal configuration, that determines how these various meanings fit into it. In reconstructing language, Joyce strives to subordinate its existing structure to that of his own memory. The relation of multiple meanings within the totality of a word, the role each plays in the overall configuration, and their influence on each other, all are determined primarily by Joyce's ideas, associations, and feelings. Any other critical approach, while it might be fruitful, would work on a secondary level, and would not be as well connected to the overall context of Joyce's work. Therefore, Joyce is present as a relation among mental parts in each significant word of his writing as he is present in the whole and in every part. Like God, he is a complex mystery deep within everything at the same time that he is high above and far beyond it.

The increase in the godlike ability to create life through Joyce's career is accompanied by an advance in the techniques of skepticism. This is primarily because the uncertainty of his thinking freed the objects of his thought from the enclosures of formulation. To assume God's point of view is to learn that every particular meaning given to things is a delusion, to deconstruct all conventional realities. Moreover, Joyce had to surround his power with a network of defenses before he could accept it. He grew more able to mobilize the process of the life he created as he girded that life with mechanisms of irony so that it would be strictly controlled by his needs. Bound in this mental armor, he gained momentum, from the bitter entrapment of *Dubliners*, to the solipsistic circles of *Portrait*, to the peripatetic movement toward inner relationship in *Ulysses*, and finally to the joyful flow of the *Wake*. At last his art succeeded through discipline in escaping every opposition that was not its own as it became a dream within the mind. Being responsible for his own world, he had to keep it alive, and he could not affirm the value of life as expansively as he does in the late works unless he filtered that affirmation through a system of skepticism which assures that the force he celebrates is insulated from adhering to any one formulation.

Skepticism is the contractile force in the fabrication of Joyce's mental world, in accord with Blake's statement in *The Marriage of Heaven and Hell:* "Energy is the only life and is from the Body and Reason is the bound or outward circumference of Energy." Through his skepticism, Joyce gave sharp outlines to his world by analyzing it into more and more minute and isolated units of inquiry. But at the same time, to keep this world from being inert and incoherent, he had to charge it with his own energy through the expansiveness of feeling.

As Joyce assembled a universe in his own image, he found himself increasingly able to believe in it and to express himself through it. He augmented its life by making its substance progressively richer and denser, more filled with possibility. The constant generation of new images, ideas, and language displaces the center of authority from the past to the future and from the surface of the text to beyond it. The focus of interest in the Joyce world shifts from the realm of actuality to that of potentiality as it moves from outside Joyce's mind to inside it.

The system Joyce elaborates is based on the peculiarities of his personality, yet it generates a world. Joyce realized that the reality of the world can be seen only as a product of interacting mental functions, and so, by concentrating on the generative action of those functions, he created a world with a metapsychological reality never before rendered, unless by the First Cause. Because this world was congruent or syntonic with his own being, it allowed him to translate all aspects of his mind into his writing. Because it is conceived as a multiple being, this system is capable of seeing itself from several opposed points of view and of animating agencies that are free to act against each other.

Through this multiplicity of ideology and being, Joyce's world approaches the complexity we find in the "real" one. A good definition of such a diverse world is given by Heidegger, who insists that relation to the world refers to beings. Here is a summary of the perspective of Heidegger:

> ... he defines "world" as the structural whole of significant relationships that Dasein [existence] experiences—with tools, things of nature, and other human beings—as being-in-the-world. "World" is that already familiar horizon upon which everyday human existence confidently moves. ... "World" names the essential mystery of existence, the transcendence that makes Dasein different from all other intramundane entities, the disclosedness of beings, the openness of Being.[44]

The world Joyce creates as a complex of significant relationships is carefully modulated to control external threats by reproducing them within the structure of his mind. This context allows Joyce to expand into pure being without fear of injury or restriction. In a world constructed by his own principles, there is no danger of transmitting himself as a distortion by synecdoche, a part standing for the whole. For every part of this world is related to every other part by Joyce's individual entelechy. By projecting the inner relationship of the parts of his soul as a macrocosm, Joyce encompasses his creation, surrounding his figures with the essential mystery of the only existence he possessed.

In the chapters that follow, I will first show how Joyce's cultural, personal, and intellectual development produced in him a drive toward godhead. I will begin by using St. Augustine—one of the main sources both of Joyce's autobiography and of the civilization into which he was born—to delineate some relevant ideas on the relation of God to man. Then I will use Aristotle's *Metaphysics* to explain the theory whereby Joyce found it necessary to cultivate the operation of his deity in his work. This will prepare for a detailed examination of how Joyce manifests himself as a transcendent function in *Ulysses* and of how his presence in this book works to activate its technique and its being. I devote a chapter to one of the most subtle images through which Joyce presents himself as a god in his fiction, the image of the sea.

My discussion of *Finnegans Wake* will center on what is perhaps Joyce's most sophisticated model for the procession of the author into his work, the kabbalistic Tree of Life. As an image of how the mind of God relates to the world by unfolding itself into a familial grouping, the Tree of Life shapes the structure of the tenth chapter of the *Wake*, the study scene, which presents theoretical statements and models central to the entire book. The advanced images of the mind in this, one of the last sections of the *Wake* to be completed, will serve as a basis to develop the validity and potential of the multipersonal model of mentality.

My theory that Joyce unified his work by dividing himself will be developed in both of its aspects: the unity of the canon and the polyphonic nature of Joycean discourse. Finally, I will suggest a few of the implications for Joyce study, for pyschology, and for critical theory of an understanding of how the artist operates as deity and multiple consciousness; and I will sum up Joyce's intention to revise our understanding of the relationship between God and man.

2 Augustine Joyce

"Apostate's creed"

The faith of an apostate rarely, if ever, stops being influenced by the sources it rejects. Throughout his career Joyce tenaciously maintained an intense, if not untroubled, faith in himself. We can see how the ideas of the church shaped this faith by comparing it to the attitudes of the great Church Father who provided Joyce's first middle name, St. Augustine. In 1902 Joyce presented to Lady Gregory a credo to which he never stopped adhering:

> I want to achieve myself—little or great as I may be—for I know that there is no heresy or no philosophy which is so abhorrent to my church as a human being. . . . I shall try myself against the powers of the world. All things are inconstant except the faith in the soul, which changes all things and fills their inconstancy with light. And though I seem to have been driven out of my country here as a misbeliever I have found no man yet with a faith like mine. (*Letters,* 1: 53)

If this seems too credulous to be Joyce, it is because of the elaborate, ironic defenses around his faith in himself that he developed. By using these defenses to make himself accountable to an internal version of the harshness of reality, he enabled himself to assimilate the world. He could accept everything because it was controlled by his mind, and so he expanded his sovereignty over vast reaches of time and articulation.

The core of Joyce's belief is shaped negatively by the template of church doctrine, for he says that he wants to be human because it is anathema. The violence of his antagonism toward established religion seems to generate the intensity of his belief in the spiritual principle within him. But this principle was nurtured by the church, and the power and scope of God's place in his world remain crucial factors in his identity after his abjuration.

The idea that all is inconstant but a faith in the soul that irradiates the world is typical of Augustine. In his *Confessions,* one of the major sources of *Portrait,* Augustine concentrates on exploring his soul in order to find God. The *Confessions* describe a childhood of anxiety and sin, and Augustine, who coined the term *soliloquy,* analyzes his senses and his mind with great penetration in a meticulous and varied style. Sometimes he speaks of an unknown power guiding him to his vocation: "In secret you were using my own perversity and theirs to set my feet upon the right course."[1] Stephen feels his own final vocation to be no less appointed, no less hidden, no less a commitment: "The end he had been born to serve yet did not see had led him to escape by an unseen path" (*P* 165).

Both men locate this unknown power in their unconsciousnesses. Augustine maintains that any truth we find in the world can be apprehended only because it is potential in our minds,[2] while Stephen says we find outside what is inside "as possible" (*U* 213). The theory of Jaynes holds that ancient man was guided in his decisions by the voices of gods that came from the intuitive right lobe of the brain. The African and the Irishman both came from spiritual cultures in which it was still possible to hear "a voice from beyond the world" (*P* 167). The potential in his mind that Stephen hears in a voice beside the sea, however, is no orthodox God, but Joyce himself, the artist he will become, who "remains within or behind or beyond or above" his world. It is Joyce who gave Stephen the name that portends his vocation. Unlike Augustine, Joyce perceives his autobiography as fiction, and so he accepts responsibility for the myth he creates.

A fine treatment of the relation of Joyce to Augustine by J. Mitchell Morse emphasizes differences between them;[3] but a recognition of what they share, if qualified by an awareness of those differences, can help us to understand what Joyce believed. It is widely felt, of course, that Joyce didn't really believe anything, and he sometimes supported such views. When it was suggested in 1907 that his obsession with religion indicated that he might return to the church, he said, ". . . in my opinion I am incapable of belief of any kind" (*Letters,* 2: 89). This position in Joyce and his followers starts by being hardheadedly realistic and ends by exceeding the conditions of life. The credo and the anticredo may be reconciled by saying that while Joyce never adhered to any fixed system after abandoning the one he always considered best, he did maintain belief in certain shifting but definable processes, concepts in progress. The most basic of these processes were art and love, but these were only the formal and material means by which Joyce expressed something more essential, the content of his soul.

In 1907, strained by working for a bank in Rome, Joyce reported that he had not written in months and had lost interest in everything:

> Yet I have certain ideas I would like to give form to: not as a doctrine but as the continuation of the expression of myself which I now see I began in *Chamber Music*. These ideas or instincts or intuitions or impulses may be purely personal. (*Letters*, 2: 217)

Joyce says here that he did not know what he was expressing of himself in the poems until after he wrote them, and the "instincts or intuitions or impulses" he aims at seem largely unconscious. This agrees with his earlier statement that ". . . there cannot be any substitute for the individual passion as the motive power of everything—art and philosophy included" (*Letters*, 2: 81), and his statement to Arthur Power during the twenties, "What do we know about what we put into anything? . . . do any of us know what we are creating?"[4] All of these statements indicate that, like Stephen, Joyce was concerned most with expressing his "inner world of individual emotions" (*P* 167).

Joyce believed, as Augustine did, that the inner world he pursued was sacred. Both men felt that in expressing themselves they were expressing God, but Augustine felt he created his being through God, while Joyce felt he created God through his being. For Joyce seems to have accepted Blake's view that God as we know Him is a creation of the human mind: "the slow growth and change of rite and dogma like his own rare thoughts, a chemistry of stars" (*U* 21). This accumulation of images, which inspired the civilization that created it, was augmented by every person with an individual vision. It is because individualism is the only source of vision that Stephen says that Ireland must be important because it belongs to him (*U* 645). In this sense Bruno united with God when he was burned because he added to God. Though the church excluded him, his heroic assertion of the right of each individual to frame his own God had the effect of multiplying the possibilities of divine existence.

Joyce's attitude may be seen as a reaction against Augustine's in that Augustine, writing in the fifth century, laid the basis for orthodox Christian philosophy. As young Stephen moves toward a life of sanctity, he finds his being under the control of alien powers, both bad and good:

"Apostate's creed" 31

> Who made it to be like that, a bestial part of the body able to understand bestially and desire bestially? Was that then he or an inhuman thing moved by a lower soul than his soul? His soul sickened at the thought of a torpid snaky life feeding itself out of the tender marrow of his life. . . . And, cowering in darkness and abject, he prayed mutely to his guardian angel to drive away with his sword the demon that was whispering to his brain. (*P* 139-140)

As a Catholic, Stephen, like the medieval Everyman, feels he must submit either to the devil or to the angel. Augustine, quoting St. Paul (Romans 7), speaks of a lower self in his body at war with conscience (VII.21). He also tends to relinquish control over virtue by asking God to direct his will (as, for examples, in IV.11, much of Book VII, and XII.11). By realizing how orthodoxy encroaches on the sphere of the self, we can see how the system of the church negatively defines Joyce's individualism at the same time that it predicates the sanctity of his soul. He had to make a world of his own out of the self that had been subverted by institutions. This imperative is summed up well by the famous line of Freud, "Wo es war, soll Ich werden," as translated by Lacan: ". . . where it was . . . I should come into being."[5]

Augustine often states that mortals can understand only parts — individual notes or words — of life, while God understands the entire composition of cosmology.[6] Stephen notices this pattern as a child when he observes that only God can think about everything: "He tried to think what a big thought that must be but he could think only of God" (*P* 16). God must be confronted as a personality before His attributes can be claimed. The page before this presents the flyleaf of Stephen's geography, inscribed with words that put him in the context of the universe. The first commentator on this inscription says that it shows heaven to be Stephen's expectation (*P* 16). His struggle to conceive of and name God leads him to realize that because the knowledge of God is given by His grace, the only way to possess Him is to take Him in.

The delight with which Joyce was filled when he appropriated the powers of God through art comes out strongly in Herbert Gorman's Joyce-approved biography:

> He had yet to realize the reason for his existence, yet to comprehend that it was the unconsciously self-dramatizing imagination of the lonely artist who enlarges himself at the expense of the apparent world that carried him from the nadir of despair to the zenith of a paradisal overlordship of the disastrous flaws of time.[7]

Joyce derived immense pleasure from the love he gave his work. This joyance is rendered in *Portrait* when Stephen on the beach is caught up in ecstasy at the thought of creating an imperishable living thing (*P* 170) and in the villanelle scene when a "glow of desire" fulfills his body at the thought of the temptress conscious of him as he completes his poem (*P* 233). In both scenes the delight depends on a sense of creating life out of the mind as another being capable of reply. Joyce enjoyed this activity so much that he gave up more and more of his life to his work as his career progressed: he relinquished such external distractions as job holding, eyesight, and all but the most controlled social relations. As Jacques Mercanton portrayed him in 1937, he tended to sigh and be melancholy when not involved in his work.[8]

The portion of his life Joyce gave to his creation was transformed into the substance of God from the point of view of the world it was sacrificed to create. Joyce was able to bear the assumption of this power only by constantly mocking it, but insofar as Joyce's belief in his work grew, fed by his opposition, he assumed godhood more fully. Now his work grew more personal and less subject to external models as he occupied it and unfolded himself in various forms and directions to expand it.

I may seem to have strayed from the purview of Augustine, but the saint frequently defined God as a mystery to be sought within. He would never claim to be God, but by his strategy of subordinating himself to an intuitively perceived God, he attained godlike powers. At least whatever spoke through him played a major role in defining our concept of God: no one, for example, did more than Augustine to develop the theory of the Trinity. William Barrett says Augustine had the greatest influence on history of any philosopher in the West.[9] Like Joyce, he not only probed his own psyche, but took it upon himself to project immense visions of an entire city (*The City of God*) and of cosmology.

The parallel between the two writers may be said to hinge on the ambiguous relation between dominance, or godlikeness, and submission,[10] the empathy or shared identity between active and passive partners. It would seem that in submitting himself to God, Augustine must in effect have been obliged to avoid noticing to what extent he was assuming God's power. In assuming that power, Joyce had to avoid noticing to what extent he was accepting the Deity. Augustine justified himself with logic and faith, while Joyce dejustified himself by disassembling logic and faith. But Augustine was haunted by a sense of sinfulness, and Joyce could hardly avoid a persistant feeling that he was justified.

The skeptical Joyce and the devout Augustine have similar views of man's earthly estate: he wants what he cannot have and what he does have is both beneath his dignity and constantly on the verge of disappearing (X.40).[11] If they did not see the situation of man as impossible, they would not be driven to transcend it by creating written worlds. Of course, Joyce maintained an earthly faith that Augustine lost when he converted—a belief in Eros. This faith liberated Joyce, but his romantic attitudes still paralleled the devotion of the saint in their emphasis on self-sacrifice leading through self-realization to transcendence. After all, Augustine was liberated by God, and if both men had faith in writing, then Joyce's faith in Nora filled the place of Augustine's faith in God.

Creation as Devotion

Augustine and Joyce both use the conflict between separate wills within themselves to balance enormous personal pride with humility. Both realized that they could be gods because they were slaves. Ellmann speaks of the link between Joyce's self-deflation and his confidence (*SL* xii), and Mark Shechner shows the prominence in Joyce's letters to Nora of the pattern of sacrificing oneself to achieve exaltation.[12] Augustine presents a parallel pattern as he alternates denunciation of his sinful nature with extravagant claims for God's grace, and a consideration of the letters to Nora in an Augustinian light can clarify how Joyce relates to authority.

Augustine repeatedly thanks God for thrusting a goad into his heart (VI.6, VII.8, IX.4) and asks God to make him suffer so that he will seek mercy: "It is always the case that the greater the joy, the greater the pain which precedes it. . . . Is this the rhythm of our world?" (VIII.3). It is the rhythm of Joyce's work after *Dubliners,* and Joyce gives Augustine credit for the idea of *felix culpa,* the fortunate fault (*SL* 321), suggesting that he knew the Augustinian basis for this rhythm of death and rebirth.

Joyce applied this pattern when he believed that the crisis in which his suspicion alienated him from Nora briefly in 1909 had the effect of solidifying their bond:

> What can come between us now? We have suffered and been tried. Every veil of shame or diffidence seems to have fallen from us. Will we not see in each other's eyes the hours and hours of happiness that are waiting for us? (*Letters,* 2: 239)

The entire relationship ran on sacrifice and regeneration, for he could submit to Nora as he could not elsewhere: "I gave others my pride and joy. To you I give my sin, my folly, my weakness and sadness" (*Letters*, 2: 243). From the time she first took the initiative with him, revealing his weakness ("It was not I who first touched you," *SL* 182; compare *U* 191), he was free to show her his faults and have them returned to him as virtues. His diffidence allowed her vitality, and his need for shame titillated her. So he gave her charge of the mechanism of deity whereby, to quote Augustine, "ex malo bonum fit" ("out of evil comes good," *SL* 321). The faults he expressed to Nora were fortunate, for now that he had revealed his worst suspicions and written out his vilest fantasies, they were more strongly united.

"I have *enormous* belief in the power of a simple honourable soul," Joyce wrote to Nora (*Letters*, 2: 243). Any soul had the potential for godhead if it could answer his own on a deep level and give him back to himself confirmed. Augustine, looking into his own soul, found a light within that was "superior to my soul, because it made me; and I was inferior to it because I was made by it" (VII.10).[13] The lovely chapter in which these lines appear uses God as a symbolic tool for self-development. The creation of his own soul is central to Joyce's adoration of Nora, which is often strongly religious:

> . . . one who held me in her hand like a pebble, from whose love and in whose company I have still to learn the secrets of life. . . . you are more to me than the world.
> Guide me, my saint, my angel. Lead me forward. *Everything* that is noble and exalted and deep and true and moving in what I write comes, I believe, from you. O take me into your soul of souls and then I will become indeed the poet of my race . . . O that I could nestle in your womb like a child born of your flesh and blood. . . .
> (*Letters*, 2: 248)

Nora generates the truth of his work by transforming and creating him. She teaches him the secrets of life that lie in his own soul by letting him express his lowest urges and get a vital response. The extreme desires at the boundaries of his consciousness can thus be explored to expand his awareness. He could not do this without a god image, another soul in whose infinity he has faith. Lacan says, "The Other is, therefore, the locus in which is constituted the I who speaks to him who hears . . ."[14] As her soul mirrors the expansion of his being, he no longer has to deny himself and be possessed by the alien power of guilt. He can reclaim with a sense of innocence the polymorphous or many-bodied potential of his personality to be what it is on the deepest level, the level that is most generative because it is least controlled. Lacan asks "where the peace that follows the recognition of an unconscious tendency comes from if it is not more true than that which constrains it. . . ."[15]

At this point a crucial distinction between Joyce and Augustine emerges from the fact that Joyce invested his faith in a physical being. As Molly Bloom and Anna Livia Plurabelle show, Joyce characterized the feminine as a principle of change. By attaching himself to a woman, Joyce released the feminine part of his personality, allowing himself to grow aware of his division and variability. By worshiping her, he prepared himself to generate a vision of a deity who would be divided and variable, in accord with Bruno's theories.[16] In fact, the divine being through which Joyce projects the last two novels is hermaphroditic, having been formed by the union of Joyce and Nora.

Ellmann says that Joyce held his two images of Nora as wife and mother "remorsefully apart, opposing them to each other so that they became the poles of his mind" (*JJ* 294). The alternation of aggressive and submissive tones in his 1909 letters to her demonstrates how she served to develop his polarization. In fact, the proud, spiritual side of Joyce and his degraded, bestial side resemble two personalities. Out of this self-division came *Exiles,* the first work in which Joyce shows a group of minds in active relation to each other. In this drama of marital crisis, the four protagonists intertwine with each other in such symbiotic and parasitic ways that they tend to be functions of one total mentality,[17] and the tendency toward a union of minds becomes clearer as the situation of adultery is carried further in *Ulysses.*

The 1909 crisis may seem more important as a turning point in Joyce's career than it is because it is so vividly recorded, and Joyce may be laying on his rhetoric to propitiate Nora; but there can be little doubt that he was basically sincere, and he was justified in believing that his artistic ability grew as a result of his connection with her. By realizing himself through contact with another soul, he established a state of communion with depths shared by humanity. The creative power of love that he got from her he passed on to his imaginary beings, able to give them what he had found in himself so that they gained life that could never have been granted by his earlier bitterness. The dynamic quality of this life was formed by the ability to hold opposed ideas in the mind simultaneously. The need for belief that Joyce focused on Nora had a parallel in his attitude toward his work. He learned to divide himself into his work as he learned to divide himself for and yield himself to another person. Nora contributed to Joyce's art by adding to his mind, but one of the main things she added was the kind of inner division described at the end of *Exiles* when Richard Rowan says he has wounded his soul for Bertha.

Being dynamic, feelings, as opposed to theories, must be based on unresolved conflict. It is, therefore, by projecting his division onto his work, as Richard projects his on Bertha, by loving his work, that an author gives pyschic life to his creation according to this sacramental theory of art. The artist should refuse to distance himself in order to avoid enclosing his characters in theories. The creative nature of God must be expressed as unresolved conflict in earthly terms. One reason for the divided nature of God's image is indicated by Aquinas's observation that virtues that are distinguished from each other in men, such as kindness and courage, are unified in God as a single complete good (Q. 13, A. 4). A mind that wants to give full vitality to a world must draw on more thoughts than can be contained within the narrow construct of a single personality. Joyce appears in his world as God does in his, as mystery, paradox, and anomaly.

As Gordon indicates, Joyce believed throughout his career in basing his books on his personal experience in such a way as to arrange significant events of his life as an antecedent substructure to the world of the fiction.[18] Perhaps all writers do this, but Joyce was more aware of it than others. He realized, as Augustine did, that life came from an incomprehensible source. So must fiction. In 1937 Joyce wrote, "The encounter between my father and a tramp (the basis of my book) actually took place at that part of the park" (*Letters*, 1: 396). We will probably never know much about the actual encounter that is parodied in the second chapter and elsewhere in the *Wake*, but Joyce here gives it absolute cosmogonic importance for the book's universe. Nora serves a similar function in *Ulysses*, which is set on the day Joyce became intimate with her; and so may Alfred H. Hunter, the Jewish gentleman who rescued Joyce from a street brawl over a girl on June 20, or shortly thereafter, if he actually did so (*JJ* 161–162, 762n).[19]

A recent revelation of biographical underpinning involves what Joyce described as his first sexual experience in a lost 1917 letter to Dr. Gertrude Kaempffer, whom he was trying to seduce. Joyce said that when he was fourteen, and a maid he was with stepped into some bushes to urinate, he heard her making water and "jiggled furiously" (*JJ* 418).

Creation as Devotion

This scene served as the basis for many references to chamber music in Joyce's work, especially the original sin in the *Wake* which is often presented in terms of HCE's misbehaving while two maids urinate (*FW* 34.12-28, 46.27-30, 98.20-25).

It was a matter of chance that this letter was recalled for Ellmann. Such cases suggest that there must be many other biographical references buried in the work never to be recovered. Much of Joyce's submerged presence will always remain unknowable. From the great deal we know about Joyce, however, it is clear that the works are built on the life not merely as autobiography, but through undercurrents of imagery whose motivation is invisible but powerful.

Like God, these images work in mysterious ways. In fact, both the tramp in the park and the maid in the bushes happen to operate as versions of original sin, and this is appropriate. These images represent archaic causes behind every point in the *Wake*, operating like genetic messages in the cells of each character. Like the original sin in Eden, these original acts took place outside the fallen world, before the text; but they condition the nature of every existence in that world.

For the reader and within the work, these prophenomena can be seen only through a glass darkly, but they are essential and we need to develop terms to describe how they operate. A useful tool for this purpose, and one Joyce was familiar with, is the Christian belief that man, made in God's image, contains the structure of his creator within his soul. One of the main statements of this concept is contained in Augustine's major work of theology, *The Trinity*. Here he says that the Father, the Son, and the Holy Ghost are reproduced in the three principle powers of the soul, memory, understanding, and will (or love). This idea of Augustine's appears near the beginning of the catechism.[20]

Augustine's discussions of the analogy between psychic functions and parts of God explore the relation between unity and division in the mind. On the one hand, he argues that memory, will, and understanding are one substance in that each requires the other two to exist. Thus, for example, memory cannot be manifested without using will and understanding. But on the other hand, he suggests that they are like separate persons, for each includes its own version of the other two: ". . . our will, when it is right . . . possesses its own kind of knowledge which cannot be there without memory and understanding."[21] Similar arguments could be made to the effect that memory has its own kind of understanding; understanding, its own kind of will, and so forth. Thus, Trinitarian theory leads to the idea of a mind made up of minds.

The theory that the human soul reflects God may serve as one indication that Joyce's mind is reflected at many points in his work. In fact, I argued earlier that the various meanings of a verbal unit from the *Wake* demonstrate that a matrix that follows the shape of his mind is contained in every point of his creation. The presence of the Joycean substructure is especially rich in the minds of his characters. As religion and psychoanalysis do, Joyce frames the mind as built on prior knowledge from which it is sundered, lost data which, whether they come from God, parents, an author, or one's past, are essentially external and irrecoverable at the same time that they are implicated behind everything.

The mind of the text, like those of the author and the reader, is suspended in an uncertainty from which it draws its substance. Riquelme suggests this when he says that we need a metaphor for textuality as consciousness that will include the unconscious and the imagination.[22] The metaphor he seeks may be the author as god. The fact that this unknown source often seems as invisible as the Deity should not keep us from realizing that it manifests itself in an elaborate and consistent structure. Emphasis on external reference is a Joycean technique that reminds the reader of the presence of an external system of knowledge at the same time that it prevents him from mistaking potentiality for actuality—for the works and days referred to cannot be recovered in the text, yet they are immanent in its sub-stance.

Joyce was being realistic about the conditions of fiction in recognizing that his characters and his creation were subject to unknown content in his mind. The tradition that is known as realism, which might be called empiricism, uses a fantastic set of conventions whereby the author pretends that his book is not written by anyone, or is written by someone else, and that his characters are uncreated creatures, independent of him in their rationality. These conventions have been mocked by many of the best novelists from Cervantes to Pynchon. Throughout his canon, Joyce moved resolutely away from these artificial strictures on his self-expression, enabled to see through them by his knowledge of Scholasticism.

Primal Matter

Augustine says that nothing can exist except insofar as God knows it (VII.4), and this statement is one indication that men in the world Augustine defines have the status of characters in fiction. In his chapter "The Godlike Artist," Morse demonstrates that Augustine tended to describe God as an artist and argues that this was a major influence on Joyce.[23] The *Confessions* says that if God does not need anything the world could give him, he must have created it purely to project his own perfection (XIII.4). Human beings thus act out the esthetic desires of their Creator; and in doing so they partake of the structure of the divine mind according to the logic of the esthetic theory presented by Stephen in *Portrait*. For this theory holds that the esthetic object shares the three-phase structure of the artist's mind just as Augustinian man shares the structure of the Trinity.

The artist as God is also like a parent, and Joyce speaks of an inverse relation between the control exercised by the artist and the expansion of his characters: "His [Hauptmann's] characters appear to be more highly vivified by their creator than Ibsen's do but also they are less under control" (*Letters*, 2: 173). One of the key ways in which the artist gives his characters life is by *not* understanding them, for understanding involves reducing them to logical formulas.

The process by which fatherhood takes on the supernatural creative power of godhead is described in *The Dead Father* by Donald Barthelme: "Fathers are teachers of the true and not-true, and no father ever knowingly teaches what is not true. In a cloud of unknowing, then, the father proceeds with his instruction."[24] A good deal of what a father conveys to his son is unconscious to both. This unknown knowledge includes whatever is beyond conventional reality, the powerful and dangerous currents of feeling and energy that make up life before rational order is imposed on it. This subjective level is what the *Wake* is referring to when it keeps insisting that the patriarch HCE is amalgamated in his descendants: ". . . he is smolten in our mist . . ." (*FW* 7.17). The obscurity that surrounds the father because his major activity is unconscious makes him mysterious and godlike, as Barthelme's reference to the anonymous fourteenth-century classic of mysticism *The Cloud of Unknowing* suggests. Life is conveyed through mystery, through uncertainty, through a shifting of meaning that avoids formulation. And the artist, as Joyce conceives him, constantly conveys to the reader important material of which both are unconscious.

While this may seem an ultra- or postmodern suggestion, a similar pattern appears in Augustine. He presents five different interpretations of the line "In the Beginning God made heaven and earth" and says that all may be valid and that the least interesting of them is the literal one (XII.17-20). One interpretation Augustine presents here is that the word "earth" refers to "formless matter," an intermediate stage between immaterial God and the world. God had to create formless or primal matter before he gave it the specific forms of creatures. Augustine's knowledge of this concept from Greek philosophy derives from his having been a classical scholar and literary critic before his conversion.[25]

Augustine's five interpretations are similar to the seven meanings Joyce presented to Harriet Shaw Weaver for an early version of a line in the *Wake,* "L'Arcs en His Cieling Flee Chinx on the Flur" (*SL* 326; compare *FW* 104.13). Augustine says the writing of Moses covers a great area of humanity because that writing divides into many streams. If people see any number of meanings in Genesis, providing that all are morally acceptable, Augustine says that they may all be there. For God transmitted through Moses a variety of truths consubstantial in the same words in order to reach the greatest possible part of humanity.

> . . . If I were called upon to write a book which was to be vested with the highest authority, I should prefer to write it in such a way that the reader could find re-echoed in my words whatever truths he was able to apprehend. I would rather write in this way than impose a single true meaning so explicitly that it would exclude all others. . . . (XII.31)

In order to write in a way that will simultaneously sustain the greatest number of theories, one must have access to the raw material or formless matter of reality before it has been mediated by any of these theories. On the diagram he sent Carlo Linati, Joyce identified the sense of the "Proteus" episode of *Ulysses* as "*Prima materia*" or primal matter,[26] indicating that formless matter is the creative principle Stephen strives to make contact with on the beach. While Joyce's polyphonic techniques work to dismantle the traditional authorities they juxtapose, they also work to promote "the highest authority" on the new level of reality constituted by Joyce, a level that harnesses the power of potentiality behind or above the conventional realities in his world.

Primal matter, as its name suggests, is immediately close to God, and the discussion of multivalent scripture by Augustine implies that insofar as it embodies primal matter, the text, like Jesus as the Word, embodies two aspects—that is, it conveys spiritual truth in material form insofar as it is extracomprehensible. Likewise, insofar as a unit of Joycean text is filled with multiple meanings, it is filled with Joyce.

The general tendency throughout the history of exegesis has been to place the most elaborate interpretations on the most sacred texts.

Primal Matter 41

Therefore (other things being equal) the more readings a passage sustains, and the further those readings are from the surface, the more spiritually powerful that passage is. Thus Christ gains authority by speaking in parables. A striking example of how radical interpretation indicates divine power appears early in the Gospel of St. John. The prominence of Johnny MacDougal among the Evangelists in the *Wake* suggests that John may be Joyce's favorite Gospel. William Barclay describes John as "The Mind of God in Human Form" because it is the Gospel in which Christ's claims and the charges against him concentrate on his role in the world as a man who takes godhead on himself.[27]

As Jesus is condemning the money changers at the temple, he is asked for a sign of his authority. "'Destroy this temple,' Jesus replied, 'and in three days I will raise it up'" (2:19). The Jews are skeptical, but he does not get to demonstrate his claim. John explains that Jesus' statement did not apply to the immediate situation, but it was later remembered when he was resurrected after being dead for three days, so that "temple" turned out to mean "body." Such delayed interpretation might be called equivocal, but John presents it with pride: Jesus gains force as God by having his mind on a larger context, a poetic context, rather than letting his mind be understood in ordinary terms.

Joyce aimed at achieving a similar authority by multiplying his contexts. By his design, his works have attracted more elaborate commentary than those of any English writer except Shakespeare. Stephen is aware of the magnitude of Shakespeare's creation, for he quotes (*U* 212) from a statement by Dumas père: ". . . in the theatrical world, everything has come from Shakespeare, as, in the real world, all comes from the sun; . . . . he was the man who had, after God, created the most."[28] Statements almost as hyperbolic have been made about the role of Joyce in modern fiction. Robert M. Adams, for example, asks, ". . . what novel of the last fifty years is *not* a post-Joycean novel?"[29] If Joyce can be located not far behind Shakespeare on the line of creators, it must be by his intention. In both Joyce and Shakespeare, the vastness of creation depends on its extension into readings generated by the swarming recombinations built into the text. The mind of God, like that of the poet, sees connections outside existing contiguities because He sees through the world He imagines—sees through it because He imagines it completely, sees every phenomenological possibility.

As Fausto Maijstral argues in Pynchon's *V.,* everyone believes in metaphors, but the poet, by knowing that they are only metaphors, can invent new ones and so create new realities for others to live in.[30] A writer can reject the forms of the given world only by aiming at a better world conceived in alternate forms, however he may define them. This is why Nietzsche, the great negator, was bound to reach the conclusion that he was God.

By moving toward the general forms behind existence in each of his works and through all, Joyce created new mental worlds for us to live in. He had to explore the uncreated realm of primal matter to achieve this, had to reach a state in which, like the God of Augustine, he included the essence of all existence in his mind, and so could not see anything outside himself but the void upon which the world is founded. He put himself in the position of God before the creation when he wrote to his son in 1935 in Italian that for over fifty years he had "gazed into a nullity" where he found "a lovely nothing" (*Letters*, 3: 361). Staring into the void that he trained himself to perceive for the sake of his creation, Joyce produced the most complete human beings ever made by man out of faith in the meaning of his own being.

The God of Augustine, like those of Joyce, Jung, and Jaynes, occupies (or shares with other supernatural beings) the part of a person's mind he is not conscious of. Realizing that he cannot understand all that he is, Augustine asks himself where the part of his mind is "which it does not itself contain" (X.8), and concludes that it lies in God. Joyce's development as a writer was based on looking into the part of himself that he did not contain or control, and he aimed at revealing the parts of his characters' souls that their conscious minds did not contain. If this unknown area is a nullity from the point of view of conventional logic, it is everything from that of creativity. It is "the divine substance wherein Father and Son are consubstantial" (*U* 38), enacting the double-aspect theory because it is the only medium that can transfer metaphysical life from Joyce to his characters. Like Aristotle's primal matter or Freud's primary-process thought,[31] it is the source of life; insofar as his characters are alive, it is by the will of Joyce.

Joyce looked at himself by projecting himself into others, just as he related to others by ingesting them. Whether or not anyone ever perceives people in any other way, these are useful vices for a novelist. Added to the alienation from his own identity expressed typically in lines like Stephen's "Other me" and "that I" (*U* 41, 45), these practices indicate the likelihood of a high degree of fusion between author and characters. Derrida observes that autobiography is more than self-analysis: it is the creation of the self for the same reason that looking into a mirror is making oneself.[32] And writing fiction is also a self-construction, for every form projected objectifies or gives form to the author's potential for thought, developing a part of what he is. At the center of Joyce's creation is the mind of the author growing to accommodate more parts and levels from chapter to chapter.

Joyce never swerved from his youthful aim—"to achieve myself." Whether he imagined himself or others, whether he projected human narrators or spoke in voices beyond human kenning, whether he expressed himself in words or artistic gestures, Joyce was continually unfolding unknown possibilities of his mind. The authorial personality he constructs is the soul of his creation, and its multiplicity fills his world with life.

The spiritual showing-forths of the early works all hinge on discoveries of personality that developed Joyce's freedom and power. The god revealed in these epiphanies is Joyce. This was no less so when he imagined himself in roles that differed from his proper being or revealed the nature of life by defining the absence of life. In his later works, Joyce concentrated on embodying godhead—not in himself, but as a presence within the increasing self of the work.

The point at which the balance shifted so that he began to give more life to the work than he took from it, the point at which he took occupancy of the world he made and so assumed divinity, corresponds to the point at which his personality shifted from the predominance of Stephen to that of Bloom. And this psychological point of commitment or conversion is reflected and recorded in the letters to Nora. His faith in love was so intense that it centered on a conversion experience that could not be repeated. Once he had made his choice in the world, he left worldly action behind and he was free to enter the world of fiction.

3   The Metaphysics of Creation

Aristotle and Bruno

The central creation of Joyce's canon was his continuous development of his own mind. The world of Joyce and its beings emerge from this mind insofar as they do emerge. They go far toward attaining independent being, but they never leave this mind behind, for it is the strength of the mind that allows them to emerge. They keep referring to the Joyce that underlies their constitution, the Joyce by whose grace they are given whatever free will they have. This expanded Joycean mind is modeled on the concept of God because God, organizing the universe on every level, is by far the most powerful image of what the mind could be.

There is an enormous development of the image of God in Joyce's mature work, and it always refers to the artist. In order to perceive the operation of Joyce's mind as a god in his work, one must examine his theory of the functions of God. Such an examination leads one to discover the presence of Joyce as god at many points in the text that seem empty. Two crucial figures to define the role of God for Joyce were Aristotle and Bruno. A correct understanding of his use of these two geniuses will recognize how he synthesized their theories, rather than insisting that one or the other was the right one.

A number of critics have presented cogent arguments to the effect that the interruptions and violations of narrative norms in *Ulysses,* such as the headlines of the "Aeolus" episode and the style shifts of "Oxen of the Sun," work to deconstruct the reality of Joyce's world by raising questions about the validity of narrative conventions. Contemporary poststructuralist philosophy, augmenting the tendency of analysis to take things apart, sometimes gives the impression that theory and skepticism are inseparable. In this light, those who try to see meaning in Joyce's work look naive and old-fashioned. Yet Joyce's effort was not merely to destroy a world, but also to create one, and to do this he had to generate a great flood of meaning. There is need for a theory of his constructive powers, and such a theory will lead to an understanding of how his constructive and deconstructive powers make each other possible.

The decreation of one world serves the creation of another. Every displacement in the assumed order comes from a new point of view that implies its own values. In Joyce's work the shift away from reality framed in empirical terms is a shift toward reality defined by Joyce's personal Scholasticism. Scholastic reality is closeness to ultimate truth, and the ultimate truth of Bloomsday Dublin originates in the mind of its creator. Despite the taboos of the New Criticism and the newer criticism, this person is an active, sacramental presence in his work. The violations by Joyce of established styles, his external references, his coincidences, and his sudden changes of rules actually function as spiritual manifestations, positive acts Joyce performs as a god—and these miraculous events in the text are sources of one of Joyce's major kinds of reality. Riquelme notices a pattern similar to this when he says that the presence of the narrator reveals itself through difference.[1]

One of the central definitions in the West of the role of God appears in a book Joyce described himself as "up to the neck in" on March 20, 1903: Aristotle's *Metaphysics (Letters,* 2: 38). His notes on Aristotle suggest a search for elements of an esthetic system that could be used to seize control of a scholastically defined universe. On March 27, he wrote of the *Poetics,*

> *e tekhne mimetai ten physin*—This phrase is falsely rendered as "Art is an imitation of Nature." Aristotle does not here define art; he says only, "Art imitates Nature" and means that the artistic process is like the natural process.[2]

This interpretation frees the artist from the obligation to follow nature and promotes him to equal footing by saying that the artist imitates the process that creates nature.[3] Because Joyce could never subordinate himself to God, he could accept the world only by making it a product of his own imaginative will. One reason Aristotle was useful for this endeavor was that he came from an age before the hierarchical distance between man and God was reified in the West. The Greeks celebrated heroes who, as Tennyson put it in "Ulysses," "strove with Gods."

Joyce's Aristotle notes also state that the "intellect separate from all things is immortal and divine" and that "the intellectual soul is the form of forms."[4] "Form of forms" is clearly a definition of godhead, the first cause of everything else, and this phrase is on Stephen's mind in *Ulysses* (*U* 26). Aristotle, who made God a mind, is here interpreted so as to make the mind God. The master, moreover, indicated to Joyce not only how it would be possible to conceive of himself as God, but why it would be necessary to do so. Finally, Joyce found with the help of Bruno how this could be done without trapping himself in a static system.

Joyce eventually passed beyond some of Aristotle's ideas, but many of them remained basic to his mentality. Gose indicates that Bruno's rejection of the simple, changeless Scholastic Deity led Joyce toward a vision of God that was dynamic and multiple.[5] J. Lewis McIntyre says that Bruno's objections to Aristotle were aimed more at narrow-minded reductions of Aristotle than at the sage himself.[6] Joyce saw Bruno as adding a new dimension to Scholasticism rather than abolishing it. His respect for the older system and his reservations about the newer one are evident in his language in a passage of the review of McIntyre in which Joyce defines his adherence to Bruno:

> In his attempt to reconcile the matter and form of the Scholastics — formidable names, which in his system as spirit and body retain little of their metaphysical character — Bruno has hardily put forward an hypothesis, which is a curious anticipation of Spinoza. . . .
> And yet it must be the chief claim of any system like Bruno's that it endeavours to simplify the complex. That idea of an ultimate principle, spiritual, indifferent, universal, related to any soul or to any material thing, as the Materia Prima of Aquinas is related to any material thing, unwarranted as it may seem in the view of critical philosophy, has yet a distinct value for the historian of religious ecstasies. (*CW* 133-134)

Note that Joyce refers to the ultimate principle as "indifferent" — the term Stephen uses to describe his role as artist-god — at the same time that it is in everything.

The hypothesis Joyce presents Bruno as advancing here is the double-aspect theory. Joyce derived the idea that Bruno anticipated Spinoza from passages like the following in McIntyre:

> There are certain general resemblances between the finished philosophies of the two authors, so far as Bruno can be said to have a finished philosophy. The first principle of both is the unity out of which

all things spring, to which all return, and in which all have their true nature, or highest reality,—a unity with which both identify nature and spirit alike, and which is for both God.[7]

Here again the double-aspect theory is described. The irony of Joyce's statement that this theory is valuable for the "historian of religious ecstasies" is that he himself was to use it increasingly. These passages, which confirm Joyce's interest in some of the ideas I mentioned earlier, make it clear that for Joyce at this point Bruno's ideas were merely speculative modifications of the prodigious structure of the Schoolmen. They also show that despite Bruno's belief in a multiple God in all things, he ultimately believed in the unity of the First Cause—though this unity was for him beyond human knowing. The authority of many Aristotelian principles remains "formidable" throughout Joyce's career. If he went beyond Scholasticism in the *Wake,* even these late developments had to be built on—or deconstructed from—Aristotelian bases.

Causality

One fundamental thesis of Aristotle's *Metaphysics* that must have stayed with Joyce is that there are four causes for everything: essence or form, matter, cause of change, and end or purpose (*telos*). In the case of a shovel, for example, its essence is the pattern it is made in, its matter is what it is made up of, its cause of change is the agent that makes it, and its end is what it is made for, i.e., to dig.[8] The last two are active in relating the shovel outside itself and are sometimes known as the efficient cause and the final cause.

Aristotle tended to blame all other philosophers for seeing only two causes. He said that some of them sometimes noticed other levels of causation, but that he was the first to formulate the last two clearly. He even blamed his dissertation director, Plato, for dividing everything into ideal (which was essentially form) and matter. Aristotle said that because Plato left out cause of change and purpose, his ideal forms were isolated from his material objects, and that because his forms were not actively related to his matter, his world had no life (988a, 990a).

I think Joyce felt the same about other novelists—with a few exceptions, such as Flaubert, from whom he got the idea of the novelist as God. A writer who governed the material of his fiction with a clear, consistent, monistic theory would typify the limitation to two causes. The essential cause of his ideology might be seen as combining with a material cause of tradition. His characters and objects would have to follow either his ideas or convention, and there would be no other dimension of causality to mediate or introduce complexity or change. Such a model tends to eviscerate the life of fiction and reduce it to rhetoric.

Joyce's objections to many of the classic English novelists, especially Scott and Hardy, may be seen as caused by their lack of spiritual complexity. His distinction between the spiritual Irish and the materialistic English (*U* 133; *JJ* 446) accords with a substantial literary tradition. Matthew Arnold, in *The Study of Celtic Literature* (1867), presented the extreme theory that any English writer who showed spiritual qualities must have Celtic blood.

Joyce recognized that it was causal complexity that made him modern: "Previously, writers were interested in externals and, like Pushkin and Tolstoy even, they thought only on one plane; but the modern theme is the subterranean forces, those hidden tides which govern everything."[9] Here Joyce's aim is the multiplication of planes. Although he fills these new fields with psychoanalytic forces, his conception of additional planes of motivation was originally derived from Scholasticism. As Father Noon observes, in Joyce's later work the unconscious fills the position of God.[10] As Joyce said he could never know any mind but his own (*JJ* 265), this unconscious must originate with him. In deifying his unconscious, he creates a god who cannot be contained by a clear, stable definition. The inability of man clearly to define God is a Scholastic tradition, and Father Boyle delineates it as a vital theme in Joyce.[11]

The power of Aristotle's system rests on its ability to define causes that are so different from each other that they occupy completely opposed planes. If these planes are at right angles to each other, as far from parallel (or commensurate) as possible, they can extend to cover the greatest area and to multiply dimensions most effectively. The reality of an object within this system depends on its being defined by different powers that cannot be bound together into a firm structure because their natures are not related. For material and form are no more commensurate with prior cause and end than matter is with spirit.

In this respect at least, Aristotle's system is not subject to Derrida's attack on metaphysics, which focuses on Plato and sees metaphysics as reducing the world to a fixed structure. In fact, Derrida's argument is parallel to Aristotle's criticism of Plato, for Derrida claims that metaphysical emphasis on form stifles the articulation of force, "the other of language."[12] By introducing his last two causes, cause of change and purpose, Aristotle allows for the operation of will and time. Moreover, by putting his unconscious in the role of God because it is the ultimate source of the world he creates, Joyce hitches Aristotle's sytem to a first cause that must perpetually recede beyond any definition. In this sense I agree with Margot Norris's unpublished remark that the god of Joyce's world is a deconstructed god. On the other hand, Joyce realized that the parts of his mind related to each other to form a structure. And however vertiginously difficult it might be to define or maintain this structure, Joyce made a great effort to do so. After all, it is no more impossible to unify the mind completely than to disintegrate it completely.

Aristotle's causes provided Joyce with a framework within which to unfold the world that expressed his mind. I have said that the development of multiple meanings in a word must be organized by the structure of Joyce's mind, and these meanings follow the concept of multiple causality. Joyce had to operate all of the causes to make his world real, for once you have trained yourself to see four causes in every object, a world with only two causes looks two-dimensional. And the need to maintain these differing forces is typical of the pressure on Joyce to multiply himself in order to expand his creation.

The sheer complexity of Scholasticism inspired Joyce to maximize his elaboration. Aristotle sees that the same object may have not only four categories of causes, but any number of causes within each category that work in different ways. For example, the efficient causes of a shovel include the tool that makes it, the man who wields the tool, and the principle that motivates the man, and each of these is caused by the one after it. In such a manner Aristotle weaves a network of lines of distinction through the space his theory fills, and this network extends in four dimensions because he makes time and depth active.

Aristotle is "master of those who know" partly because of the scale on which his intellectual structure is built and its vitality. Stephen implies that Shakespeare animated such a world of causality with his soul. Joyce intends to go further by a conscious and specific articulation of his personality that multiplies causes, changes rules in progress, and activates a spiritual presence. There are thousands of voices in the late work that cannot be clearly identified until they are seen as coming from Joyce, and one of these voices claims of HCE that few cared to doubt "the *c*anonicity of *h*is *e*xistence as a tesseract" (*FW* 100.34, my italics). A tesseract, in projective geometry, is a four-dimensional analogue of a cube. The statement is partly motivated by HCE's insecurity about whether he does exist, but its main effect is to represent the elaborate way that he is enclosed by a multidimensional system of mental causality that extends through the entire Joyce canon.

Joyce's concern with all aspects of causality in his world is reflected in his use of etymology, allusion, and psychological motivation. These are so employed that words tend to be alive with earlier and later forms, while psychological impulses tend to be seen as reactions to other impulses. Every event and detail in Joyce's universe is linked to a matrix of symbolic systems that surrounds it with a web of connections. These connections operate causally to create this point in the text through the agency of Joyce's mind, which readily causes connections that no one but Joyce could understand.

Causality is carried beyond Aristotle in the *Wake*. David A. White argues that because the *Wake* is a repeating cycle, no event in the text can be distinguished as either before or after any other, and therefore causality breaks down.[13] This is true in terms of conventional causality, for particular causes in the *Wake* cannot be identified in any exclusive way. On the other hand, the *Wake* multiplies causality in specific ways. It places emphasis on teleology in that every event is caused as much by what comes after it as by what comes before, and the final cause has always been linked to God. Moreover, the boundaryless flux that White sees resembles primary-process thinking, which Freud sees as timeless. It may stand for the pure expression of the mind within itself, unrestricted by external forms.

There is a cause for the breakdown of causality in the *Wake*, and that cause is Joyce. He operates from the mental world behind the *Wake* as the dreamer of the dream. Within a dream, causality is not an empirical reality, as it is for us, but a set of names, a sequence of images proceeding from an unknowable power, as it was for Aquinas. Moreover, conventional causes are particular causes with particular points of view; but in the dream of the *Wake*, as I will show, the mind of the dreamer assumes multiple points of view. Dreamers often feel capable of seeing things from several points of view at once. This is because they project every element in the dream, and because the idea of a discrete single point of view is something they had to learn in infancy. The omniscient viewpoint of dream is the point of view of God.

Polyphonic Discourse

The Joycean development of multiple causality, liberated from the requirement to maintain or to try to grasp the simplicity of the first cause, led to the construction of a discourse in which several voices spoke at once. I have suggested this in looking at the word "gnawstick" from the

Polyphonic Discourse 51

Wake; now I will show how it works in a more substantial passage that involves more definable voices.

In the seventh chapter or Shem section of the *Wake,* Shaun presents a questionable female companion that Shem dreams of as "of the flushpots of Euston and the hanging garments of Marylebone" (*FW* 192.29). In *Ulysses (U* 131), Joyce made the watercloset a symbol of British imperialism, and the English toilets and the French prostitute in this line from the *Wake* stand for the state and the church (embodied by St. Mary). On a second level, the implication is that Shem dreams of the corruptions of power. On a third, the line sounds like "the fleshpots of Egypt and the hanging gardens of Babylon." On a fourth, it refers to the opening of the second chapter of Blake's *Jerusalem:*

> The fields from Islington to Marybone
> To Primrose Hill and Saint Johns Wood:
> Were builded over with pillars of gold,
> And there Jerusalems pillars stood.[14]

These lines describe an area of London blighted by industrialism, another aspect, for Joyce, of the corruption of empire.

The presence of multiple levels below the surface gives the text a depth that imitates the substance of life. The spatial aspects of these connections, such as physical parallels to other texts, are formal and material causes. But the temporal aspects are efficient and final causes because they involve change. Insofar as he motivates cause of change and purpose in the text, Joyce introduces his will in an active way. Moreover, once he has done this at a given point, he remains present and capable of doing it again. The text changes meaning as one thinks about it, and Joyce often programs the text to change in a certain order. For example, the reader of the above passage is likely to see it as referring to Egypt and Babylon before he sees it as referring to Blake. Joyce may have indicated that he intended the Blake reference, which has not been mentioned before, to be discovered late by making "jesusalem" appear seven lines below.

The language of the late Joyce is haunted by its causes and yearns for its ends. Phrases in the *Wake* are frequently suspended between the previous level they arise out of and a new, incomplete level toward which they may be described as moving. For example, the phrase "on the flounder of his bulk" (*FW* 6.31) includes "on the flat of his back," and "flat" appears in a manuscript.[15] The latter phrase gives birth to the former, an image of a supine person turning into a fish, through the imposition of a mind below the surface of the text. Joyce creates the original etymology that derives *flounder* from *flat* to express the psychic reality of the dream of HCE.

The two levels of this phrase imply two speakers, blending states of the mind of HCE in this case, and thus the passage is an analogue, on the simplest level, to the frequent passages in the *Wake* in which it is hard to distinguish who is speaking. The most prominent of such confusions is the frequent indistinguishability of Shem and Shaun. The line on Euston and Marylebone is relatively clear in that Shaun seems to be describing Shem, but even here ambiguity creeps in. For if Shaun is a clergyman denouncing Shem's sinfulness on one level, on another, he is Blake denouncing an attraction to imperialism. Thus, the identities of authority and rebel are confused. The rationale for mixing Shem and Shaun up involves the fact that they are conceived of as parts of one mind. After all, when one is engaged in the ordinary activities of life, it is often not possible to tell whether one's right or left brain lobe is dominant.

The simultaneous presence of more than one speaker that is so prevalent in the *Wake* is widespread in more subdued forms in *Ulysses*. For if Shem is usually seen from Shaun's point of view, and Shaun from Shem's, then it is also true that the irony surrounding Bloom expresses Stephen's perspective, while the pathos with which Stephen is seen relates to Bloom. Once the second three episodes, describing Bloom, are established as simultaneous to the first three about Stephen, *Ulysses* becomes a book that expresses two minds at once. And just as Stephen and Bloom, as has often been observed, are aspects of Joyce, so the multiple minds that are usually being expressed simultaneously in Joyce's mature work are aspects of one mind, his mind.

Many of the later techniques of *Ulysses* add voices to the minds of the characters, such as the satirical, parodic voices added to the mind of the narrator in "Cyclops," the various styles in which the thoughts of the characters are expressed in "Oxen of the Sun," and the hallucinatory projections in "Circe." These express the moods of the characters as they could not otherwise be expressed. One of the most precise developments of polyphonic discourse in *Ulysses* occurs in "Sirens" as the people in the Ormond bar are listening to songs. Music breaks down the logical continuity of language and replaces it with a sequence of immediate impressions. As a result, the thoughts of a character tend to mix two tracks of discordant discourse at once and to interrupt each other. For example, here is Bloom listening to Richie Goulding whistling:

> Richie cocked his lips apout. A low incipient note sweet banshee murmured all. A thrush. . . . Is lost. Rich sound. Two notes in one there. Blackbird I heard in the hawthorn valley. Taking my motives he twined and turned them. All most too new call is lost in all. Echo. How sweet the answer. How is that done? All lost now. (*U* 272)

Bloom, meditating on the idea of two notes in one, is experimenting with language in the line "All most too new call is lost in all"; but that line is no more abstract in its mixing of discourse than other lines in "Sirens," such as "Cross Ringabella haven mooncarole" (*U* 279). The line Richie is whistling, "All is lost now," is mixed with other phrases passing through Bloom's mind. Throughout this section of "blending . . . voices" (*U* 279), there is constant observation of how the perception of music influences and is influenced by other levels of the mind. Bloom is trying to listen to the music, eat, avoid thinking of Boylan, talk to Richie, and write to Martha Clifford, sometimes all at once. The narrative emphasizes contrasts between levels of his mind. At one point, for example, he murmurs as if writing a business letter while writing to Martha: "Bloom mur: best references. But Henry wrote: it will excite me" (*U* 280). Joyce described "Sirens" as a fugue, and the technique and subject of this episode accentuate the idea that mental discourse is not merely a voice, but a group of voices.

The use of polyphony in Joyce indicates a crucial difference between him and Aristotle, who emphasized a unity at the center of things. The center of consciousness that speaks in the mature works of Joyce is generally divided, expressing more than one mind at once. This results from the process described earlier by which he divided himself into his work. It accords with the poststructuralist view of Norris, who describes the *Wake* as decentered, or empty at the center.[16] Moreover, recent critics have traced the divided center back to Joyce's earliest works. MacCabe shows how Joyce began to break up the fixed meanings of words as early as *Dubliners,* and Gordon says that the *Dubliners* stories are dialogues divided between their protagonists and distanced narrators.[17]

In putting a relation between voices rather than a single voice at the center of his fictional discourse, Joyce follows the principles of Bruno, who insisted that every unity was made up of opposites. "Poor Aristotle," says one of the speakers in *Cause, Principle and Unity,*

> He failed to arrive because he halted at the genus of opposition and remained shackled by it; he thus did not go down to the species of contrariety, did not break through and set his eyes on the goal. Instead, he strayed wholly from the way by stating that contraries cannot actually come together in the same subject.[18]

Stephen presents a similar criticism when he says that Aristotle's whole system rests on the idea, presented in the *Metaphysics* (1005b), "that the same attribute cannot at the same time and in the same connection belong to and not belong to the same subject" (*P* 208). Joyce moved away from this position toward a Brunonian recognition that only by its opposite could any quality be constituted.

The failure to realize that what is usually speaking in the mature Joyce is not a voice, but a combination of voices, a polyphonic discourse, helps to explain the difficulties many critics have had in trying to define Joyce's narrative methods. It means that the center of consciousness at any point is not an intelligence in the ordinary sense, but a space between intelligences. This space, however, is not empty. It is as full as a chord, filled with the relationship between the beings that surround it. And these beings are not mere fragments: they are parts of a whole, shaped by their connections with other parts to make up the total entelechy of Joyce's mind.

It is not necessary to abandon the idea of unity at the center of Joyce's work, but only to recognize a Brunonian unity made up of conflicting parts. The presence of multiple causal agents does not overthrow Aristotelian causality, but complicates it. If consciousness is divided in the work and truth is a balance of differing forces, nevertheless, the multiple elements are so organized as to show forth the unity of Joyce behind them. Neither the Scholastics nor Bruno doubted the unity of God, but that unity was recognized as beyond human perception. Even in the *Paradiso,* Dante gets to see only symbols of God. Similarly, Joyce does not seem to have doubted his own unity, but he recognized that the totality of Joyce could be manifested only in parts — in both his imaginary and supposedly real worlds.

The concept of the mind as a relation among parts has been developed by psychoanalysis because it is dynamic. Even the body has to be seen as made up of parts in order to recognize its movements and changes. Joyce's will is therefore manifested most precisely through the interaction of parts. This will is a force that works through the time of narration to dictate changes of level, point of view, style, or language, and shifts in the balance of combination of Joycean parts from one section or word or moment to the next. And all of these changes, all of these levels, and all of this personal involvement were necessary for the accurate representation of the only thing Joyce could represent, a phenomenon with two aspects — the world that he saw through his mind's complexity, which was also the mind that he saw through the complexity of the world.

Authorial Action

Joyce aimed to add to the reality of his cosmos by generating its causes of change and its ends or purposes. He was ill-suited to pretend he did not exist. Moreover, the idea of the mind as the cause of motion for the universe, as expressed in the twelfth or lambda book of the *Metaphysics,* would lead Joyce to see the need for a mind behind the efficient and final causes. And so he would be obliged to yoke his mind to his work in order to operate causality.

Aristotle, in proudly expanding human consciousness by delineating his last two causes, was constructing the idea of God. His system is the backbone of the immense definition of God drawn up by Aquinas sixteen hundred years later. In shaping God, Aristotle assumed His identity as first maker of the First Maker. In the traditional novel, the efficient and final causes, the active functions of God, are operated by the silent literary deity of convention. Anyone who follows rules without knowing why is following an unknown god, but this is how we spend most of our time, as Joyce knew:

> When we are living a normal life we are living a conventional one, following a pattern which has been laid out by other people in another generation, an objective pattern imposed on us by the church and state. But a writer must maintain a continual struggle against the objective: that is his function.[19]

In the conventional novel, decisions about appropriate style, turns of plot, and denouement are dictated largely by traditions within which ancient religious principles are buried. Insofar as a novelist chooses to intrude his personality on his work by violating narrative conventions, he takes upon himself the role of creator in a universe made in the image of his soul. The Joycean artist does this as much as possible. And by constituting himself in opposition to the most easily grasped reality, he commits himself to inevitable divarication.

According to Aristotle, whatever an author creates must have the same composition as his mind:

> Things generated by art are those whose form is in the soul. By "form" I mean the essence of each thing and the first *substance,* for even contraries have in some sense the same form . . . (1032b)

The primary substances or inner forms of the artist and his characters are the same; and opposites share their essence because they are based on what they oppose. Even an antithetical figure such as Blazes Boylan has the form of Joyce's mind because he is an anti-Joyce conceived by Joyce. Stephen says a man of genius makes "his own image . . . the standard of all experience" (*U* 195).

Aristotle says that being requires identity because it "signifies whatness and a *this*" (1028b). It follows that the being of what the artist creates has his identity, that the mind of the book is his mind. Nothing exists in his world but the marks made by the conscious or unconscious action of his mind; and even external source materials are transformed by passing through his mind to become part of that world. Joyce is related to his created figures as an unattainable cause prior and subsequent to what they are able to perceive. As Gordon indicates, however, this does not stop Joyce from making his characters refer to him continually.

Aristotle says that if change moves through contraries, there must be something underlying to connect them (1069b). Thus, if an element of Joyce becomes an element of his fiction, they must have substance in common. Aristotle defines substance as the cause of being or ultimate substratum (1017b). The idea of a substratum would also suggest subjectivity for Aristotle, whose word for subject, *hypokeimenon,* literally means "underlying."[20] The common substance between artist and art, as I have indicated, suggests primal matter, the intermediate between spirit and matter. Bruno calls primal matter the "substratum from which all things and beings arise and into which they return."[21] As God conveys primal matter into form, Joyce conveys his undifferentiated primal thinking into his work insofar as the forms he creates enact the potential in his soul. This substance, shared by the author and his creation, is enclosed by the form of his personality in the extra-Joycean world; but it is formless in the world formed by his mind.

With relation to immaterial objects, Aristotle says that thought and the object of thought are not different (1075a); and this presumably applies to Joyce's imaginary creations. When thought shares the nature of its object, it becomes that object and thinks of itself, and this unity of thought and object is the permanent state of God. Insofar as man's thoughts succeed in satisfying him he temporarily approaches the divine state. For this reason, "being awake, sensing, and thinking are most pleasant, and hopes and memories" (1072b). This fully waking or mentally active state cannot be maintained, but it can be preserved and concentrated by art. From this perspective, the work of art is excellent insofar as it contains the soul of the artist completely. This explains why Joyce felt that the goal of art was, without losing sight of the external world, to be as subjective as possible—and why his career progresses through a steady multiplication of the parts of his mind.

Aristotle held that all motivation had to start with a prime mover. Trying to define an entity that moved others without being moved, he observed that the objects of desire and thought work in this way, so he described God as the object of all desire and thought (1072a). This perception remains true psychologically in that people constantly want and think about what they cannot reach. As Aquinas says, the idea of God is so close to the idea of the best that it is hard to reject one without the other (Q. 1, A. 2). In this sense, the image of satisfied desire is the purest image of God man can see. But the ultimate object of desire and thought for Joyce's creatures has to be Joyce himself, for God enters the works only insofar as Joyce conceives and embodies (or enminds) Him.

What Aristotle said about the location of the prime mover, or movers, was wrong because at this point he depended on contemporary astronomy rather than his own logic (1073b–1074a). But the prime mover remains an inalienable goal of human thought, whether one locates it externally or internally. Many writers popularly supposed to have passed beyond the prime mover, such as Nietzsche and Beckett, are intensely obsessed with it, as their projections of themselves as gods in *Thus Spake Zarathustra* and *The Unnamable* indicate. As Jung recognized, the concept of God is the main tool of human creation because no one could go beyond what is already known unless he aimed at such a transcendent goal.

It may seem that Joyce dismantled the agency of the first cause as he multiplied epistemological difficulties in his late work, where sources of truth conflict, personality is divided, and words grow more inscrutable as they are examined. But these disjunctions serve a unified creative principle. They are tools Joyce uses to extend the reality of his world by giving it the accidental density of life. Insofar as he succeeds in creating the impression of a conflict between different systems or minds framing the work, he frees the work from the authority of a single author, expanding its being into multiple dimensions.

One paradox of this situation is that it is precisely by the disjunction of the writing, by the loss of a particular viewpoint or language, that the work becomes most Joycean. The straightforward initial style used at the start of *Ulysses,* as Kenner points out, resembles that of a standard Edwardian novel.[22] But the later episodes, with their stylistic transformations and multiple levels of discourse, are unlike anything written previously. No one before Joyce had expressed such a plural consciousness or taken such a multiphonic point of view. The sudden jumps from one style to another and the discordances felt in simultaneous opposed meanings are the truest expressions of Joycean individuality. The voice Joyce labors to articulate speaks from beyond the world as it speaks from outside organized thought. Lacan sees subjectivity as defined by disjunction. He says that when the subject is expressed, "the place of the 'inter-said' . . . is the very place in which the transparency of the classical subject is divided. . . ."[23]

4 Consubstantiality

"A being again in becomings again"

Recognition of Joyce's immanence in his work clarifies his narrative method and lights up formerly invisible elements. This chapter and the following one will consider how Joyce's presence in *Ulysses* is described and manifested. Understanding of this presence, however, not only illuminates details. It alters the nature of Joyce's work for us by showing that it is conceived as containing a soul and therefore may be entitled to be regarded as a living being.

The interface of the double-aspect text resides in the area where the mechanical figures in the text meld with the psychic being that generates them. If we observe with an oscilloscope the activity in the area around the interface between Joyce and his work as his career proceeds, we will find that the area grows wider and more active. As Joyce moves from the early naturalism to the late symbolism, he becomes more personally involved in his work, and more turned into it. Joyce is present in his works not as a clearly formulated obituary, but as a changing mind in progress, swelling to fill a growing creation.

The dynamism of Joyce's deity conflicts with the traditional definition of the First Cause as immovable and inseparable. As Gose points out, Joyce explained his relation to the First Cause when he told Mercanton that he labored "as the Demiurge goes about the business of creation."[1] When Stephen, in "Proteus," remarks that the solidity of the world he occupies is "made by the mallet of Los Demiurgos" (*U* 37), he is referring to Blake's blacksmith Los, a symbol of human creativity. Stephen continually refers to — or oscillates with — Joyce, the demiurge who is making him.

Joyce was aware of two versions of the demiurge. The original one, who acted as a creative extension of God in Plato's *Timaeus* by constructing the universe, was turned into a negative figure by the Gnostics, who hated the world. The Gnostic demiurge is an antithetical parody of God, and makes a universe of evil.² In his more ironic moments, Joyce, who portrays Shem as "a gnawstick," may have thought of himself as such a misguided, demonic creature; but it is unlikely that he continued for long at a time to think of himself and his world as essentially evil. The primary role of the demiurge is that of a cosmic artificer, and Joyce as a demiurge gave his works whatever positive being they have insofar as he embodied the constructive power of God.

The definition of the demiurge that Joyce was probably most familiar with was Bruno's, which, as McIntyre explains it, goes back to Plato:

> The *efficient cause* of the natural world is the universal intelligence, "the first and principal faculty of the soul of the world." This *intellectus universalis* is to natural things as our intellect to the thoughts of our mind, and Bruno identifies it with the Demiurge. . . , for it impregnates matter with all "forms": it is an *artefice interno* [Italian, internal artificer], for it works from within in giving form and figure to matter, as the seed or root from within sends forth the stem. . . .³

Here the universal mind and efficient cause of nature acts toward the world as the artist does toward his creation, as the generator of forms. If natural objects are his thoughts, then he resembles Aristotle's prime mover. While he is not God, he is the main agency of the part of God mortals can perceive, and so God reaches His world through him.

Etienne Gilson defends the unity of the First Principle by arguing that if identity is reality, then being cannot be subject to change.⁴ Joyce, however, was influenced by Blake's belief that it was unsound to define or stabilize a deity beyond human conception. He included in a sermon in *Portrait* a powerful demonstration that the mind cannot conceive of eternity (*P* 131–132). He must therefore have known that being can be perceived only in the act of becoming, just as life can be seen only in changing parts. Yet he did not want to deny his creatures the possibility of partaking of being.

Joyce provides being for his becomings both in the changeless, inconceivable form Gilson describes and in the dynamic form Joyce found more controllable. He provides his characters with unified form insofar as he is felt from within the work as the being who has died to give them life; but he also arranges, by a more complex procedure, to live within his work as seen from outside. Moreover, it is his living form that makes his dead form meaningful. His absence is felt best through his presence and by his presence, and this active awareness of the lost Joyce generates the completeness of his reality.

The concepts of being and identity Joyce believed in were accessible to human perceptions. He realized that pure being and identical identity were unknowable, for identical things did not exist in nature. Science was beginning to suspect in Joyce's day that no two atoms either are or remain the same, and Joyce suggests this by having Bloom think of blood cells as universes (*U* 699). The convention of simple identity was far from Joyce's conception of the mind, which he saw as a shifting interaction rather than a monad.

When Stephen speaks of "the first entelechy, the structural rhythm" (*U* 432), he equates the most elementary conceivable form of God or the mind with Joyce's definition of rhythm, a relation between parts. From the 1904 essay "A Portrait of the Artist" on, Joyce intended to portray his personality as a state of flux, a series of parts of an assemblage that could never be total at once: ". . . a fluid succession of presents, the development of an entity of which our present is a phase only . . . a portrait is not an identificative paper but rather the curve of an emotion" (*P* 257–258). What is portrayed cannot be represented in static form. The curve image implies that any point in life has to be defined as a movement between two coordinates. Moreover, any discrete definition of personality must always be a part of something larger.

In the Aristotle notes, Joyce said that sculpture contained movement because of its rhythm, and he intended to instill his works with inner movement as Aristotle's first cause conveys internal principles of motion to nature. This internal principle, as substance, may be linked to the *prima materia*, intermediate between God and the world, and it may be compared to the will that creates Joyce's creatures.

Joyce complained to Mercanton that as a demiurge he had to obey laws he did not choose. But his activity as a dynamic prime mover is one indication that he struggled to repeal some of those ancient laws. In 1937, in a less modest mood, and probably later than the "Demiurge" statement, Joyce said of the *Wake* to Mercanton, ". . . I am making it out of nothing."[5]

Instead of opposing unity to dynamism, Joyce saw unity as composed of movement. The Paris Notebook of 1903 says, "Parts constitute a whole as far as they have a common end."[6] They are united by shared dynamism. The unity of Joyce's god-in-progress works through inner principles of expansion instead of being imposed from without by restriction, because unity has no value without life. To unify something by exclusion is to cut off part of it. Unity can exist positively only by a sharing of qualities among different things. This is why Bruno said that ten is a greater unity than one.[7]

From this perspective, God is unified by the uni-verse he creates, the mind is unified by the body it moves, and the immanent Joyce achieves "uni-fication" by his works,[8] which are remarkable for being tightly bound together by the inherence of Joyce's personality in them even though no two works of Joyce resemble each other in form or manner. Just as the canon of Joyce gains magnitude by its variety, so the human mind is alive insofar as it is moved by conflicting desires; and God is real for us insofar as he conflicts with His own infinity by being incarnated in finite form.

One consequence of the unity of parts is that each part is incomplete and bound to the others in dependency, the normative state we spend our lives denying. Joyce's effort to achieve independence by enlarging the unity of his work began with volumes of isolated lyrics and stories, and the apparently shapeless *Stephen Hero*. In his next phase, from about 1908 to about 1918, Joyce imposed the strict bindings of autobiography and the Aristotelian unities of drama. This produced two works, *Portrait* and *Exiles*, that are excessively unified in formal terms, but not successfully unified, because they are not complete. *Portrait* and *Exiles* are not held together by inner forces because Stephen is satirized, and Richard idealized, so that Stephen's need to be Joyce and Joyce's need to be Richard stick out with nothing to balance them. Here Joyce is not communicating with himself.

In order to make his work complete, Joyce had to make it contain its conflicts by locating himself in a divided position between his characters. In doing this, he accepted the world he created, and subjected his mind to it. Once his mind had conquered this world by being conquered, his old limits dropped away and his works gained independence. They were now powered by oppositions between forces within themselves.

Once Joyce had constituted the complex creative core of opposition at the center of his cosmos, it began to assimilate all elements of his works. The earlier works were retroactively fused into the single work which is the canon. Thus *Ulysses* contains not only characters from *Dubliners*, but something very like the author of *Dubliners*, as Stephen's story "A Pisgah Sight of Palestine or the Parable of the Plums" (*U* 145–149) suggests. The earlier book thus becomes an extension of the later. And in *Portrait* Stephen was the kind of youth who wrote *Chamber Music*. The

Wake refers to the earlier works so often that they become elements of its mythology. *Exiles* is not referred to much in other works, but it is the silent center of the canon as the work in which Joyce learned to divide himself and accept his world. The differences among all of Joyce's works make their unity especially strong because each work fills a different role in the entire organism.

The generative core of this expanding being is not only composed by Joyce, but composed of Joyce. His greatest work grows out of his certainty that he would live in it, and the thoughts and feelings of Joyce should not be amputated from the flesh of characterization in *Ulysses* or the metabolism of transformation in the *Wake*. Distinctions between Joyce, the text, the characters, and the reader, considerable though they may be, should be handled with caution to avoid underestimating Joyce's art. For his effort was to make use of such differences, seeing through them to incorporate them productively among the apparent disunities of his mind and style. Riquelme recognizes the scope of the unity Joyce aims at: "It would seem excessive to claim an absolute identification of teller with character and of character with reader for any literary text. But Joyce's texts tend toward excess. . . ."[9] The ideal Joyce pursued was a consubstantiality of his mind, the minds of his characters, and our minds that would include both knowledge and doubt; and it is on such a basis that interpretation lives, when the reader sees either meaning or obscurity in the text generated by Joyce's mind. No other writer used obscurity as successfully as Joyce, and he used it so that it promises that answers can be found by careful effort. He achieves this effect of "seek and you shall find" by playing off multiple levels of meaning against each other to give the text subterranean depth.

Artefice Interno

The discovery of meaning or its possibility in the text is generally a discovery of part of Joyce's mind. When we are carried from one track of that mind to another, we may become aware of its scope as a principle that includes more than one consciousness. For this reason, Joyce is manifested as a superhuman force every time the text, in Karen Lawrence's phrase, violates a narrative contract. Every change in context, every new style, every surprising word and every external reference is an intervention from outside the established world of the text, an action that has no cause in that world and so must derive from a source prior to that world, a miracle. These causal manifestations of Joyce tend to be concentrated in passages that deal with birth, death, art, and sex —transcendent experiences that take the text to the margin between the world of Bloomsday and its other world, the Joycean mental world within or behind or beyond or above it.

These marginal experiences evoke the souls of the characters or the depths of their minds, and Joyce has to manifest himself in the text in order to reveal such inner levels. After all, many emotional elements that psychoanalysis sees as coming from within are seen by religion as coming from above or beyond; and the demiurge is an internal principle that represents an active force beyond the world. Theories in themselves cannot serve to create the spiritual or unconscious lives of the characters, for theories merely restrict being by containing it within principles. Joyce's characters can live only insofar as he animates them or transmits his soul into them. To give them being, he must assert the force of his creative will in violation of whatever framework of ideas exists at the moment of creation. Therefore, this creative force must come from the unconscious, from a level beyond ideas.

Joyce maintained that his work expressed elements of his mind that he was not aware of:

> Though people may read more into *Ulysses* than I ever intended, who is to say that they are wrong: do any of us know what we are creating? . . . After all, the original genius of a man lies in his scribblings: in his casual action lies his basic talent. . . . Which of us can control our scribblings? They are the script of one's personality like your voice or your walk.[10]

Joyce did not see the distinction between his intention and his work as a justification for severing his mind from it, for he recognized that they remained connected on deep levels. Whatever observations can be derived from his work, insofar as they correspond to that work, express the structure of his mind. His mentality grows into the work not as any particular desire, but as a general will that includes many particular desires in its organization. This general will breathes life into Joyce's souls, and the dispensation of souls is one of his central aims. Stephen says that the artist strives to perceive the whatness of the esthetic object, and the essential whatness of a living thing is Aristotle's primary definition of the soul (*De anima,* 412b).

A brief example of a marginal experience that reveals the soul of a character by passing near the border of his existence occurs when Bloom remembers how he and Molly conceived his lost son, Rudy:

> Must have been that morning in Raymond terrace she was at the window, watching the two dogs at it by the wall of the cease to do evil. (*U* 89)

The reader is lifted out of the story by the last four words and obliged to think about where they come from. He may determine by research that a building across from the Blooms' had "Cease to do evil . . ." written on it.[11] In doing so, he refers to a connection in Joyce's mind. The sudden turn of the language toward the unknown is more realistic than a conventional phrase would be for several reasons. In the naturalistic sense, it is realistic as a particular association in Bloom's mind based on a physical fact of his world. On the subconscious level, it gives Bloom depth by capturing a nuance or undertone of his mind that he could not explain, a sense underlying his sudden transition—that the generation of life is an escape from corruption. Because this transition cannot be conceived by Bloom's conscious mind, it requires intervention from another level. This realism in depth is realism in the Scholastic sense of closeness to the Creator. Like the realities of psychoanalysis, it depends on contact with fundamental causes.

Joyce expands the soul of his character here by adding a voice out of the imaginative depth of his mind. He specializes in expressing for his creatures the parts of their minds that they are not cognizant of, the parts Augustine defined as God. In Joyce, these parts contain not only a highly developed version of the Freudian unconscious, but a Joycean unconscious that includes elements of Joycean myth that the characters express without being aware of them. "A character in *Ulysses*," Kenner says, "is an interference phenomenon between 'his' language and language not his, sometimes other characters', sometimes the author's";[12] and the language of the others reaches the character through the author.

When characters refer without knowing it to each other, to Homer, to Shakespeare, to Joyce, or to the structure of the work, they express Joyce as well as themselves. The overlapping of author and characters is sometimes so pervasive that the characters seem to be extensions of the author. Their existential umbilici play active roles in transmitting being from Joyce to them. Above "Wandering Rocks" in the Linati schema, Joyce wrote, "*Finito Antiali-Ombelico.*" This means that the first nine episodes built up the umbilicus and the opposing wings (*antiali*), presumably those of Stephen and Bloom.

The *omphalos* is Joyce's idea at the same time that it is Stephen's, and common substance between Joyce and his character appears whenever Bloom thinks of seafaring, wind, temptation, food, and other symbolic images—and when the rhythm of his thought imitates such symbolic patterns as incubism, peristalsis, musical development, and detumescence in various episodes. Joyce used his techniques to add spiritual substrata without which his characters would lack the mythical resonance of immortal beings. Joyce's novels all concentrate explicitly on creating immortal beings, souls to animate his creatures, and such an aim can be accomplished only by great investments of being and meaning.

Some of the central processes in Joyce's work operate through the implantation of the unknown content of his mind into the indwelling essence of a character's life so as to communicate with the soul of the reader, without any awareness of what that essence consists of on the part of the three participants. A major example in *Ulysses* is the love that binds together Bloom, Stephen, and Molly. Facts about this love may be cited and insights may be gleaned, but we cannot determine what this love actually consists of, essential though it is to the book. And similar statements could be made about any of the dense symbols of the book, such as the apparition of Rudy Bloom in Nighttown. Every moment of the entire narrative built around these symbols has an unclear component, as life does and well-made fiction does not.

This unclear aspect is not peripheral: it is the heart of Joyce's aim. It is why all of the central issues of human relations and metaphysics in Joyce's works are developed with such careful balance that they are insoluble. All of the novels are designed to lead to conclusions of maximum uncertainty on their last pages. Stephen is going to encounter truth and to avoid it; Molly expresses love and infidelity; and ALP is dying and being reborn. The divisions in these endings are lyrical because they express the generative depths of their creator.

The most important truths are ungraspable in Joyce's work because if the main characters, their situations, and their relations were reduced to clear statements, they would lose the potential functions of their lives. If personality is a flow, the characters have a right not to be fixed. The final balance among possibilities that the books all end with is the pure revelation of Joyce's being, freed from the imposition of ideas by the perfect harmony of his union with his creation. As an overdetermined, indefinable essence outside patterned thought, that being corresponds to the formless matter that in religious tradition gave birth to the world. In fact, it is designed to give birth to a mental world—and it has done so.

Life in Print

When a writer introduces uncertainty, he thrusts something of himself into his work as an unresolved conflict, an opposition between voices. In fact, no writer can give his work life without hinging that life on his own uncertainty. For it is when we are uncertain about an object of perception that we recognize its life. This pattern is illustrated in "Sirens" when Bloom first hears the singing of Simon Dedalus that will have such a powerful effect on him in succeeding pages: "Through the hush of air a voice sang to them, low, not rain, not leaves in murmur, like no voice of strings or reeds or whatdoyoucallthem dulcimers, touching their still ears with words, still hearts of their each his remembered lives" (*U* 273–274). Bloom's uncertainty about the voice, illustrated by his rapid series of six interpretations of what it sounds like, shows that it reaches him on a deep level, a level capable of calling forth multiple responses.

Joyce's avoidance of stable formulations is crucial to his success as a writer because it allows for the constant development of new interpretations without which his works would ossify into antiques. And this use of obscurity is no mere modern foible. Kermode says of St. Mark, the oldest Gospel, that its power depends upon its multiple obscurities: ". . . mystery, what cannot be reduced to other and more intelligible forms . . . that is what we find here: something irreducible, therefore perpetually to be interpreted; not secrets to be found out one by one, but Secrecy."[13] As Augustine indicated, multivalent language is essential to the ability of Scripture to perpetuate itself. Such language is produced by a divided mind, and Christ was at least technically divided by his dual nature as the evangelists were by the transformation they lived through. Joyce also abandoned the world he grew up in, in order to make a new one.

Of course, the use of uncertainty may easily lead to esthetic problems in a writer whose deity is not adequate to handle it. The writer must have the authority to develop simultaneous, opposing aspects of his personality, giving them the freedom they need to interact productively. If each is given his own independent world of values, as Stephen and Bloom are, they may constitute a self-perpetuating dialectic whose differences will be virtually inexhaustible. The center of this creative principle disposes itself in the space between the two figures in Joyce's mind.

Because this space is shared by both figures, it is freed from clear definition by either. The best model for the creative process involved here is D. W. Winnicott's theory of shared space between mother and child. Within this space, the child need not worry about the distinction between what is himself and what is not himself (the reality principle), and so he is free to expand his primary-process thinking (dream). Winnicott says that such generative space is always involved in creative thinking.[14] In Joyce, its most particular location is at the heart of each word, where it activates the various meanings involved. This creative space within the text is designed to generate meaning perpetually.

There are images and patterns potentially present in Joyce's work that are not now demonstrably present and have never existed in the sense of being conscious, but will exist when they are discovered. Instead of being unusual, such nascent patterns pervade many areas of current study. A psychoanalytic critic may see the forces of obsession operating in Joyce's work, a structuralist may see *bricolage,* a phenomenologist may see a "gaze of petrifaction," and a deconstructive critic may see sliding signifiers.[15] And a reader-response critic will see in Joyce's work the minds of his readers.

All of these approaches are likely to discover points that did not occur to Joyce, but all of these points will be related to each other by Joyce. For example, the order of principles that Joyce believed in gave him a support that allowed him to open himself to the structural method of free improvisation known as *bricolage.* In this respect he was parallel to the natives studied by Lévi-Strauss whose basic faith allowed them to originate *bricolage.* Moreover, Joyce's existence, like that of God, is manifested through the interpretations of a group of believers who take sustenance from his texts. Even systems he could not have access to (except by influencing them) can be inspired by the breadth of his vision.

Nor is it probable that Joyce was cognizant of all of the more-than-a-hundred synchronicities in *Ulysses*. Jung uses this term for meaningful coincidences or psychic phenomena which, by going beyond cause and effect, indicate a principle of psychic causality in life.[16] Many examples of this pattern remain to be discovered, but many have been noticed by critics. When Stephen says, "Return, return, Clan Milly" (*U* 393), using the name of Bloom's straying daughter, of whom he has not heard, or when Bloom thinks, "*Hamlet, I am thy father's spirit*" (*U* 152), they refer to each other without knowing it, prefiguring their communion. Synchronicities are also constituted by references to systems outside the naturalistic world of the book, such as the *Odyssey,* Shakespeare, and Joyce's life. Insofar as these references have no actual cause in that world, they are generated by a mental structure inherent in the book, the book's entelechy.

While Joyce could not have been conscious of all of the constellations of verbal configuration that extend across the firmament of his work, he did not deny his connection with their possibilities: he believed that they would express him, for he regarded the potential aspect of his work as primary. Referring to the author's survival in his work and to his future as his own creator, Stephen points out in "Scylla and Charybdis" that the artist transmits into his creation ideas that cannot be known until later:

> In the intense instant of imagination . . . that which I was is that which I am and that which in possibility I may come to be. So in the future, the sister of the past, I may see myself as I sit here now but by reflection from that which then I shall be. (*U* 194)

Stephen is certain that he will become his own creator in the sense that what he is will not be clear until he looks back on it. He would like to become Joyce and write *Ulysses*, but he doesn't know what Joyce or *Ulysses* are. These ideals are potential in him, but they are beyond his conscious mind, in the realm of destiny. They are also partly outside the text, and by referring to them Joyce makes this passage indicate the inevitability of Stephen's becoming Joyce and creating himself beyond his imagination. The passage reveals an enormous potential in Stephen that he has only an intuition of. Moreover, Stephen says that the mind the artist projects in his work contains truths that can be revealed only in time. Joyce implies here through Stephen that theories about his work that go beyond his conscious intention may still express ideas that come from his soul.

The new images and patterns that will appear in Joyce's self-supplementing work will be born out of the life of his mind that goes on living in the text. The substance of this life is a mental primal matter created by overdetermination. The causes behind this substance are so many and so inscrutable that they cannot be clearly defined. Thus, this substance does not have specific form, and so it resembles Freud's primary-process thought, the infantile mental formlessness out of which all ideas are generated. To ignore the life of Joyce's work is to kill its Joycepossibled soul by a failure to have intercourse.

Joyce saw life in Scholastic terms as incomplete without a goal or a potential for change. Jung says that symbols are energy-generating devices because they give us goals beyond fixed reality to aim at.[17] Joyce inserted his mind into *Ulysses* in the indeterminate form of symbols charged with his own uncertainties, and these symbols energize the lives of his characters. Joyce informs the unconscious of his creatures with image clusters that configure his own essence.

Stephen Dedalus is described by Suzette Henke in existential terms as constantly recreating his identity moment by moment in *Ulysses*,[18] and he feels that art should recreate the artist over and over. It does so in a book that changes technique and style often. Narrators in *Ulysses* take different sexes and temperaments, and they increase and decrease such factors as size, age, and person. Moreover, they are often inanimate, a pattern that first becomes evident in the tramlines and headlines of "Aeolus": "Right and left parallel clanging ringing a doubledecker and a singledeck moved from their railheads, swerved to the down line, glided parallel" (*U* 116). The voices of things, expressions of the demiurge, speak at frequent intervals from here to "Ithaca," adding supernatural variations to the changes in the Joycean narrator. Just as the cells or units of our lives are constantly dying and being reborn, "their molecules shuttled to and fro, so does the artist weave and unweave his image" (*U* 194). The movement of molecules, like the similar unconscious movement of trams, suggests the Brownian movement of primal matter below the forms of consciousness. As Gose suggests, the artist lives in his work in the process of constant transformation.

Stephen says that the substance of the author passes into his work when he says that Shakespeare survives as a spirit in *Hamlet:* "a voice heard only in the heart of him who is the substance of his shadow, the son consubstantial with the father" (*U* 197). Robert Kellogg says that Stephen's theories here imply that Stephen and Joyce are consubstantial.[19] The Joycean protagonist is son by analogy with Christ as the Word of the Father. He parallels Christ's dual nature, divine and human, by being consubstantial with Joyce in spirit and with the other characters in imaginary matter.[20]

Stephen is closer to Joyce than a son, as Christ is closer to God, for two reasons. The first is that he follows Joyce's biography. This is especially pronounced in Stephen's case, though all of Joyce's main characters follow his biography to some extent by sharing his thoughts. The second reason is that Stephen is likely to have less chance than an actual son to resist Joyce and develop his own proclivities. Perhaps it is his bond to Joyce that makes Stephen see the mystery of fatherhood as the central power of the universe (*U* 207).

According to Stephen's model of consubstantiality, the voice in which the artist speaks to his son can be heard only by Stephen. Moreover, as I will show, the term "son" here refers not only to the protagonist, but to the work; and the series of voices through which the artist speaks to *Ulysses* can be heard only by the book. We outsiders, being on a lower level in the Joycean universe, can hear only variations on the original choir. In this sense, Joyce's consubstantiality is ideal rather than actual, but it nevertheless motivates Joyce's creation. Divergence from the ideal is a common religious problem, and the Creator has to appear to us in imperfect form.

The Wounded God

Whether or not there is a First Cause in the real world, one certainly exists in frequent manifestations for the creatures who inhabit Joyce's fiction. If this god cannot manifest himself clearly in the forms of happiness, purpose, and truth, it must be because he is faulty. As he manifests himself to us, a wound is built into him, the stigma of the artist, caused by his cause: "And as the mole on my right breast is where it was when I was born, though all my body has been woven of new stuff time after time, so through the ghost of the unquiet father the image of the unliving son looks forth" (*U* 194). As a father's flaw appears in his son, so an artist's is reflected in his work. The "mole of nature" Hamlet originally spoke of (I.iv.23 ff.), a vice for which one is not guilty by one's own act, is associated with the tragic flaw. In Joyce, it may not be more serious than the peculiarity of an individual identity, but Stephen's lecture makes it clear that this flaw is essentially neurotic, a spot of bitter alienation. It is the part of the author that is too weak, too bound to convention, to give itself to the creation.

If Stephen judges from the plays that Shakespeare never freed himself from this "note of banishment," the young Joyce seemed inclined to pass a similar judgment on "God and his theatre." Stephen criticizes God as a playwright by observing that He created light before the sun (*U* 213). According to judgment of this sort, neither Shakespeare, God, nor Joyce seems to be able to believe in the perfection of life sufficiently to sustain on his earth the communion of the family trio at the center of his work.

One use Joyce makes of the unwieldy role of deity is to criticize what is sacrosanct. He suggests that men continue to believe God perfect despite evidence — which Joyce acts out with emphasis — that He is either following rules He cannot control or neurotically alienated. The figure of the guilty, flawed god is developed extensively in the *Wake* through the portrayal of HCE. Joyce's constant preoccupation with this image begins with the first two stories in *Dubliners*. The first portrays a paralyzed priest, and the second presents two boys on a quest for "the Pigeon

House." In Joyce's Dublin, instead of the home of the Holy Ghost, they find a sadist. One of Joyce's persistent themes is "There but for the grace of man goes God."

The human side of Joyce's conception of the artist-god is the analogy of parenthood. Parents and writers struggle to give life to their creations by being aware of them and responding to their needs. But the artist is more limited than the parent (as God is) by the tendency of his figures to have no life but what he gives them. He may father them too strongly, pushing forward his own ideas to make them rigid, or he may mother them too softly and so inflate them to vagueness. The effort of sensitive attention by which he delineates them drains away his own life. When he pays attention to himself instead of them, however, he violates the contact with them that gives them the freedom to grow, and transmits to them his own neurosis (the ghost of the unquiet father), the inherited or dead part of birth, the conventional part of writing (the unliving son).

Like God or a parent, the artist needs to be able to see the shape of the future in the past to know what he is doing. He must match the shape of his thought to that of his creature so that the interface or overlap between them is smooth and conflict-free. This is the kind of relation Winnicott describes when he speaks of the zone of free play between mother and child: it allows the created being to expand and release the material of primary-process thought without losing contact.

If the creator's vision is too limited by his flaws to allow him to see truly, if he subjects his world to convention or abstraction, this does not mean he is not responsible. He is more responsible than he can realize, for the harmful contact will remain imprinted on his world. Therefore the artist must struggle to see the mole of personality that ties together the past and the future, the hidden part of the soul that shapes what will be created.

Future possibilities not only come from present and past, but also transform present and past, which are empty unless they have an aim. The meaning of the present cannot be understood until it is looked back on from the future, so a writer must avail himself of divine knowledge. And a character can understand his problem, his unliving aspect, only insofar as his author gives him insight: "But those who are done to death in sleep cannot know the manner of their quell unless their Creator endow their souls with that knowledge in the life to come" (*U* 196–197). Shakespeare had to be the ghost in *Hamlet*, whether or not he formalized the role, in order to give the play meaning. He is the being whose destruction generates the imaginary world, and none of his creatures can escape his spirit.

Reconstruction

The roles Joyce plays in *Ulysses* are connected to each other in functional ways in a relationship that may be called familial. Though Lacan says that fatherhood can only be a name,[21] Joyce defines a relation between Stephen and Bloom that is more real than this. Bloom is not Stephen's father in name, and the connection between them operates outside of any clear or official definition. The mystery of its psychic reality must be defined in stages.

Stephen's phrases "unquiet father" and "unliving son," like many things he says about his cuckold Shakespeare, refer to Bloom. And Stephen's discussion of the connection between past, present, and future, like many of his ideas, is balanced by Bloom's expression of the opposite notion elsewhere: "But tomorrow is a new day will be. Past was is today. What now is will then tomorrow as now was be past yester" (*U* 515). Bloom does not want to carry the past into the future: he slips more easily through a temporary acceptance of inconstancy. The ideas of Stephen and Bloom on such subjects as paternity, ontology, and mutability are designed to interact with each other, constrained by Aristotle's idea of unity even when they do not match.

The mental lives of Stephen and Bloom arch toward each other like flying buttresses on the cathedral of *Ulysses*—an edifice that changed form as it was being built and has many gargoyles and empty niches. In the obscure central nave is suspended the totality of Joyce constituted by the combination of their two extremes, the sides of his mind that could never be reconciled. The extremes in the passages contrasted above, for example, are youthful idealism and middle-aged accommodation, the worship of ideas and the worship of matter, both present in the author.

The action of *Ulysses* is the confrontation between these two sides of his mind that resulted in the generation of the mature Joyce. Its causes come from outside the realistic world in which it is set, and so it is thoroughly coincidental. In the Linati schema, Joyce refers to the technique of "Ithaca" as "fusion," and the joining of Stephen and Bloom, which visually constitutes Shakespeare in Nighttown, must be said to constitute Joyce. This joining may have been influenced by the Jew who may have rescued Joyce, but his Stephen side had to be brought in contact with his Bloom side before he could write the book. In view of this, the Eucharist of hot cocoa that Bloom and Stephen share must be seen as the substance of Joyce in *Ulysses*. Christ said he would be present whenever two or three people got together in his name (Matt. 18: 20), and by their communion the two protagonists generate their own first cause. Their union in his name is what creates them.

The spiritual potential generated by Stephen and Bloom cannot be physically manifested in their world precisely because it is numinous. As a transcendent principle, Joyce cannot appear directly in the work he makes continuously; like God, he can be manifested only by signs. Stephen and Bloom drift apart with so little apparent interchange that it is easy to see irony as the main motive for their juxtaposition. But irony is not an active enough motive for such vital figures or for the resonance with which they collide.

Joyce creates Stephen and Bloom and juxtaposes them in order to express his mind fully. Only by representing the parts of his mind as living beings, by drama, can he make the interacting impulses capable of qualitative changes and complex reactions. A feeling like anger has its own personality. It is falsified by being denied its full range of personal connections. This is why a person is made up of people. Joyce wrote to Linati in 1920 (in Italian) that each episode of *Ulysses* was "one person although it is composed of persons—as Aquinas relates of the heavenly hosts" (*SL* 271).[22] Here, because it is alive, is a more sophisticated psychic apparatus than the various hydraulic devices, flow charts, and electronic gadgets science has come up with.

Joyce knew that the best way to develop the mind was by giving it the richest content and the most activity, and that the most complete model of the mind was God in that every detail of the universe and all forms of life were His thoughts. Joyce was aware of the extent to which the concept of mind inherited its dignity and vitality from religious thought. He saw that every connection between human minds formed an enlarged portion of the mind of God. The only way to understand this incomprehensible mind, he knew, was to assume it, to fill it by making the greatest possible number of connections center on the only mind he knew. This is not very far from what Aristotle, Augustine, and Aquinas did in less personal ways in their virtually endless writings.

Without their external faith, Joyce had to approach godhead through the generative power of uncertainty. Using the modern tools of analysis and self-dismemberment to penetrate illusions, Joyce girded himself in the defenses of negation in order to reach the absolute incerti-

Reconstruction

tude through which his deity could be manifested by an entire fluctuating world of doubt. And so, divided among his projections, listening inwardly from all sides of himself, he proceeded unremittingly toward fulfilling the dream of his adolescence in the last two-thirds of his career by uniting with God.

The medium through which he achieved this union was language, and the great strength of language for Joyce's purpose resides in the unbridgeable gap between the signifier and the signified. Because of the sacred origin of language and how widely it is used, even simple phrases tend to have so much meaning and so many meanings in relation to human feelings that their truth can never fully be captured. The progressive movement away from fixed meaning in Joyce's work described by MacCabe is not only a release of sexual and revolutionary forces; it is a shift toward the realm of spirit, of ideational potential that is not fixed in material form.

In order to show how Joyce uses deconstructive techniques constructively to generate spiritual content, I will focus on the episode in the middle of the book, "Oxen of the Sun." Wolfgang Iser has pointed out that the various styles in the hospital scene undercut each other to demonstrate that no perception can ever be free of the imposition of stylistic convention.[23] This is sound, but the denial of any particular truth always has to aim at a higher truth, and the styles of "Oxen" not only conflict, but work with each other.

For one thing, they form an organic structure. A given phrase in "Oxen" will simultaneously represent a phase of the history of English prose style, an author in that history, a stage in the development of a foetus, and the feelings of the characters involved in the scene. By working in several ways on several levels, such a phrase acts like a living cell, which may function as connective tissue at the same time that it contributes to digestive, respiratory, hormonal, and other systems.

Consider, for example, the line "Stark ruth of man his errand that him lone led till that house" (*U* 385). By imitating Anglo-Saxon poetry, this line evokes the intense but simple concern with destiny and the endurance of suffering in such works as "The Wanderer" and "The Seafarer." It is an effective way to present the awe that Bloom feels at the mystery and pain of childbirth in extremity. The syntax imitates the not-yet-organized structure of the early embryo, and the primitiveness of Anglo-Saxon culture corresponds to the early embryo in other ways. For example, an organism with a small number of cells will be one in which every part will die and be recombined in a short space of time.

This is equivalent to the instability of Old English civilization, which was constantly subject to waves of invasion and war. Moreover, the Anglo-Saxon passages, like the Latinate ones at the start of the episode, do not yet have English syntax. They still retain the word orders of Old German and Latin; and their lack of syntactical differentiation corresponds to the fact that Bloom, on first arriving at the hospital, cannot yet see what is happening clearly. And the substance of a foetus, in the earliest stages, may retain quite a bit of the substance of its parents. These are only some of the ways in which this sentence functions. The mystery of life is approached through the ability to sustain many vital functions at once, and Joyce was constantly trying to make his works complete organisms.

Moreover, the juxtaposition of fifteen hundred years of prose styles in "Oxen" produces a tremendous density—exactly the density needed for the scene in which Bloom makes the strange decision to follow Stephen. A biblical feeling of casting perception through distant ages contributes powerfully to the evocation of something being born. And the elaboration of a mind that includes vast stretches of history serves to draw out what is really being born here—a mind that includes two personalities. This episode activates the process that leads to what Joyce called the "fusion of Bloom and Stephen" in the last four episodes.

Finally, if each style in "Oxen" is selected as the right one for its moment, then Joyce, by taking upon himself a power to change styles that extends virtually beyond human ability, actually eliminates the interference of style. That is, the total vision constituted by all of the styles is virtually free of stylistic limitation, a pure representation of the thing itself. Iser does say that Joyce's multiple perspectives allow the reader to see the phenomenon itself, but for Iser, this phenomenon does not express anything outside itself.[24]

If the purpose of "Oxen" were simply to show the phenomena of the scene, then its many styles would be mere imposition. This is why S. L. Goldberg objected to "Oxen" on a naturalistic level.[25] But the subject of "Oxen" is not merely a group of people in a maternity hospital: it involves the roots of birth. The question of to what extent birth is a separation and to what extent it is a continuation has been on Stephen's mind since he thought of his parents conceiving him in "Proteus" (*U* 38). This question, which pervades both the content and form of "Oxen," involves the ultimate cause of birth. If the creation of something new must come from outside existing physical causes, the cause of birth must involve God, or at least an author on a higher plane. Therefore, it is appropriate that the millennial perspective of "Oxen" represents the viewpoint of God.

If "Oxen" represents the perspective of God stylistically, it is parallel to "Wandering Rocks," which represents the perspective of God spatially. When "Rocks" is acted out, as it was in Dublin in 1982, even someone in a helicopter cannot take it all in because he cannot hear it. An attempt to capture the action with a panel of video screens would illustrate how God's viewpoint has to appear in fragmented form to mortals (who can watch only one screen at a time) because their perceptions are all parts of His. "Circe" develops God's view in psychological terms by creating beings who embody subconscious impulses, thus turning omniscience into omnipotence. And "Ithaca" renders God's view scientifically, as a catechism should. But in presenting God's outlook stylistically, as "Oxen" does, one of the first aims Scholasticism would dictate is to show the falseness of any particular style. For God would be bound to see beyond any specific system or set of values. Yet the broadness of God's perspective apparently has never kept Him from exerting pressures on human beings.

Imposition

The stylistic variations in *Ulysses* are supposed to express the feelings of the characters and their world at the same time that they serve the structural purposes of the novel's oversoul.[26] Joyce represents the minds of character and author as a seamless continuum in each one of thousands of words because he believes that the author, as first cause, is contained within the minds of the characters. For Joyce to be aware of his controlling presence in each of his creatures is realistic not only in the Scholastic sense of seeing the reality behind appearances, but also in a psychological sense. It is unrealistic to pretend that either characters or people are independent entities, whether the dependence we must face is caused by God, history, or parents.

The issue of dependence is developed in the passage in which Stephen imagines his parents conceiving him. Here he speaks of himself as "made not begotten." In theology, these terms mean he is a man rather than the Son of God, but they may also be taken to mean that he is a product of art rather than natural reproduction:

> They clasped and sundered, did the coupler's will. From before the ages He willed me and now may not will me away or ever. A *lex eterna* stays about him. Is that then the divine substance wherein Father and Son are consubstantial? (*U* 38)

The active force that created Stephen, the will of the father and of God as they are here conflated, continues to be present in him. Semen is equated with God here as "the divine substance wherein Father and Son are consubstantial" because it performs a miracle by reversing time when it is transformed from an adult's substance to the substance of an infant. Science has no way of explaining this reversal of time. The primal matter or intermediate substance between God and creation stands for the creative principle the author shares with his characters. Whenever an idea or reference enters a character's discourse without his understanding or awareness, this generative principle injects new possibilities into the known world of the text.

One of the images used to represent the awareness the characters have of an external consciousness inhabiting them is the "tenebrosity of the interior" (*U* 393). Gose demonstrates that Joyce refers to the mystical tradition, associated with Dionysius the Areopagite, that God is an obscurity within.[27] Thus, Stephen sees in his "mind's darkness" the shadow of Christ over him (*U* 26, lines 1, 13), and thinks of himself as having been "made" "in sin darkness" (*U* 38). Stephen's concern with "darkness . . . in our souls" (*U* 48) is paralleled when Bloom, at the end of "Lestrygonians," speculates that the blind see objects as "something blacker than the dark."[28] These negative images reflect (or fail to reflect) Joyce's divine obscurity as a tendency to appear to his creatures as an imposition, an undercurrent of incomprehensible inevitability.

The population of *Ulysses* is preoccupied by the feeling that they are being controlled by some external force. Stephen's antagonism toward the collective unconscious makes him fear that the books in the library itch to "urge me to wreak their will" (*U* 194). Bloom reflects, "If we were all suddenly somebody else" (*U* 110), and repeats to himself variations on the phrase from Mozart's *Don Giovanni*, *"Vorrei e non vorrei"* (*U* 64, 77, 93, 445), or, as Stephen puts it, "what he would but would not" (*U* 197). The normal state of mind in Joyce is an opposition between at least two minds within the individual, and since both of these can't be equally conscious, a feeling of external influence is bound to recur. Joyce has to operate this otherness for his characters by projecting himself into complementary mentalities.

The theme of external control is prominent in "Wandering Rocks." This episode begins with Father Conmee's walk and ends with the viceregal procession, so that it frames Dublin with the external controls of a Roman church and an English state. Stephen is frightened by a sense that God may be watching him in "Wandering Rocks" (*U* 242), and Bloom is overwhelmed by the authority of the author of *Sweets of Sin.* In fact, the god who is watching Stephen is the author of *Sweets of Sin,* for even if this was a real book by someone else (which it apparently was not), Joyce makes it his in *Ulysses* by his use of it.

A striking example of external control occurs in the scene of "Wandering Rocks" that shows Mulligan and Haines in the Dublin Bakery Company tearoom (*U* 248-249). Mulligan says that Stephen's wits were driven astray "by visions of hell." "—Eternal punishment, Haines said, nodding curtly. I see." Actually, Mulligan and Haines are in hell in this scene: for the crime of doubting Joyce's art, they are condemned to go on for eternity repeating Stephen's announcement that he will write a book in ten years. Near the end of this scene in which they are used to demonstrate the intensity of Joyce's faith in himself, Haines says, "I don't want to be imposed on." And on the following page, Cashel Boyle O'Connor Fitzmaurice Tisdall Farrell suddenly mutters, "*Coactus volui.*" This means "I willed it under compulsion" or "acting with someone or something else." His lack of control over his mind makes him a suitable spokesman for the unknown, and schizophrenics are often regarded as seers in primitive societies. These lines contribute to the thematic picture of a city full of people activated by external will in accordance with Joyce's theory. But in seeing this or any other *theme,* we are seeing Joyce's will in action.

All thematic content is a manifestation of Joyce in the sense that when words become thematically significant, they stop functioning as ordinary words in the fictional context and become visible as signals organized by an external will. They are lifted above the created world into a proximity with their creator. Of course, the writer should harmonize his will with the independent consciousness of his fiction, but they remain two vectors in one substance even when they are parallel; and theme does not become visible as such until they diverge. Joyce chose to emphasize their divergence by such methods of personal manifestation as the theme of external will, which grows more prominent in the *Wake.* The difference between the mind of Joyce and those of his characters does not mean that they can be separated, but rather that the characters contain another mind within themselves. Their situation corresponds to Derrida's argument that whenever we speak, we are expressing another voice that reads an older text: "Inspiration is the drama, with several characters, of theft . . ."[29]

Joyce was heavily ironic about the imposition of his presence on his creatures, for the mole that one inherits is after all a cavity, a blind spot, a dependence. And so he represents the implanting of grace through sardonic sexual images. One of the chief religious instruments of Bloom's life, the "thaumaturgic" Wonderworker, serves Bloom's worship of Nature by promising to make "a new man of you" when you insert it in yourself (*U* 722); it represents his need for author-ity, for someone to tell him what to do, as a need to be violated.

In "Circe," when Elijah tells everyone in the bordello that they are all part Christ, the divine component in them is identified with guilt: "Miss Higgins and Miss Ricketts got religion way inside them. . . . I don't never see no wusser scared female . . ." (*U* 508). The girls proceed to tell how they lost their virginities, a process here equated with the injection of godhead. Joyce uses them to express his belief that guilt is what keeps prostitutes at their trade; and so he takes charge of the areas of their minds that they do not control.

Elijah, however, also indicates that the Joyce embedded in each character has two sides when he says, "Are you a god or a doggone clod," prefiguring the apparition of the twin black and white masses at the climax of "Circe." Just as the conflicts that make up life combine the possibilities of salvation and damnation, just as God is creator and destroyer, so the Joycean component in each character is, like the unconscious, both a limit on the individual's life and a source of the possibility of his extending beyond himself. For if it is from Joyce that they come, it is also toward Joyce that they go.

The technique of "Circe" is based mainly on Flaubert's *Temptation of Saint Anthony* and Goethe's *Faust*. The revelations of the unconscious in both of these sources are not directly psychoanalytic; they are divine. It is not a human mind, but a higher power, that organizes and delivers their visions—or rather a lower power, for in both the *Temptation* and the *Walpurgisnacht*, the guides are satanic. The model of knowledge dispensed by superhuman authority is also basic to the catechism of "Ithaca." Here again we are flooded with information the characters are not aware of that purports by its thoroughness to embody the ultimate truth about them. "Circe" and "Ithaca," which add up to almost a third of the book, are the climactic episodes, the ones toward which the others move. If Joyce allows the possibility of transcendence to be muffled in "Circe" and apparently defeated in "Ithaca," nevertheless, he takes the form of a revelator. He can allow himself to play God only as an apparent failure for the same reason that Stephen cannot believe in a father more manly than Bloom. It may be argued that God himself seems to show a tendency to play dead in the material world.

If Joyce plays God in order to maximize his creation, he also intends to indicate the limits of His position as defined in human terms. This god, like the Savior with whom he is not below identifying himself, seems as ambivalent about his powers as any sensitive being would be in his position, as parents often are. He holds out to us the ideal of unselfish love, yet he has his moments of wrath, and he seems to have created a universe to generate admirers for his incomprehensible self. He appears to show antisocial tendencies by hardly ever manifesting himself to anyone except in such abstract forms as mathematical singularities and violations of his own rules.

He dwells in what Joyce, speaking of love in his notes for *Exiles,* calls "the region of the difficult, the void and the impossible."[30] He sacrificed himself for us while feeling superior and started a revolution that cannot be completed, for modernism has not transformed the world any more conclusively than Christianity has. If Joyce's work is infected by his limitations, he uses this condition to imply that the world suffers from those of its Prime Mover. For if Joyce's deity is absolute to his creatures, outside his work, he himself was subject to a higher power that he did not consider flawless.

Ordinary people do not consider the difficulties of godhood, but great writers must. Jorge Luis Borges tells of a man born with a deep sense that he was nothing. He tried to convey the emptiness he felt inside to others through conversation and sex, but no one understood. So he practiced pretending to be someone, and this led to a career on stage in which he created a vast, expanding series of false selves. Finally, he grew horrified at all this illusion and fled to the country to be nobody again. At his death, he said to God,

> "I, who have been so many men in vain, want to be one man; myself." The voice of God replied from a whirlwind: "Neither am I one self; I dreamed the world as you dream your work, my Shakespeare, and among the shapes of my dreams are you, who, like me, are many persons—and none."[31]

As Stephen's theory of Shakespeare suggests, Joyce knew that the power he held over his work sprang from his powerlessness in the outside world. Therefore the impulsion that created the new, Joycean world was bound to infect it with the deprivation of the pre-Joycean one. Men are obliged to see God in human terms. Insofar as He does not seem to have motives, He loses vitality for us because we tend to see Him as inanimate. Yet insofar as He can be said to have motives, He must include division and privation, for motives are dynamic, moving from one mental image toward another. Thus, for example, in the Miltonic tradition, God makes the world to compensate Himself for the loss of His rebel angels. Aquinas put God above such dynamism, but Bruno did not; and Joyce worked in the margin between what could be known of God and what could not be known of Him.

The representation of God as human or neurotic that Joyce carries out through his own presence is developed most extensively in the figure of HCE, who is constantly presented as God through a wide range of mythological references even though his substance is largely composed of weakness and fallibility. Note the capitalization: "Well, Him a being so on the flounder of his bulk" (*FW* 6.30). By humanizing God and pursuing him into the unknown, Joyce extended the human realm of perception and reason, obliging the unknowable aspect of God to retreat into further levels of incomprehensibility.

Joyce's criticism of God was accompanied, in fact, by a growing into the role as he settled into more and more of God's territory. If one central tenet of Joyce's youth was that God must never be forgiven, his view of the Deity in the *Wake* can well be described as sympathetic. Joyce never resolved the conflict and lack of integrity that resulted from combining human limits with the role of God. But he realized that because identity was created, it was always based on disjunction, and because he was able to accept the fact that he was "many persons — and none," he was able to use his conflicts to grow.

While writers who tried to preserve a unified truth by avoiding self-contradiction tended to stop advancing, Joyce cultivated his personal division as a tool for generating complex substance through a dynamic polarization that unfolded his consciousness into the far corners of a psychic cosmos. As he advanced through his career, he multiplied the parts of the mind at the center of each of his works, shifting from nullities to an individuality, a duo, a trio, a quartet, and a quintet. Only by this process of fission could Joyce stay in progress not only before, but after, the death of his body.

The multimind that Joyce elaborated through his canon is his most essential creation: out of its self-involvement the fullness of his world springs. Through his myriad minds, Joyce constitutes an integrity based on the relation of his own parts, the morality of a god who is both creator and destroyer. If Stephen were to accept the world and be born, or if Bloom and Molly were consciously reconciled, the reality and vitality that depend on their opposition would diminish and the novel would flatten out into an unreal, idealized picture of life ruled by one idea. Neglecting to invest himself fully in his several opposed selves, the dreamer would remember that he was only dreaming. This is why God must remain indifferent and transcendence must remain potential: because the reality of the world consists of the difference between our understandings and the unknowable nature of their causes — the difference between reading and writing. If we cannot know this reality, neither can we avoid studying it, for we cannot see anything else that is active.

Every person who imagines a new set of conditions or connections or a new level of life is taking upon himself the power of God to create being, to constitute the difference between reading and writing. Joyce derived from Aristotle and others — and from his own feelings — the idea that a man can partake of godhood through his mind. Having embarked on this course and accepted letters as his medium, Joyce used every means he could devise to equal God's creative power in every possible dimension. He even used his bitterness to represent the mockery he saw in God's administration, for he aimed to use every part of himself to avoid projecting himself as a fraction.

Joyce respected God sufficiently to suspect that the Deity might value his honest emulation more than his slavishness. The rapidity with which he changed the rules on virtually every page of the *Wake* suggests that he was trying to surpass God in pace and virtuosity. By expanding the possibilities of human perception and knowledge, he would oblige God to take a more active role. In fact, the strongest thing God (or Joyce) can do is to allow His world to deconstruct itself. To do this, He must have enough control to give the text its independence.

Joyce's failures in his competition with the Deity are less astonishing than his successes. The recent centennial of 1982 left the Joyce world more active than ever, and when future centennials roll around, readers will still be discovering new levels and principles in his creation. At the center of this expanding universe will be the presence of Joyce in his work, the being from which it derives its becoming. The life of Joyce's work depends upon the inherence of its soul, the consubstantiality of Joyce in his world.

5 The Sea of Joyce

The Sea's Voice

The most capacious image of depth for Joyce was the sea. Freud describes it at the start of *Civilization and Its Discontents* as the most powerful of all images of God. Here Freud presents the theory that religion has its origin as an attempt to explain an oceanic feeling that he traces back to infancy.[1] Early in *Portrait,* when Stephen sinks into his depths at the start of a dream, he hears the voices of waves "talking among themselves" (*P* 26), the sound of an interior sea. The roaring of the sea is the voice of God that resounds most resonantly through his works; and in all of the novels, this voice is identified as that of Joyce.

In "Proteus," as Stephen walks by Dublin Bay, making contact with what the Linati schema refers to as "Prima materia," he refers to "signatures of all things I am here to read" (*U* 37). In *Signatures of All Things,* Jakob Boehme argues that every being is informed by God with an innate pattern that contains the complete image of God. When a person speaks, the voice of God is heard in the rhythm of his particular identity, a formlessness manifested through form.[2] This reference suggests that "signatures" is an appropriate term for points in the text at which Joyce is heard speaking.

Signatures are signs of authorial intervention in the form of words—or other signs, such as the black dot at the end of "Ithaca" (*U* 737)—that do not fit previously developed contexts. They include changes in style, unexpected words, external references, and material that is thematic or self-reflexive. Every signature is an injection of Joyce's mind into the text that changes its identity; and whenever a voice speaks or a sign appears that cannot be identified, it is Joyce's. Signatures are more frequent in "Proteus" than in any other early episode, partly because "Proteus" sounds the depths of Stephen's thoughts and partly because signatures have a special frequency in proximity to the sea.

Hayman sees "the narrator's signature" in this line from "Aeolus": "A smile of light brightened his darkrimmed eyes, lengthened his long lips" (*U* 133). The narrator whose signature Hayman sees is not the narrator of "Aeolus," a curious individual who is obsessed with rhetoric and speaks in headlines, but a larger narrator whom Hayman sees behind the first eleven episodes.[3] I believe that the realistic narrator and the inventive arranger Hayman distinguishes are not two people, but poles of one mind. This is indicated by the fact that, as Hayman recognizes, both are often present at once. In "Aeolus," for example, the arranger seems to be reflected in the headlines, the rhetorical games, and such effects as the trolley language noted earlier. Hayman says that the narrator "gradually" metamorphoses into the arranger, suggesting their common identity. If the presiding intelligence in *Ulysses* may be eighty percent narrator and twenty percent arranger near the beginning, but eighty percent arranger and twenty percent narrator near the end, with varying ratios in between that tend to shift steadily, then he is continuous and unified.

An indicator of signatures that has not been mentioned — one that suggests divine qualities, as all such indicators do — is excellence. In the line Hayman cites above, the phrase "a smile of light," which he focuses on, stands out among the rhetorical tricks of "Aeolus" because it is unusually brilliant. It is outside the usual range of the "Aeolus" narrator, and insofar as he is inspired beyond himself here, he expresses Joyce.

The narrators of *Ulysses,* who personify the spirits of various sections, are specialized functions of Joyce's mind — only partly (in varying degrees) differentiated as characters, and completely dominated by the Joycean vision they express. Joyce as writer exerts more than one personality, and so he can change from narrator to arranger as he moves away from a *Portrait* and toward the *Wake.*

Synchronicities are signatures in that coincidences make the reader think of the author, and signatures are synchronicities in that they come from and aim at a realm outside the naturalistic Bloomsday. Every structural literary reference is a coincidence and every coincidence refers to a spiritual principle insofar as it is meaningful. Nevertheless, it is possible to distinguish two kinds of manifestations of Joyce in his texts: synchronicities, which are predominantly coincidences of plot, and signatures, which are predominantly turns of style. Signatures are typical of the narrator, who speaks through nuances of style, while synchronicities typify the arranger, who represents a shift toward the mentally controlled world of the *Wake*.

When Stephen says in "Proteus" that he is "here" to read signatures, it raises the question of why the sea is the place for such reading. This question was also suggested in the fourth chapter of *Portrait,* when Stephen turned seaward while asking himself why he had rejected the priesthood. If Stephen cannot explain why the sea exerts such power over him, it must be because the source of this power is beyond his knowing.

Boyle detects images from the *Paradiso* in the *Portrait* beach scene, and suggests that when Stephen finds his vocation, he achieves a contact with God.[4] This god, however, seems to be the "eternal imagination" of which Stephen later proclaims himself a priest (*P* 221), a god of art. The sea god is linked to Stephen's future as Joyce. Stephen speaks in his esthetics lecture of the personality of the artist flowing around the characters "like a vital sea" (*P* 215). In the vocation scene, he hears "a voice from beyond the world . . . calling" (*P* 167), and this voice can be identified with the artist, who, as Stephen later says, remains present "beyond" his handiwork. After all, it is Joyce who gave Stephen the name that makes him wonder what it means.

Something like what happens to Stephen in the fourth chapter of *Portrait* is described in Joyce's Blake lecture of 1912, in which Blake's soul "finds itself renewed and winged and immortal on the edge of the dark ocean of God" (*CW* 222). Such a transcendent experience should be accompanied by supernatural signs, and Joyce was able to provide them insofar as he was prepared to assume the godlike position of seeing his whole career as simultaneous.

Stephen's scene in the "Telemachus" episode of *Ulysses,* which Joyce had already sketched for *Stephen Hero,*[5] is prefigured here as Stephen looks toward his future. Here he sees clouds voyaging over the sea, through which "a veiled sunlight lit up faintly the grey sheet of water where the river was embayed" (*P* 167). This is similar to a passage in "Telemachus" in which Stephen watches the shadows of clouds moving seaward over the mirror of bay water (*U* 9). In both scenes the water is flat, and in both Stephen perceives something invisible running over it. In *Portrait,* ". . . he saw a flying squall darkening and crisping suddenly the tide." In "Telemachus," ". . . the mirror of water whitened, spurned by lightshod hurrying feet." The image of the spirit of God moving on the face of the waters is one of the most poetic in the opening of Genesis because it suggests the contact between thought and matter. When Joyce uses this image, he gives us a subtle view of the motion of his mind.

Within a few lines of his perception in *Portrait* of what he will experience in *Ulysses,* Stephen has a vision of Dublin: "Like a scene on some vague arras, old as man's weariness, the image of the seventh city of christendom was visible to him across the timeless air, no older nor more weary nor less patient of subjection than in the days of the thingmote." All of this passage is paraphrased in the third chapter of the *Wake* (53.1–6). Stephen, then, sees his future as an artist at the sea. He cannot know this in clear terms, yet there must be a sense in which he does know it, for the subject of this scene is revelation. He knows it insofar as it is dispensed by Joyce, the cause toward which he moves insofar as he wants to become immortal.

That the sea is Joyce as God is suggested on the first full page of *Ulysses,* when Mulligan whistles for a Eucharist, and "two strong shrill whistles" answer "through the calm," leading Mulligan to say, "Thanks, old chap. . . ." Eighteen pages later we are presented with some nearby bathers who might have provided the answering whistles, but on the first page these whistles carry a definite suggestion of the supernatural. The line about the two answering whistles was added after the publication of "Telemachus" in the *Little Review* in 1918,[6] and if Joyce decided to announce his active presence at the start of the book, it would make sense that this should be a late decision.

The voice an author has in his work is described by Stephen in a passage I touched on earlier in which he tells how Shakespeare, after his corporeal life is over, "passes on towards eternity in undiminished personality." Personality requires life, but the life of the author in his work is not physical, but spiritual: "He is a ghost, a shadow now, the wind by Elsinore's rocks or what you will, the sea's voice, a voice heard only in the heart of him who is the substance of his shadow, the son consubstantial with the father" (*U* 197). At first this statement seems to contradict itself: first it says that Shakespeare is heard in the wind and sea at Elsinore (possibly in any sea), and then it says he is heard only in the heart of his son. In fact, the son Shakespeare is consubstantial with is not merely Hamlet the prince, but *Hamlet* the play. He exists in the heart of his work, speaking in its wind and sea. He has also planted himself in the hearts of his readers as "what you will," the object of their desire.

But what is the voice of the sea that resounds in the heart? In "Telemachus," Mulligan cites through Swinburne the convention that the sea is a mother (*U* 5), but Stephen, in "Proteus," calls it "Old Father Ocean"; and it is as Neptune that it arises at the end of the *Wake* to end Joyce's canon as well as it can be ended. The sea in "Proteus" is thought of also as primal matter, intermediate between God and man. The edge of the sea is the border of chaos, the boundary of life and of fiction, and in *Portrait* Stephen dreads the sea's "cold infrahuman odour" (*P* 167). How can a voice from such an alien source be heard in the heart?

What the Waves Are Saying

The link between the sea and the heart is developed in "Sirens" when Lydia Douce listens to a seashell. She thinks she hears the sea, but it is actually the sound of the sea of blood within her, the sound of her being. At this point, George Lidwell asks her, "What are the wild waves saying?" (*U* 281). By following Joyce's associations, we can answer this question, at least in part.

Gifford and Seidman point out that "What Are the Wild Waves Saying?" is a song in which a brother asks a sister this question, and a songbook of 1881 adds that it is based on "the well-known scene" in *Dombey and Son*.[7] In Dickens's novel, the rigid businessman Dombey has a frail son, Paul, whose mother dies from giving birth to him. Paul is haunted through his brief life by the sound of water, especially the sound of a river flowing. This is a symptom Joyce presents in the thirty-fifth of the *Chamber Music* lyrics, where he recognizes the sound as internal:

> All day I hear the noise of waters
>   Making moan,
> Sad as the sea-bird is, when going
>   Forth alone,
> He hears the winds cry to the waters'
>   Monotone.
> The grey winds, the cold winds are blowing
>   Where I go.
> I hear the noise of many waters
>   Far below.
> All day, all night, I hear them flowing
>   To and fro.[8]

For Joyce here, as for Paul, the noise of waters suggests a sad going forth, though exile is not death. The pathetic chapter in which little Paul dies, essentially as a result of his father's coldness, is called "What the Waves Were Always Saying." As Paul passes away, he embraces his beloved sister Florence:

> "How fast the river runs, between its green banks and the rushes, Floy! But it's very near the sea. I hear the waves! They always said so!"
> . . . the swift river bears us to the ocean!⁹

This scene must have made an enormous impression on Joyce, who probably read it when he was about twelve, and who lost two brothers in his youth. It is one of the few major representations in literature of death as a river flowing into an ocean. The same image is used for the death of Paul's mother in the first chapter: "Thus, clinging fast to that slight spar within her arms, the mother drifted out upon the dark and unknown sea that rolls around the world." Here, as in Joyce, the ocean tends to be associated with what is beyond life. Mrs. Dombey clings to Florence just as ALP thinks of her daughter, Isabel, when she reaches what Joyce called "the dark ocean of God."

In the choruses of "What Are the Wild Waves Saying?" Paul and Florence conclude that the sound of the sea is more than the noise of waters:

> "No! It is something greater,
> That speaks to the heart alone;
> The voice of the great Creator,
> Dwells in that mighty tone."

The voice of the sea, which Stephen identifies with the voice of the artist in his work, is thus equated with that of God as the voice of the unknown that corresponds to the depths of the soul. The fact that the saline solution in the body was originally derived from the sea means that the voice of the sea within us is primordial, and "Oxen" describes "the plasmic substance" as "immortal" (U 419). Stephen refers to the song "What Are the Wild Waves Saying?" when he says that his godlike Shakespeare survives as the voice of the sea "heard only in the heart." This particular reiteration of the idea that the artist remains present in his work as God implies that the personality of the artist is submerged in the depths of his work and transmuted into extrahuman forms.

As a roaring voice at the heart of his work, Joyce speaks not only through characters or narrators, for his experimental techniques allow him to express what is intangible. His headlines speak for the public mind in "Aeolus," as Karen Lawrence points out.[10] In "Lestrygonians," his rhythms give voice to the intestines. In "Scylla and Charybdis," the self-reflexive nature of the subject of poetic creation manifests the author behind and above the dialogue. The discontinuities in "Wandering Rocks" speak through separation for the stones, the dead blocks of Dublin, that Protestant-designed city referred to in the Linati schema as "The Hostile Environment."[11] In "Sirens," Joyce's sound effects express the ambience of music. In "Cyclops," his parodies evoke the spirit of power. "Oxen" expresses the development of a foetus. "Circe" speaks for the unconscious by personifying its impulses. "Eumaeus" gives voice to the state of exhaustion through clichés and solecisms. The catechism of "Ithaca" evokes destiny through an image deeper than the sea, outer space; and the rolling of "Penelope" imitates the earth. While all of these effects point to their origin, they also contribute substance to the scenes involved. Joyce makes these scenes more real by incarnating their atmospheres or souls.

Two Views of the Sea

Joyce's oceanic presence in his work does not provide easy comfort to his characters. Stephen is in dread of his creator, as he is in dread of the sea. He cannot bear to recognize the element in himself that he does not possess because it was implanted in him by another: "My father gave me seeds to sow" (*U* 26). When he confronts the watery margin of existence in "Proteus," he thinks of his beginning and his end with loathing. The image of his parents conceiving him is oppressive because it is encased in the "*lex eterna*" of God's will. And his goal is seen no less morbidly: "*Omnis caro ad te veniet*" ("All flesh comes to you," *U* 48). His vision of God here is a dreadful "pale vampire" in accord with his hatred of his efficient and final causes. The god who creates him limits his possibilities because this god is Joyce, to whom he must inevitably come, at the expense of his independent existence.

One reason Stephen feels guilty for the death of his mother is that he suspects that he is bound to create a world in which her death is accomplished and accepted. "None wed the second but who killed the first" (*Hamlet* III.ii.186; *U* 203, 568), and Joyce is the obscure power behind the drive that compels Stephen to destroy the real mother earth in order to create an imaginary one. As Lacan observes, one must always mentally destroy an object in order to create a symbol of it.[12]

Stephen's fear of the unknown within that creates and determines him was indicated by his definition in *Portrait* of one of the two feelings required by tragedy, terror: "the feeling which arrests the mind in the presence of whatsoever is grave and constant in human suffering and unites it with the secret cause" (*P* 204). This secret cause combines cause of change and end because it both creates and destroys. It is God, the primal, archaic, invisible object of terror. The most terrible thing about the self-annihilating union with the secret cause is that one is drawn toward it by the desire for absolute being.

The distrust Stephen harbors toward God or the constructive aspect of Joyce tends to make his signatures negative ones. That is, the expressions of his individuality through Joyce tend to be morbid. It is typical of him in *Ulysses* to look at the sea and see a bowl of his mother's vomit (*U* 5) or the decay of low tide (*U* 37). *Ulysses* as a whole, however, is dominated by a more positive set of transitions, the movement from Stephen to Bloom. Bloom enjoys change and is attracted to fate. For him, the sea represents possibilities of voyage. The irony of this contrast is that Stephen's morbidity is the other side of his vital idealism, while Bloom's acceptance of an inconstant world is self-obliterating.

While Stephen is at the beach, around eleven A.M., Bloom is at Glasnevin cemetery for Paddy Dignam's funeral, so that the young man confronts the symbol of birth at the same time that the older one encounters those of death. The Linati schema lists the sense of the "Hades" episode as "Descent to Nothing," while one of its symbols is "The Unknown Man." This suggests that Bloom is to encounter some opposite of existence that corresponds to "The Unconscious," another symbol of "Hades." At the climactic moment of the funeral, as Bloom watches the coffin enter the grave, an image of union that leaves the surface of the world behind, he descends to nothing by vicariously entering Dignam's nonexistence:

> He doesn't know who is here or care.
> Now who is that lankylooking galoot over there in the macintosh? (*U* 109)

The appearance of the man in the macintosh seems especially appropriate at this point if we accept, as Brook Thomas does, Vladimir Nabokov's argument that this "selfinvolved enigma" (*U* 729) is Joyce: "Bloom glimpses his maker!"[13] Herring thinks that the word "*Tarnkappe*" (Ger. "invisible cloak") in *Ulysses* Notebook VIII.A.5 refers to the macintosh.[14] Joyce found this term in use for an attribute of the god Hades. This impermeable coat may be linked to the "diaphane" Stephen refers to on the beach (*U* 37, 48). It is the veil that separates Bloom's world of appearances from what lies beyond it in Joyce's mind.

After seeing the unknown man, Bloom seems to receive a high concentration of psychic transmissions from Stephen on the beach. He thinks, "The Irishman's house is his coffin" (*U* 110) which parallels Stephen's vision of "houses of decay" (*U* 39); and he speculates, "If we were all suddenly somebody else" (*U* 110), as Stephen imagines his uncle Richie Goulding saying, "We thought you were someone else" (*U* 39). And Bloom's comparison of the rope that lowers the coffin to a "navelcord" (*U* 112) harks back to Stephen's umbilical telephone wire (*U* 38).

Passage into the other world is again represented by going into a hole when Bloom sees a rat wriggling into a tomb, while Stephen thinks of "the stoneheaps of dead builders, a warren of weasel rats" (*U* 44). The rat makes Bloom think of methods of disposing of corpses, including a "Parsee tower of silence" (*U* 114), parallel to Stephen's "silent tower entombing their blind bodies" (*U* 44). And Bloom's "saltwhite crumbling mush of corpse" echoes Stephen's "corpse rising saltwhite from the undertow" (*U* 50).

Bloom and Stephen contact each other when they approach the limits of conscious life because the same mind lies under the surfaces of both of theirs. A similar psychic structure is indicated in the *Confessions;* Augustine looks into the depths of his soul and sees with his inward eye a light: "It was above me because it was itself the Light that made me, and I was below because I was made by it. All who know the truth know this Light . . ." (VII.10). Stephen and Bloom both gain spiritual life by finding each other in themselves through Joyce. The depth they come into contact with creates them by uniting them.

This mental depth is defined by the organization of synchronicities that relates Stephen to Bloom. The skill Joyce devoted to this organization is illustrated by the intertwining of the terms "word" and "world" in *Ulysses:* Bloom overlooks the spiritual word because he is lost in the material world, while Stephen rejects the world for the word. And so Bloom gets a letter from Martha Clifford containing the misprint "I do not like that other world" (*U* 77); and when Stephen asks the object of his spiritual desire for "the word known to all men" (*U* 49, 581), his ghostly mother answers contrarily, "I pray for you in my other world." May Dedalus, "folded away in the memory of nature" (*U* 10), speaks to Stephen from the place in which she is remembered best, the mind of Joyce.

The subject of *Ulysses* is neither the word nor the world, but something between them, just as it is neither Bloom nor Stephen, but someone between them. On a note sheet for "Eumaeus," Joyce wrote, "SD & LB = iden."[15] He saw them as making up one person. In fact, the subject of *Ulysses* is not any of the beings in the book, who can only be becomings, but a being made up of all of them. Each, however major or minor, plays his role in the whole mental structure. The nature of this great being is hypothetical and heuristic, for all of it cannot be seen at once by any person; but it is conceived of as alive rather than dead, and it resembles Joyce more than any other individual.

When Bloom, in "Nausicaa," appears on the same beach Stephen visited in "Proteus," he unsuccessfully attempts to write, as Stephen did. And as Bloom drifts out of consciousness in a postsexual reverie, his mind is flooded with images from Stephen's in a passage of remarkable coincidensity:

> I.
> Some flatfoot tramp on it in the morning. Useless. Washed away. Tide comes here a pool near her [Gerty MacDowell's] foot. Bend, see my face there, dark mirror, breathe on it, stirs. All these rocks with lines and scars and letters. O, those transparent! Besides they don't know. What is the meaning of that other world. I called you naughty boy because I do not like.
> AM. A. (*U* 381)

In the earlier episode, when Stephen confronted the edge of the sea, he feared his ashplant would be washed away as the tide from a tidal pool called Cock Lake, combined with his urine, formed a pool near his foot (*U* 49). In that scene he thought of his urine as a "floating foampool, flower unfurling," thus prefiguring the image of Bloom's penis in the bath as a "floating flower" in "Lotus Eaters" (*U* 86). Stephen also bent over the darkness of his shadow, as Bloom does, thinking of his breath and wondering who would ever read his signs (*U* 48). The letters Bloom senses on the rocks are Stephen's disorderly "signatures of all things," while Gerty's transparent hose recall Stephen's translucent diaphane, and the question at the end, paraphrased from Martha's letter, parallels the one Stephen asks his anima: "What is the word known to all men?" (*U* 49).

In a passage of "Scylla and Charybdis" that will appear in print for the first time in the forthcoming Critical Edition, Stephen identifies the sought-after word: "Love, yes. Word known to all men."[16] This discovery should not lead critics to assume the answer is simple, for the "bitter mystery" of love is beyond Stephen's knowledge, a mystery he broods on all day. He is still asking this central question, which delineates Bloom's commonness, in Nighttown: "Tell me the word, mother, if you know now. The word known to all men" (*U* 581). He asks this continually, and he always asks it of his dead mother, a being who may be located in a superego that he shares with Joyce.

Clearly, the "word known to all men" must have subordinate aspects that are spiritual as well as being erotic, and the phrase appears in spiritual contexts Joyce was familiar with. Gifford and Seidman gloss Stephen's "word known to all men" as "the 'word' that is revealed to each individual after his death" and say that it can be known only as mystery in life and cannot be known as reality until death.[17] The last clause could be applied to many Romantic and spiritual concepts of love, and I pointed out in the previous chapter that Joyce, in his notes to *Exiles*, says that love seeks "the region of the difficult, the void and the impossible." Moreover, Cheryl T. Herr observes that Madame Helena Blavatsky, whom Joyce read, spoke of the word known to all men as "an unknown word equivalent to the true name of God. . . . which identifies the 'Unknowable Cause' of the universe."[18] Here again, such terms may be applied to love, and in my first chapter I argued that the process whereby Joyce divided himself to enter into and enrich his work was a process of love.

These readings suggest what the other world is that Bloom speculates on as he drifts in his reverie. Like that of Gabriel Conroy in "The Dead," his soul approaches "that region where dwell the vast hosts of the dead" as he feels his identity fading. Joyce might call this realm the universal memory, or Akasic records in theosophical terms: it is the repository of all souls. But where is it that Bloom and Stephen connect with the finality of death? In the place where they connect with each other, the place where they were born.

Bloom is fading into the mind of Joyce, which includes both him and Stephen. And this "dark mirror" is the night of eternity that Stephen feared being caught in when he closed his eyes on the beach: "If I open and am for ever in the black adiaphane" (*U* 37). Where else could Stephen go if he lost consciousness but into the mind that projects him?[19] His touching this Proteus by following his associations freely is likely to lead him to Bloom. For the substance wherein he and his literary father are consubstantial is predicated on the relation between him and his complementary opposite. And though the "centrifugal" Stephen is driven by a dread of reaching any completion, he knows that we move ineluctably toward our final selves.

Further correspondences between Stephen and Bloom on the beach may be noted. At several points in "Nausicaa," Bloom sees a bat. This matches the vampire image of God as devourer that Stephen imagines in "Proteus," and there is a "Proteus" manuscript that includes the word *bat*.[20] Hayman has argued that Stephen masturbates in "Proteus,"[21] and Kenner accepts his argument.[22] If this were true, it would link "Proteus" and "Nausicaa" solidly; but I doubt it, for Stephen's supposed self-indulgence (*U* 49) is awfully inobtrusive. It is true that Stephen, like Bloom, is in an expansive, autoerotic mood.

The paragraph of Bloom's thoughts blending with Stephen's is preceded and followed by two short paragraphs that add up to three words: "I. . . . AM A." These are the words Bloom writes on the beach, but God may be speaking through him, for they seem to refer to "I am Alpha and Omega, the beginning and the ending, saith the Lord" (Rev. 1:8). This line identifies God as the cause of change and purpose. Riquelme demonstrates that the letters "A . . . O" form a motif in the *Wake* that refers to "jas jos" (*FW* 184.2).[23] If anyone were ever to fully grasp his origin and his destiny, he would transcend humanity and pass into a heavenly state.

Within the paragraph, Bloom comes close to grasping his own first cause by naming the book in which he appears: "Useless." The pun is extended when the *Wake* refers to "his usylessly unreadable Blue Book of Eccles" (*FW* 179.26). Bloom's transcendent state here derives from the fact that he earlier grasped his first cause during his public relations with Gerty. Joyce regarded sex, like art, as a path toward godhood. In the *Ulysses* note sheets, for example, he says that in the act of intercourse, a man "obliges God to create."[24] Bloom thinks here of one of the primal images of the creation of life, stirring water with breath. This image harks back to Genesis and to the wind on the water that Stephen noticed in the two beach scenes I discussed above; it also reaches forward a few pages to the birth process that gets under way when Stephen and Bloom, in "Oxen," grow attached to each other in their symbolic roles of embryo and sperm.

These hints of the uncanny, while demonstrable, are so subtle that they must be described as concealed. In view of the facts that Joyce considered not publishing his schema for *Ulysses* and that he produced this diagram in varying forms, it is easy to believe in a great depth of undiscovered systems. Discoveries within this creative compages are motivated by faith in its hidden meaning. This faith constitutes a granting of life to the text; for even if the reader is not supposed to behold the systemic anatomy of the work, he is supposed to perceive the vitality of the work made possible by that anatomy.

If Joyce's godhead is partly a joke, it also has its dreadful aspect, for Freud has shown that a joke is a way of handling something disturbing. Stephen defines terror as union with the secret cause (*P* 204) because fear of the unknown is fear of losing control, fear of being taken over by an alien power that corresponds to the other within. Stephen and Bloom confront such terror when they get closest to each other in Bloom's kitchen. Stephen's fear of Bloom leads him to sing an anti-Semitic song (*U* 690–691), but if Bloom does not earn such dread, then what Stephen fears in Bloom is really in himself.

Bloom's consideration of whether Jews could be guilty of ritual murder, spurred by the song, centers on whether he could be doing things he does not know about. The situations in which he seemed to be under the power of an alien mind that he remembers include hypnosis, somnambulism, and more than one occasion when "waking, he had been for an indefinite time incapable of moving or uttering sounds" (*U* 692). Such helplessness on the edge of being is frightening. Insofar as its intensity corresponds to Joyce's knowledge of the submerged part of his own mind, Bloom makes a strong contact with Joyce at this point.

A "cognate phenomenon," one born in the same place, "declared itself" in a member of Bloom's family when Milly "uttered in sleep an exclamation of terror" and answered subsequent questions" with a vacant mute expression" (*U* 692). This suggestion of a demonic force within accords with the archaic culture of Eastern European Jews at the turn of the century, who were rife with demonology, as the works of I. B. Singer show. But Joyce, as we have seen, was not above taking on a demonic role. One indication that the fears that afflict both protagonists are fears of their unity in Joyce is the presence of the eucharistic cocoa they have just drunk "in jocoserious silence" (*U* 677).

Joyce's activity as a deity sometimes generates the kind of terror one feels in the presence of a supernatural being. If terror addresses the unknown, then the Joycean text is surrounded by terror because, building on the void, Joyce gives us more of the unknown than any other writer. The hidden, unknowable meaning that remains buried in the text, potentially able to speak over and over, can give the impression that it is alive and watching us.

Submerging

Joyce's presence in his work is "something blacker than the dark," seen through blindness because it is made manifest by the negation of the fictional world. It is a sort of antimatter that must be approached, like

God, with dread because it signals the dissolution of the self in a larger mind. The course of Joyce's career is a constant expansion of his presence by which he assumes increasing dominance over a world of ever greater complexity. He controls this world so well that he often frees it from the knowledge of what will happen next from word to word — like an improvising virtuoso who can decide each note.

Robert Martin Adams says that once Joyce's mind passes through the black hole at the end of "Ithaca," it is never a daylight mind again.[25] I would add that once Joyce's fiction passes through this aperture, the individual characters in it are absorbed by Joyce's mind and become parts of a larger being. After this the problem of freedom, which haunted the early works, scarcely exists for Joyce's protagonists. They play their roles without question, for they are given to their world, as Joyce is given to his fictional creation. The movement toward subordination to a larger consciousness advances when Bloom swoons away after his consummation with Gerty. Gordon observes that after Bloom slips into a trance at the end of "Nausicaa," he stays in it for the next three episodes. His half-conscious state plays a role in generating many of the techniques of "Oxen," "Circe," and "Eumaeus."[26]

The dissolution of Bloom's mind and syntax on the last page of "Nausicaa" reduces the text to the level of primal matter, the chaos of substance without form: ". . . years dreams return tail end Agendath swoony lovey showed me her next year in drawers return next in her next her next" (*U* 382). I have compared primal matter, the intermediary between God and His creation, to the primary-process thinking Joyce transmits from his own unconscious into those of his characters and his world. The unformed mental substance at the end of "Nausicaa" leads directly into the shapeless language of the unborn unconscious before conception at the start of the succeeding "Oxen." Thus, the field of Joyce's mind becomes visible at the interstice between episodes. It maintains its visibility for the rest of the canon, which never again encloses itself in the convention of a "direct view" of the external world.

The union of Stephen and Bloom to form Joyce is parallel to the union of Shem and Shaun to form HCE. In his unconscious form as the atavistic dreamer Finnegan, Earwicker makes explicit Joyce's role as the mind that contains the work, and he is continually associated with God. His sons try to keep him at rest because he has to remain outside of the dream world of the *Wake* for that world to exist. They ask him to stay in his role of alpha and omega or *a* and *z*: "Now be aisy, good Mr. Finnimore, sir. And take your laysure like a god on pension and don't be walking abroad" (*FW* 24.16). He is asked to remain in the realm of possibilities beyond the world, "remembering your shapes and sizes" (*FW* 24.29), rather than take definite form. The conscious identity that has to be withdrawn in order to dream is compared to the God whose absence is the basis of physical existence. Joyce appears in his work as antimatter because contact with God is death to mortals: "*Prepare to meet your God,* says he" (*U* 628).

St. Paul describes God in the First Epistle to Timothy as "dwelling in the light which no man can approach unto: whom no man hath seen, nor can see" (6:16). Augustine comments: "In these words neither the Father, nor the Son, nor the Holy Spirit is mentioned especially by name, but 'the Blessed and Powerful One, King of kings, the Lord of lords,' which is the one, the only, the true God, the Trinity itself."[27] The individual Persons of the Trinity can be visualized, or at least the Father and the Son can. The Trinity itself, however, like the Holy Ghost, can only be represented symbolically. Augustine implies that the unity behind the Trinity is beyond human perception. Likewise, the identity of Joyce cannot be seen in any of his projections in the book or through the book to its readers. Yet this greater self is constituted by the work.

When it takes up a question that occurred to Bloom (*U* 274), the problem of what is behind music, the *Wake* refers to a traditional system whereby the mind of the author is the ultimate truth to be found in a work of art: ". . . for the melos yields the mode and the mode the manners plicyman, plansiman, plousiman, plab" (*FW* 57.2). Roland McHugh says that this refers to the stages by which Confucius learned to play the zither. First he learned the melody, then the rhythm, then the mood, and finally he knew the man who composed the music: ". . . his eyes when they looked into the distance had the calm gaze of a sheep."[28] And the *Wake* asserts repeatedly that its author can be perceived by careful attention to the text: ". . . if you are looking for the bilder deep your ear on the movietone!" (*FW* 62.8). He is to be found in the depths of the text that embodies his personal rhythm.

Yet the builder can be seen only as a *Bild* (Ger. "representation"), and there are many passages in the *Wake* that deny that the unifying factor, the identity above the book, can ever be located:

> Anyhow, somehow and somewhere, before the bookflood or after her ebb, somebody mentioned by name in his telephone directory, Coccolanius or Gallotaurus, wrote it, wrote it all . . . O, undoubtedly yes, and very potably so, but one who deeper thinks will always bear in the baccbuccus of his mind that this downright there you are and there it is is only all in his eye. Why? (*FW* 118.11-17)

Here the original identity of the author is lost in the complexity of the book as world; but it is only by being lost that he can gain the full authority of a creator. For the reality of a world depends on the subsidence of its god from its surface.

The end of this passage implies that the presence of the author is inseparable from the minds of his readers. If the reality of the *Wake* is located in the minds of its readers, this is because Joyce inhabits those minds through his ability to speak to and for them. He claimed this power aggressively. "Really, it is not I who am writing this crazy book," he said to Eugene Jolas during the thirties, "It is you, and you, and you, and that man over there, and that girl at the next table."[29] This story has been cited as an example of Joyce's humility,[30] but humility cannot exist without pride, and this is really an assertion of godhead. If I hand you an evelope and tell you that it contains a letter you have written, I am assuming authority over you. And if I add that you have never seen this letter, that you do not understand it, and that I inscribed it, but that it expresses your innermost being, then I am claiming absolute supernatural power. Joyce's conviction that he could speak for every person in the extra-Joycean world as well as the Joycean one is fundamental to the *Wake*.

The inevitability of misreading is, as Thomas indicates, a major theme in Joyce, but it does not seem that he believed that his text could be so misunderstood that its integrity could be lost. Rather, every misunderstanding is part of the total *Wake* structure that Joyce envisioned. After all, the culture Joyce shares with his readers must motivate them to make the effort necessary to read difficult texts. One of the elements that populate the *Wake* is a group of twelve jury members or pub customers whose function is to misunderstand. Presumably the book could not work without them.

Claude Lévi-Strauss holds that every version of a myth is part of that myth.[31] If, as I said earlier, the most sacred texts are those that support the widest latitude of interpretation, then the most unlikely interpretations of Joyce's text are the ones that show its maximum authority. The use of the term *quarks* (*FW* 383.1) for subatomic particles is one that Joyce could not have predicted. But he welcomed any suggestion that his work could be prophetic, as illustrated by his reaction to the resistance of the Finns to the Russians in November of 1939: "the Finn again wakes" (*JJ* 730). There is no book from which it would be more appropriate to take terms for newly-discovered phenomena than the *Wake*, which is written in newly-made words because it is designed to generate new meanings.

The paragraph following the passage cited above gives further reasons why it is virtually impossible to pin down the author of the *Wake*. It describes him as "the continually more and less intermisunderstanding minds of the anticollaborators" (*FW* 118.24–26). The idea that authorship of the *Wake* is confused among several people, which recurs (for example, *FW* 114.33), indicates that Joyce sees his mind as divided among conflicting beings. His critique of mental unity is psychologically valuable, but the parts of the mind cannot be seen as completely separated. For Joyce to actually abolish his own unity would be equivalent to a successful revolt of Shem and Shaun against their father. The *Wake* demonstrates that no matter how the sons try to eliminate HCE, that haunting choice encirclement keeps coming back.

The doubts and divisions that interact with each other so productively are precise expressions of Joyce's unique personality. The *Wake* uses a hiatus or separation as a signature of that projection of Joyce into the world of ordinary men which is HCE, for every time a stutter appears in the text, it indicates his presence. And discontinuities in the fabric of the text summon forth the presence of Joyce. He is articulated by this shifting congeries of interacting parts more fully than he could be by any stable monad, for the process of his mind is enacted by this verbal mobile that proceeds from his mind.

"Moving and changing every part of the time" (*FW* 118.22), a mobile is essentially a group of connections, and Joyce may be said to survive in his work as a string of transitions. But this image also incarnates one current scientific view of God, dramatized in Arthur C. Clarke's *2001: A Space Odyssey* — that our world could have evolved from a cloud of dust with the help of a few brilliant mutations. It is difficult to avoid attributing to these changes a good deal of power and purpose.

Without such an attribution, one cannot justify creative writing, which has always been an imitation of God, even when it was confined to monks. In fact, every kind of recreation, generating oneself, has been well understood as an imitation of a god. This is especially obvious in the arts, but it is true of all forms of enjoyment. The Greek idea of athletics, for example, was understood to refer to people imitating gods in the hope of becoming gods. It follows from the Scholastic definition of the Prime Mover that to strive for excellence is to strive for godhood.

Why then does Joyce deny his authority so emphatically in a voice he himself projects? A dreamer cannot be located as an actuality in his own dream. Why did Christ force his disciples to deny him by leading an unsupportable course? Because he represented something mysterious which was not, perhaps, beyond him, but beyond his conveying to men in explicit terms. Even if they share the same substance, the spiritual principle must be distinguished from the material one and kept unattainable because spirit must be perceived in the world through opposition. To grasp the ultimate presence of the author in a single statement would turn him from a being perpetually streaming with meaning to a statue, from a creator to a creature.

The aspect of Christ that is inaccessible to formulation is his divine aspect; and as George Herbert indicates in "The Pulley," it is the part of man that cannot find rest that binds him to the First Cause. The denial of formulation, the undertaking of the rigors of perpetual service to reformulation, is a gesture of spiritual obligation, a devotion to the abstract that removes one from the accepted world. Merely to designate something as unknowable is to shift it into the realm of the numinous, and the breaking of idols always implies that they fail to match the reality they aim at embodying. The more abstract the image of God, the more ineffable it is.

The indefinite descriptions of Joyce from within the dream of the *Wake*, of which the ones cited above are typical, match a mystical image of God evoked continually from Xenophones of Colophon to Borges, an infinite sphere whose center is everywhere.[32] No matter how far the characters may peer, even with the powerful telescope of "Ithaca," they can never see outside Joyce's circumference. And although they can hardly detect it, his center is in virtually every phrase of the *Wake* as a signature balancing the parts of his mind through opposed meanings.

The *Wake* is filled with recognition that the creatures who inhabit it are projections of a primal mind beyond their knowing. With every word he writes, the author is finished as a unity and wakes as a disinherited, partial being. Lost in the confusion of his dismemberment, the characters strive to reconstitute him. Their learning, for example, is an epistemological effort devoted to "establishing the identities of the writer complexus (for if the hand was one, the minds of active and agitated were more than so)" (*FW* 114.33).

By defining the minds of their author, the author of the letter that is equated with the *Wake*, they hope to identify themselves. But his real existence, the unity behind the multiplicity of his manifestations, is in another world that they can reach only by leaving their lives behind. The unified identity behind the dream is associated with the gigantic forefather, Finn MacCool, who usually has to be perceived indirectly through HCE because he is antecedent to the world of the *Wake*. The beings who inhabit the book are well described by the song title applied repeatedly in distorted form to HCE, "wather parted from the say" (*FW* 371.7, 371.30, and on the following two pages).[33] Like water parted from the sea, man yearns perpetually for return to the substance from which he emerged. Moreover, he is caught in a state of uncertainty ("whether") sundered from the affirmation of definite truth ("say").

The religion of these creatures aims at serving the mind containing minds that precedes and follows all of their history and includes their universe. Yet they have an underlying fear of his waking because if he united, he would stop projecting them, as Augustine says God projects all beings constantly, and they would be reabsorbed into him. Like Freud's totem sons, as the agents and creatures of his demise, they have high stakes in his death even while they feel him as the absolute source of life within themselves.

In the end, Finn awakes: the dreamer ends his dream and the cosmos he projects is reabsorbed into the infinite ocean of God. ALP, weary of the dream world she has been living in, feels herself drawn rushing back into her father to end the narrative universe until she emerges again with the force of a new cycle of emanation. The expanse of mind she lapses into may be applied Aquinas, for St. Thomas, quoting John of Damascus on God, says, ". . . *he comprehends all in himself, he has his existence as an ocean of being, infinite and unlimited*" (Q. 13, A. 11).

Among the various images of Joyce's creative action, the sea represents its fullness and inaccessibility. The image of the procession of the author into his work as a mental family, which I will consider next, represents the complex interactions of Joyce's mind in his creation. All of these images must be seen working in concert to understand how Joyce functions in his work. Attempts to describe how Joyce's world operates that ignore the superhuman forms of his personal activity are neglecting something essential.

Moreover, because Joyce was so knowledgeable about his divine role, principles may be derived from the study of his immanence that will apply to other writers who freed themselves from conventions. For whenever a novelist rejects the silent gods of convention, he puts his personality in a position to dictate the metaphysical laws usually enforced by tradition. The personal images of divine creation in many novelists can be examined in order to show the systems by which they operate their worlds.

6   The Mind as Family

The Ancient Giant

Finnegans Wake is about a mind that contains all of history in a dream. The essentially religious nature of the image of dreaming an entire world is suggested by its appearance in Dostoevsky.[1] The dreamer projects his mind as a group of individual beings bound together as a family that tends to fuse into a single multiple personality. Part of this concept is really new and part seems new because it is old. The spirit of all of the members of a family (including both participants in a patricide) is after all hailed as a unity at the end of Dostoevsky's most fully elaborated work: "Hurrah for Karamazov!"

The mind made up of a family of minds is an image of divinity, the ideal mental structure Joyce strove to unite with in adolescence. Though the church holds that the three Persons of the Trinity have the same mind, this is officially recognized as a difficult truth for men to grasp. Joyce was attracted to heretics such as Arius and Origen, who distinguished the minds of the three Persons. If these three differ, they are capable of relating to each other in complex ways; and if their relation is familial, it is generative, capable of creating new mind or minds. *Ulysses* presents a familial relationship between three people that is mentally generative in a way that is quite unconscious to the characters, though the reader may bring it to his consciousness if he exerts himself.

The mind that contains the universe of the *Wake* must be that of a god. In order to succeed as a god, it must create life, and so it enters the *Wake* by dreaming of itself as a family. The mind of God enters the world through a holy family not only because the fullness of life always arises from a family, but because only through a family can the mind be represented in its completeness. For each member of a close family contains each of the others in his mind as an introjection, and thus he includes the whole. He can refer to, let us say, the hardness of father, the softness of mother, the innocence of a daughter, or the eagerness of a son.

Joyce, a believer in what social scientists refer to as Irish familism, felt that the mind had to unfold itself into a series of minds in order to develop. Moreover, it is logical that the structure of Joyce's god should be the structure of the family because in Irish society God was most often manifested through the family organization He supported. He was frequently invoked through family rituals and restraints.

The most elaborate model in the West for the unfolding of God's mind into the world is the Tree of Life, the main pictogram of the Jewish system of knowledge of God called the Kabbalah. The ten intelligences that make up the Tree are arranged in a pattern that resembles a family, with power flowing downward from a male and female couple under a crown at the top. The Tree plays a key role in defining the structure of the letter in the *Wake*, which is the structure at once of the book, of God, of the eternal family, and of Joyce's presence in his work.

Cope claims that *Ulysses* reflects extensive reading in the major work of the Kabbalah, the *Sepher ha Zohar* (Book of Splendor), and in the many theosophical works on kabbalism available to Joyce.[2] Cope effectively expands our recognition of Joyce's knowledge of the Kabbalah, but some of his observations are more suggestive than conclusive. Actually, the work containing an account of the Kabbalah for which Joyce's use has been most solidly demonstrated is Helena Petrovna Blavatsky's *Isis Unveiled*. Clive Hart shows that the *Wake* paraphrases this bulky theosophical synthesis, which Joyce recommended to Stuart Gilbert.[3]

It may be that Joyce's knowledge of the Kabbalah was spotty, for he is not accurate in developing the system. What he presents is a personal elaboration of certain features of the tradition. After all, the mind that contains this particular universe is his. But this mind is developed through the content of its book, and the Kabbalah shapes and animates the most systematic presentation of God and humanity as a unified structure in the *Wake*, in the tenth chapter, also known as II.2, "The Study Period," and "Night Lessons," the subject of this chapter.

To construct the human mind through his own is a goal Stephen Dedalus announces, referring to the mind of man in the singular: ". . . to forge in the smithy of my soul the uncreated conscience of my race." This consciousness, however, is not something that has never existed, but something that has been uncreated by denial, by the unfairness of history, and by the fallen nature of the world, factors Stephen sees most directly in Ireland.

Fundamental to the concept of the multipersonal mind in Joyce is the myth that all of humanity was originally united in one giant being who included the universe within himself. This myth is actualized in the *Wake*. Many theories of multipersonality may be traced back to kabbalistic sources, and the major ancient version of this myth to which Joyce refers is the figure of Adam Kadmon, the primordial or heavenly Adam, who is mentioned in *Ulysses* (*U* 38). The body of Adam Kadmon is equated in the Kabbalah with the Tree of Life, which contains and gives birth to the world, and this equation is found in *Isis Unveiled* (2:213, 270).

Similar suggestions of archaic expansiveness appear in Vico, who says that heroic education brings forth "the form of the human soul, which had been completely submerged in the huge bodies of the giants."[4] The main literary embodiment of this theory for Joyce, however, is Blake's Albion. According to *Jerusalem: The Emanation of the Giant Albion*, the world we live in was formed when this giant fell asleep and divided himself into a fallen state of alienation, separating his parts. Thus, Blake addresses the Jews on their kabbalism, which he assumes to be derived from Celtic sources:

> You have a tradition, that Man anciently contain'd in his mighty limbs all things in Heaven & Earth: this you recieved [*sic*] from the Druids. "But now the Starry Heavens are fled from the mighty limbs of Albion"
> Albion was the Parent of the Druids; & in his Chaotic State of Sleep Satan & Adam & the whole World was Created by the Elohim.
> The fields from Islington to Marybone,
> To Primrose Hill and Saint Johns Wood:
> Were builded over with pillars of gold,
> And there Jerusalems pillars stood.
> (Plate 27)

A statement Joyce made in 1907 helps us to see how the Kabbalah could be conceived of as having originated with Celts: "The religion and civilization of this ancient people, later known by the name of Druidism, were Egyptian" (*CW* 156). I indicated in my third chapter that the *Wake* refers to this passage from Blake. Upon the body of Blake's sleeping giant the slums of London extend from Islington to Marybone, replacing the lost city of Jerusalem in which humanity was united. As Joseph Campbell and Henry Morton Robinson point out, this pattern is reproduced in the *Wake,* which opens with Tim Finnegan laid out as landscape from one end of Dublin to the other.[5]

The myth of Albion and other myths that suggest a submerged universal consciousness (as all myths do) are not merely adjuncts or targets for the world of the *Wake:* they are its substance. They form the absolute basis of its reality because it is a dream. All myths tend to be true in the archaic world of dream, and the uncertainty and negation with which they may be surrounded are defenses used to conceal a truth whose full realization would end the life of the dream by bringing about a waking. The creator of the dream is involved in it, drawn in different directions within its imaginative space by its various images of desire, and anxious to be overwhelmed by the randomness of its reality. But his visionary aspect, seeing beyond the created world, wants to use this world to awaken Finnegan by reconstructing the lost unity—to awaken humanity by building the most complex possible image of the human mind, an image to show that we are both one and many.

In fact, the idea that all of humanity would unite if the giant would awake from his slumber is, for those who live in the *Wake* world, as undeniable as mortality is for us. The unique form of the *Wake* as a dream of cosmic extensiveness entails extreme metaphysical conditions. The characters are parts of the mind of a gigantic being who includes the entire vertiginously complex universe they live in. Time, space, identity, and causality are created for them moment by moment by the mind that activates them.

This mind that is a universe must certainly be identified with God. In fact, dreaming is a godlike experience, and as such, it has always provided a foundation for perception of the reality of God. If the dreamer is God, it is also true that several authorities, influenced by hundreds of relatively noticeable biographical references, have identified the dreamer of the *Wake* as at least on some level Joyce.[6] To me, it seems significant that Joyce's mind, which is unlike any other mind, is the system that generates every detail of the *Wake.*

I have suggested that Joyce's remark to Jolas that his work was being written by "you" reflects a conviction that he could speak for all human beings, a tendency to claim omniscience outside his work as well as within it. Writers who offer readers choices of interpretation frequently are taking authoritative, if not authoritarian, positions. If I give you a model kit to construct, I subject you to more restrictions by far than if I gave a finished model. The author who gives a choice of two readings is controlling his reader on two sides by taking both into account.

This tends to have the effect that there is nothing the reader can do to avoid his grip without leaving the text, and even that suicidal gesture may not help.

At the same time that Joyce gives the reader freedom in areas that he defines, he implants himself in the reader's mind as a principle that is active because it is divided. This process is like the mechanism whereby the humility of Christianity engages converts. When someone turns the other cheek on you, your feelings about him become ambivalent and hard to forget. As Joyce withholds his authority, you are released from your world into his; and by union with his mind, you develop part of your own.

As a creative principle in the mind of every man (Augustine, *Confessions,* VII.10), God must be enmeshed in a system of substitutions that keeps human godhood from consciousness. The original sense of infinity that we are born with is held under by a series of rational compromises with the outside world; and if this sense of infinity is our deepest reality, then our ordinary reality is a dream. The conscious mind that substitutes material objects for subjective reality is driven by a pride that withholds us from recognizing our dependence on a principle of prior causality within or behind or beyond or above us as the Joycean artist-god is above his work. This spiritual perspective on the human situation, which Joyce learned in his youth, defines the status of the characters in his mature work.

Individuality is a delusion for the creatures of the *Wake:* the very words with which they keep asserting their properties and proprieties are continually reversing themselves as they are uttered. Thus, HCE describes his innocence as "the lilliths oft I feldt" (*FW* 366.25); Shaun says his brother "ought to be . . . asamed of me" (*FW* 489.18); and Isabel protests that she will "betrue" her lover (*FW* 459.20).

The delusion of individuality, however, gives them the power to contribute to the unique totality that propels and is propelled by them. Insofar as they escape from Joyce's mind, that mind adds to itself. The characters animate the totality in which they move, and this overall being is the focus of the book. Immortal and suprahuman, it extends beyond the limits of individuals and across the range of their faculties. It is the mind of God represented as the context of life through the shape of an eternal family of interacting parts.

The Mind Factory

The most graphic and systematic representation of this mind in the *Wake* is the tenth chapter, which has a theoretical importance for the book parallel to that of "Scylla and Charybdis," another seminar, for *Ulysses*. "The Study Period" is about the development of knowledge, but it is also about the making of a world: "CONSTITUTION OF THE CONSTITUTIONABLE AS CONSTITUTIONAL" (*FW* 261.23). Thus, the chapter is loaded with references to cosmological systems that are also systems of the formation of the mind, the most important ones being the Kabbalah, Plato's *Timaeus,* and Yeats's *A Vision.*

I have already suggested that the Tree of Life is both the universe and the mind. Thus, for example, A. E. Waite supports the claim that "there is nothing in the Kabalah which is not found also in the nature of man."[7] In the *Timaeus,* the orbits of the Same and the Other are found both in the heavens and in the soul; and Yeats's gyres are images both of history and of psychology. Moreover, these are not three separate systems for Joyce, but aspects of one system. He had read in Blavatsky that the *Timaeus* was based on the same sources as the Kabbalah (1:7–8), and he was aware that when Yeats put *A Vision* together, his head was filled "with Cabbalistic imagery.[8]

The form of this chapter, with its separate discourses in three columns and its footnotes, may be seen as embodying an interaction between parts. The wide central column bears the continuous action of the scene, a process of mental development in which the male and female principles, HCE and ALP, work together. To the right and left of this column are comments by the pompous son, Kevin (Shaun), and the rebellious son, Dolph (Shem), and under it are uninformative footnotes by the flirtatious daughter, Isabel. Thus, every member of the family has a role in this quadrophonic text.

The fact that the separation of these voices was a late development in the composition of the *Wake* indicates that this step was one of the most sophisticated in the progress of the work. Joyce began working on manuscript versions of this section in 1926, but he did not divide the manuscript into columns until 1934.[9] It took him years to educe the polyphony underlying this discourse, but when he did so, he was only clarifying what was already implicit in this section and in the whole *Wake.* For the idea that HCE is capable of generating the other characters, as he does on the first page, and the idea that the letter was written by "a multiplicity of personalities" (*FW* 107.24) were established in Book I. Though some of the material in Issy's footnotes and elsewhere is drawn from other notes,[10] the fact that Joyce was able to separate four discourses out of one shows that they are all parts of one mind. It is usually not one person who is speaking at any point in the *Wake,* but a group of people. The different meanings simultaneously present in each word constitute different voices. By saying different things in the same situation, they act like different people. The interaction of these congruent voices is analyzed in II.2.

It seems that each of the four voices but Shem's is capable of taking over the narrative that is usually controlled by the central column, the column of love. At one point, after the mind of the text has been stirred (and disturbed) by a long erotic passage, one of Issy's footnotes swells to take up most of a page (*FW* 279). At another, when Shem's revelation of the origin of life in ALP's primary point of emptiness has stirred the anxiety of the Shaun aspect of its mind, the text is taken over for a six-page parenthesis by the authoritarian mind of Kevin (*FW* 287-292). Both of these interludes are distractions from the main process of development in this episode. Issy's little romp (enough to make one a footnote fetishist!) is announced as an intermission (*FW* 278.7); and when Kev takes over, the mind grows abstracted and stops moving.[11] These interruptions represent unbalanced states of mind—as well, perhaps, as historical periods of cultural aberration, such as degeneracy and puritanism. Neither of these voices is capable of carrying on the narrative by itself, for the full life of the human mind demands the activities of all five functions.

During his parenthetically muted solo, Kevin presents in Latin a specific statement of the relation between the two brothers in this chapter:

> . . . *totum tute fluvii modo mundo fluere* . . . *quodlibet sese ipsum per aliudpiam agnoscere contrarium, omnem demun amnem ripis rivalibus amplecti.* (*FW* 287.25-28)

Gilbert Highet translates as follows:

> . . . that the whole universe flows safely like a river . . . that anything recognizes itself through some contrary, and finally . . . that the whole river is enfolded in the rival banks along its sides.[12]

The image of the two brothers as banks of the stream of life was prominent in the ALP section. And just as Shem and Shaun join to make HCE, so the main narrative here is defined as a constant compromised between their two extremes: "*The Twofold Truth and the Conjunctive Appetites of Oppositional Orexes*" (*orex* means longing or appetite, *FW* 305.12). The penultimate Latin word above reinforces the universality of this image of dialectic by reminding us that *rival* is derived from riverbanks. Thus, the mental development of humanity, which is referred to here as *totus mundi* because it provides all knowledge of the world, is defined by the opposition between internal rebellion and external authority. The learning experience in this chapter is a dialogue in which the twins meet in the center column — presumably on the basis of a harmony established by their parents. What is learned depends on what the boys are capable of communicating to each other.

Current brain lobe theory implies that in much of its activity, the mind does not express one consciousness — it expresses a compromise between two very different kinds of thinking. The rational left hemisphere and the sensual right hemisphere cooperate in ordinary mental activity. If Shem and Shaun fit this theory neatly, it is because the theory itself matches ancient traditions.

Freud believed that all civilizations went through early stages in which every quality was seen as composed of opposites. That is, there was one word for cold and hot, one for early and late, one for live and dead, and so forth. Such dual meanings, for Freud, remain operative in the modern mind on the unconscious level of primary-process thinking.[13] Freud's main examples are from ancient Egypt, and this definition by opposition is a key principle of hermetism, which claims to be descended from Thoth, the Egyptian god of writing to whom Stephen ironically devotes himself in *Portrait* (P 225). The right and left lobes control the left and right sides of the body respectively, and the physical branch of hermetic science, alchemy, uses a sophisticated system of right-and-left symbolism.[14] Hermetic science is the basis for much of Gnosticism, the Kabbalah, and Bruno's theory of coinciding contraries. Gnosticism, which influenced kabbalism, posited a structure called the Pleroma that resembled the Tree of Life.[15] It is through such sources that Shem and Shaun embody the right and left hemispheres, thus predicting recent discoveries.

In addition to being hemmed in by the brothers, the central column is continually interrupted by the underlying insouciance of Issy and preoccupied with the relation between HCE and ALP. It is therefore presented as a mode of development and expression constituted by the interaction of five forces. Thus it resembles one of the most sophisticated psychic apparatuses developed by psychoanalysis, Robert Waelder's principle of multiple function. This theory sees the ego as mediating among four powers that shape it: the id, the superego, the reality principle, and repetition compulsion.[16] One could relate Issy, Shem, ALP, and Shaun, respectively, to these agencies; but the main point here is that in both systems the discourse of mental life is an interplay among multiple functions, as reflected by the way these four figures give to and take from the central column.

In Joyce's system, however, not only the ego, but all of the functions are persons, and this makes their totality more complex than that of Waelder's system. Because Waelder's functions are not given specific personalities, they tend to devolve into mere mechanical devices. People can change and interact qualitatively, while machines cannot, and so no mechanical device can approach the complexity of a person. Joyce's five-being mind may seem more than human, but his aim in such constructions is to make humanity more than it is.

The possibility of expanding the psychoanalytic model toward the fullness of the *Wake* has been suggested without reference to Joyce by the pure phenomenology of Edmund Husserl. The essences Husserl values are drawn from various types of intuition interacting with each other. In his system, every perception has a zone of background intuitions, and a thing can be given consciousness in only one of its aspects, a part of its complete being. White points out the parallels between these ideas and the operation of the *Wake* world. Husserl, however, was not describing a psychic apparatus, and he denied the dynamic nature of the unconscious. His intuitions, like Waelder's functions, are not personalities, and by the same token each is not divided into interacting parts. These intuitions are defined through a series of procedures for reducing perceptions to purity, and so they tend to appear as mechanical abstractions.[17]

The kind of vital multiple being presented in the *Wake* and an explanation of how it works are central subjects of the study chapter. And the main system Joyce uses here to represent the development of this mind is the Kabbalah. The existing works of the Kabbalah go back only to the tenth through thirteenth centuries, but it is generally regarded as a far older system. Joyce, as I have suggested, saw it as predating not only Christianity, but Judaism. He was aware of Bruno's statement that the wisdom of the Kabbalah "derives from the Egyptians, among whom Moses was brought up."[18] Similarly, *Isis Unveiled* sees a connection between the Kabbalah and "the cosmological theory of numerals which Pythagoras learned from the Egyptian hierophants" (1:7). Because the Kabbalah is such an ancient and technologically developed system for describing the operation of God before creation and the operation of the mind before reason, it is given a primal role in the night lessons. It provides the framework whereby a volition coming from outside the created world is shown to generate all of the personalities of the family out of itself.

According to the Eleventh Edition of the *Encyclopaedia Britannica,* one of Joyce's probable sources, the Kabbalah begins its cosmology with a formless principle of infinity called the Ain-Soph:

> In this boundlessness He could not be comprehended by the intellect or described in words, and as such the Ēn Sōph was in a certain sense *Ayin,* non existent. . . . As creation involves intention, desire, thought and work, and as these are properties which imply limit and belong to a finite being, and moreover as the imperfect and circumscribed nature of this creation precludes the idea of its being the direct work of the infinite and perfect, the Ēn Sōph had to become creative, through the medium of ten Sephiroth or intelligences, which emanated from him like rays proceeding from a luminary.[19]

Because this principle is equated with nothingness, it may be said to correspond to Stephen's statement that the world is founded on the void. The ten *sephiroth,* or "zephiroth" (*FW* 29.13), are complex beings: each has a number, a name, an angel, and a series of qualities. They form the geometrical diagram known as the Tree of Life, or *Etz Haiyim,* which, by a further series of emanations, constitutes the universe in the form of Adam Kadmon and then makes man.

The Tree is itself divided into three columns. Waite, who presents the Tree as the frontispiece of his *Doctrine and Literature of the Kabalah,* indicates that the three *sephiroth* on the right are called the Pillar of Mercy, the three on the left, the Pillar of Severity, and the four in the center, the Pillar of Benignity (see figure, p. 126). The central column of the Tree, which is associated with equilibrium,[20] is understood to be balanced between the two outer ones, which match the mercy and justice of Shem and Shaun. This suggests the way in which the central column of Joyce's structure is balanced between the outer two as a compromise between Dolph and Kev.

McHugh's *Annotations* point out that the ten *sephiroth* appear in the form of ten questions early in the tenth chapter (*FW* 261.28–31). Campbell and Robinson see references to the *sephiroth* in the three triads of qualities listed in the middle of the chapter (*FW* 270–271) and in the list of ten syllables at the end (*FW* 308).[21] McHugh identifies these syllables as based on the Gaelic numbers from one to ten. The marginal comments on these numbers, which include such terms as "Bimutualism" and "Interpenetrativeness," suggest awareness of the extremely complex modes of interaction among the elaborate beings who make up the Tree.

Two of the most prominent references to the Kabbalah in II.2, the presentation of "Ainsoph" (*FW* 261.23) and the vertical list of ten numbers at the end, both appeared for the first time in the 1934 manuscript in which Joyce first divided the text into columns.[22] The decision to use the columns was thus accompanied by a decision to emphasize the Kabbalah, and this tends to confirm the likelihood that the Pillars of the Tree were a source for Joyce's columns. Incidentally, another possible source for the three columns, which were eventually to be imitated in Derrida's *Glas*, was Abel Gance's triple-screen film *Napoleon* (1927), which had a long run in Paris.

The Family Unfolds

Having suggested how significant the Kabbalah was for II.2, I will turn to a detailed reading of the opening of this section, using psychological concepts informed by kabbalistic principles. "Night Lessons" starts with a consciousness that finds itself talking to itself without knowing who or where it is: "As we there are where are we are we there . . ." (*FW* 260.1). As it grows aware of itself, it realizes how little it knows about its ontological status. Its lack of context serves to illustrate the idea that thought cannot exist without coming from somewhere and being aimed at something. This idea appears in the first marginal gloss, Kev's "UNDE ET UBI," for *unde* means "from where"; and while *ubi* simply means "where," it is often used to mean "to where," as it does in Swift's epitaph, and it probably tends to have this meaning when juxtaposed with *unde*. The disorientation in the first pages of this chapter represents the process of leaving the chaos of the ordinary world behind to create the mental world of study. It is parallel to the linguistic chaos that precedes birth at the start of the "Oxen of the Sun" episode of *Ulysses*. The creation of the world of knowledge in the *Wake* illustrates kabbalistic principles of emanation.

We cannot be conscious of ourselves without talking to ourselves, and so the mind must be divided into active and passive or subject and object or masculine and feminine in order to exist. This is why "primal made alter in the garden of Idem" ("first made other in the garden of the Same," *FW* 263.20). The image of the first men building an altar to worship part of themselves fits in with Jaynes's thesis that the gods were projections of the bicameral mind.

Volition requires a human object to complete it: "Whom will comes over. Who to caps ever" (*FW* 260.4). The will is conceived of as movement toward a goal, and this goal has to be alive, for inanimate objects of desire can only imitate animate ones. Therefore one must have another person in one's mind to be fully alive. The idea is similar to the ego ideal that Heinz Kohut believes one must introject in order to have a solid identity, but the Joycean version is considerably more active.[23] Only by attaching its motivation (or uplift) to a living object can the mind make a local habitation for itself: "And howelse do we hook our hike to find that pint of porter place" (*FW* 260.5). As this line appears, Dolph comments on "*his broad and hairy face,*" and Campbell and Robinson see this as a reference to *Makroprosopos,* the kabbalistic image of God before the Creation as a great bearded face.[24]

The *Zohar* says, "When the Holy Aged, the concealed of all concealed, assumed a form, he produced everything in the form of male and female, as things could not continue in any other form."[25] This corresponds to the hermetic principle that "no creation, physical, mental or spiritual, is possible" without "the principle of gender."[26] In order to create, the Joycean mind has to divide itself into male and female sides so that it can interact with itself; and Gershom Scholem points out that the Kabbalah emphasizes "the distinction between the masculine and feminine, begetting and receiving potencies in God."[27] The Eleventh *Britannica* and Blavatsky both stress the ways in which the *Ain-Soph* projects female forms in the *sephiroth* in order to draw itself into creation; in fact, Blavatsky identifies the first *sephirah* as female (2:213), an unusual claim.

As soon as the mind hooks its hike in our *Wake* passage, it is stricken with libido: "Am shot, says the bigguard." And at this point a footnote summons Issy forth for the first time to say, "Rawmeash," a combination of the Irish *raimeis,* its English equivalent, "romance," and its naturalistic equivalent, raw meat. Most of the points at which Issy's voice is heard seem to be occasions of desire or anxiety, so that one of her main functions for the multimind of the text seems to be related to the release of energy. The surge of desire at this point causes a rapid movement of the mind in the center column through a series of streets named for the achievements of civilization in various fields, a movement that leads, at the bottom of the page, to the idea of union with a female. Like the ego, the center column is the arena of progress.

The image of the big god shot is connected to Cupid's arrows, which symbolize the tendency of desire to strike or attack. Lacan asks why man must assume the attributes of sexuality "only through a threat."[28]

In *Portrait,* Stephen is first attracted to Emma Clery immediately (in the text) after he is mistaken for a woman, an event likely to threaten his manhood.[29] And in the present *Wake* passage, the movement of the imagination toward the female image is preceded by "But fahr, be fear!" which includes the German *fahren,* "go towards," and is followed by a list of kinds of fear (*FW* 260.15-16; see McHugh's *Annotations*) and then by the image of marriage with a "moll." The Kabbalah portrays the *Ain-Soph* as prior to sexual division, but Joyce portrays it as male. In both, the Ain-Soph's attraction to the feminine principle causes him to divide himself into the *sephiroth,* and perhaps the reason desire tends to be preceded by anxiety is that it is a self-division. As an artist must be discontented with his world before he creates a new one, so a lover must be motivated to project his soul into another being.

The *Ain-Soph* is drawn to emanate the *sephiroth* by an attraction to the female ones, especially the third, Binah, who completes the first triad at the top of the Tree, and the tenth. The tenth *sephirah,* Malkuth, is probably referred to by the "moll" above. She is equated in some states with the material world and in others with the Shekinah. The Eleventh *Britannica* describes the Shekinah, the Divine Mother, as a halo encircling the whole. Waite refers to her as the point of contact between matter and spirit, "the place of the manifestation of the Deity."[30]

As the last of the *sephiroth,* Malkuth is the intermediate substance between God and His world. In *Ulysses,* she is manifested as Molly Bloom, and the black hole through which the text slips into Joyce's mind at the end of "Ithaca" is hers. The feminine opening into nothingness is one entrance of the creator into his world, a place of manifestation of his deity; and we will soon see this focal point of expressive strokes identified as the scene of writing.

As the marriage images proceed in II.2, Malkuth recurs as the bride: "Ainsoph, this upright one, with that noughty besighed him zeroine" (*FW* 261.21). It is she who is later diagramed (*FW* 293). The fundamentality of the female's drawing the male into existence is a key point in this chapter, the one Dolph tries to teach Kev. The active defines itself through the passive, exists by pursuing the passive, as Joyce exists by filling the space of his world. As the voice of the maternal power puts it, "To me or not to me" (*FW* 269.19). Being manifests itself by moving toward her, so that his becoming depends on her becomingness.

The essence of feminine attraction is seen here as an emptiness that summons forth possibilities. As McHugh notes, the tag from Euclid, "*quod erat faciendum:* which was to be done," is rendered through the Latin *fossa,* "ditch," as ALP's sex organ: "Quicks herit [her it] fossyending" (*FW* 298.4). Being a generator of potentiality, ALP is decked out in uncertainties: "while still the maybe mantles the meiblume or ever her if have faded from the fleur" (*FW* 267-268). Her power to motivate emanation is such that she is portrayed as sauntering around the *Etz Haiyim:* ". . . she shall tread them lifetrees leaves . . ." (*FW* 280.29).

ALP as alma mater is the "ondrawer of our unconscionable, flicker-flapper fore our unterdrugged" (*FW* 266-267). Drugged by his underside (Issy), HCE is dragged forward to make the narrative. His unconscious, the Freudian *Unterdrückt,* is drawn forth in his actions—and the more unconscionable they are, the more active it is. Yet she pulls his unconscious into consciousness by making him manifest his desires. The action of humanity in this section is specifically learning, but the argument assumes that all human activity is learning because the value of such activity is limited to what it contributes to the mind, if only through sensation. The essence of learning is seen here, as in Augustine's (*Confessions,* X.11), as a drawing forth of what is potential in the soul, a development of godhood implanted within.

According to the Eleventh *Britannica,* the interaction of the male spiritual principle and the female material one generates the world: "The conjunction of the Sephiroth, or, according to the language of the Kabbalah, the union of the crowned King and Queen, produced the universe in their own image." This union is the ongoing process of life, the interplay between minds, both interpersonal and intrapersonal. The children as emanations carry this process on here. Not only do their parents recur in the subjects they study, but the learning process parallels the union of the parents by uniting the spirits of the children with the material world.

HCE himself does not appear in this episode except as a monument or an old story. In realistic terms, he is not present at the study session, but he is also absent because the thinking in this episode approaches his spiritual meaning, his ancient form, which cannot be apprehended directly. Here, as in most of the book, he is a substratum beneath the world he created. The first person plural in which this section tends to speak—when it is not taken over by one of the children, such as the professorial Kevin—is panoramic and tends to be universal. Insofar as this voice stands for everyone, HCE is omnipresent in his children. As a creative principle, he cannot be contained in the dream world he creates: his essence, identified with Finnegan, cannot be manifested in actuality any more than the *Ain-Soph.* When HCE does appear, as in the following chapter, it is as a feeble, incompetent shadow of the real power he represents.

The abstraction and dispersal of HCE's name indicate that he represents a principle, a structure that recurs in myriad forms. This group of three letters could be called a kabbalistic triangle, a group of three *sephiroth* that function as an active group. When the mind is functioning creatively, HCE is congruent with ALP's triangle and in contact with it. The interface they share is the meeting place of spirit and matter, corresponding to the substance with two aspects, where creative action or emanation takes place. The sexual nature of the process of emanation is indicated by the fact that each of the *sephiroth* is male in relation to the one it creates, but female in relation to the one before it (*Isis Unveiled,* 2:267-268). But emanation is more than sexual — it is the creation of spiritual life. The *Zohar* calls on married couples to enjoy each other because the Divine Presence is constituted by the union of male and female (I.49b). Hart identifies a description of emanation in Blavatsky that Joyce uses: "Imagine a given point in space as the primordial one; then with compasses draw a circle around this point; where the beginning and the end unite together, emanation and reabsorption meet" (1:348).[31]

Joyce's version aims at maximizing interaction through sex. It says that if you want to know where your partner is located, first make contact with one of her orifices, and then with the other, and you will have a tumultuous, cyclonic experience.

> And to find a locus for an alp get a howlth on her bayrings as a prisme O and for a second O unbox your compasses. . . . (*FW* 287.8-11) With Olaf as centrum and Olaf's lambtail for his spokesman circumscript a cyclone. (*FW* 294)

By making the spokesman here a finger that reaches around (*circum*) to inscribe, Joyce makes this act of sex and geometry resemble fingerpainting gestures that are basic to all writing. The passage seems to use the compass image to imply that to express one's individuality fully, one must supplement normal behavior with perversion. This arrangement confirms and expands the idea of the black dot, which ends the action of Ulysses, as a major point of emanation between Joyce and his world. If this spot, which is evidently the anus, is thought of by Joyce as the place where he expresses himself most vividly, then all of his writing, because it parallels these ideal strokes, is imaginatively located at this aperture into the unknown. But the spot may also be the vagina, and the two-point model in the *Wake,* by covering both possibilities, is more complete. By presenting a sex act that involves two different movements at once in two different places, it represents an act of writing that involves two voices and two minds.

Joyce's tendency to "multiply the inlets of happiness" (*U* 402) enriches his contact with his creatures. Riquelme, taking an image from Freud's dream theory, says that Stephen is connected to the artist in his future by a navel.[32] In fact, every opening into the interior of Joyce's characters is likely to lead to a substratum of Joyce. This pattern is parallel to Blakean mythology, for Blake, in *The Marriage of Heaven and Hell,* speaks of the five senses as "the chief inlets of soul in this age." He believes that the expansion of the senses and of sexuality leads toward a return to the original state of infinite possession. On a more realistic level, Joyce locates knowledge within the body because he wants to focus on the mind of the body, which is one of the most complex and active of the minds that make up personal totality.

Both Joyce and the Kabbalah use sexuality as the most concrete and vital model of the give and take of creativity, but intercourse does not have to be sexual. I have mentioned how Winnicott describes the creative interface as based on the intermediate zone between inner and outer that a mother maintains for her child. Because the distinction between what is him and what is not is abolished in this area, the child can play with reality to expand his perceptions without worrying about his limits. Winnicott holds that all creativity makes use of such free space.

The image of the Tree as a mind made up of interacting minds allows Joyce to conceive of such spaces as working on various levels and at various angles within the mind when the parts of the mind relate to each other creatively. Within such areas, the spiritual or Joycean potentiality of HCE is free to manifest itself: he can realize Joyce by realizing himself. Thus ALP's ability to yield, as it operates in the feminine aspects of the mind that contains both protagonists, is what creates HCE. He is presented as a product of her soft concavities: "*Her*cushiccups' *c*are to *e*duce" (*FW* 355.12, my italics).

The mental principle generates itself by generating the external world as "maker mates with made" (*FW* 261.8). The more the maker imagines, the more he exists, but as he extends himself into his creations, his original formlessness is left behind. He gives up his freedom with the imagination he projects onto the objects of his attention, fixing his mind on them. By the fertility of his union with the world he dreams, he articulates and multiplies his personality at the expense of unity, giving himself to humanity to become "a manyfeast munificent more mob than man" (*FW* 261.21).

This expansion results in polarization, introducing elements of male competition. On the level of the dream narrative, the union of male and female creates a child, resulting in father-son conflict. On the level of action and reaction within the mind, any contact with the world creates a new image that competes with prior ones. As Derrida puts it, every impression has to follow a previous trace.[33] In this way, Joyce sees a structure resembling the oedipal complex as built into the mind. The composite image formed by the interplay of the old, established view and the new, importunate one is our image of the world, the only world we know.

The localization of a specific world in the clutch of such interaction serves to reify the spiritual being that existed before that consolidation. Thus we are taken through the seven wonders of the ancient world, the imagination made concrete, only to end with HCE in a mausoleum, the spirit reduced to matter: "Length Withoght Breath" (*FW* 261.13). On the following page, as we enter the house, the same steps that lead to the social world of the pub bury HCE as "Hoo cavedin earthwight," a line soon followed by echoes of the Mass for the Dead (*FW* 262.11–17).

Active connection with the world disintegrates the original unity, for possessions inevitably lead to projections that tend to have independent beings. As the mind of the author grows involved in his work, it becomes divided by the conflicts necessary to make that work live. The early descriptions of the Earwicker household in the course of this progressive constitution of "IDEAREAL HISTORY" (*FW* 262.7) are attended by "ARCHAIC ZELOTYPIA" or jealousy (*FW* 264.1) and by social distinctions such as "LATIFUNDISM," the ownership of large estates (*FW* 264.20), and father-son conflict: "*Move up, Mackinerny! Make room for Muckinerny!*" (*FW* 264.22). The *Makroprosopos* is replaced by his earthly emanation, but he remains present above and below the surface reality of the text as Finnegan, the absolute aspect of HCE that his sons continually try to suppress because his waking will dissolve them. Though this dreamer seems, from the point of view of a world formed by his mind, to be beyond form, it is possible to identify quite specifically the one mind that contains all of the material in the *Wake* as potential. The book is an expression of the mind of Joyce, and it develops that mind to a unique extent by representing it as a population.

Cerebral Conversions

The overall movement of chapter 10 involves a first half that is mainly concerned with attraction to the female, the force that draws the mind into learning (*FW* 267–281), and a second half concerned with the brother conflict that follows from the resultant specification of knowledge. The goal of truth that such precision aims at is defined here as ALP. Not only does male conflict always imply a female prize, but desire always precipitates male conflict — for even within a single mind, the energy of desire is always based on internal opposition. In view of this, desire that does not involve inner conflict is likely to be paltry.

The major action of this chapter is the interaction of the two brothers. Dolph, who is turned inward, reveals the secret of their origin to Kev, bringing him into contact with the spiritual; and Kev, who is turned outward, punches Dolph, bringing him into contact with the physical. In order to make contact with each other, they have to transform themselves into active and passive principles in the middle column; but their identities as incomplete offshoots lie in their remarks on the sides.

The point at which Dolph reveals that they come from and go to the mother is a moment of self-consciousness when the mind that contains them becomes aware of its dependence on the unknown, on unconscious roots that reach back before formed identity. At this point of education ("drawing forth") or civilization, the inner side of the mind is externalized as the external object is recognized as expressing what is within. This is one reason why the outer columns of Joyce's text change sides at this point of insight. A suggestive parallel is found in the study of the Tree of Life and its columns of *sephiroth*.

The central column of the Tree, which represents the path of spiritual progress, as the central column does in Joyce, is balanced between columns of Mercy and Severity. This structure represents the universe, but it is also a diagram of our own natures, for the *Zohar* says, ". . . everything is comprised in man. He unites in himself all forms" (III.48 as cited in the Eleventh *Britannica*). And when we use the Tree to look inward at ourselves rather than outward at the cosmos, we are told to reverse the order of the columns.[34] The reversal of the columns that occurs when Dolph conveys to Kev the truth about their origin is also caused by a turn inward. At this point man becomes aware that God is not some external object — for there is nothing out there but a point of emptiness that draws him to fill it — but a principle planted within him by the power that created him.

The pattern of reversal here exemplifies the figure of chiasmus, which Riquelme has shown to be prominent in all of Joyce's novels.[35] The crossover of chiasmus corresponds to the shift from outside to inside, in that when an image passes through the eye it is reversed. The switching of right and left is attributed to the internal experience of dreams in the thirteenth chapter of the *Timaeus:* ". . . the visual stream is reversed at the point of coalescence . . ."[36]

During the interval in which Kev takes over the narrative in an effort to drown out what his brother is telling him (*FW* 287-292), he finds himself continually drifting so far into thoughts of sex and metaphysics that he defeats his own effort to maintain propriety. Confusing St. Patrick with Tristan, he begins turning into Shem. I said earlier that Shaun seems to take over the narrative, while Shem does not, but one brother cannot be present without the other, and Shaun is reacting here to the exposition of the mother's parts by Shem. As Shaun gains knowledge of ultimate causes, he takes over Shem's role of seeing through the limits of official definition, and so the right column takes over the left's irreverence. Meanwhile Shem becomes Shaun because he assumes the role of instructor, an authority fatal to Shem's spiritual independence.

The interchange of brother principles represents the point in history when theology is overshadowed by psychology as man comes to feel that the mysteries of life are generated not by external causes, but by internal ones. It is a shift toward the modern. It also corresponds to the movement toward objectivity in Yeats's *Vision* because from here on, while the internal world will be dominant, it will also be reduced to a systematic authority, a set of principles. By being blazoned forth in definite formulations, it will be drained of its spirit, its mystery. Meanwhile the external world, though losing its claim to divinity, will come to execute the supernatural power that materialists like Leopold Bloom invest in matter. There will be no living—or unknown—internal power to oppose it. Hart says that the crossing of Dolph and Kev at this juncture is a turning point for the whole book because in the first half of the *Wake* the spiritual Shem dominates, while in the second, the materialistic Shaun does.[37] Yet because the ironic principle takes charge of the external world, Shaun will be seen from Shem's point of view.

The crossing of Dolph and Kev corresponds to Phase 22 of Yeats's *Vision,* which begins the ascendency of the objective or primary tincture, "that primary tainctute" (*FW* 286.5). This phase brings on "an interchange between portions of the mind."[38] McHugh points out that

"From here Buvard to dear Picuchet" (*FW* 302.9) refers to a sentence from *A Vision* that appears during the explanation of Phase 22 and follows immediately after a description of Dostoevsky's broken will: "His characters, in whom is reflected this broken will, are aware, unlike those of *Bouvard and Pécuchet,* those of the *Temptation* even, of some ungraspable Whole to which they have given the name of God."[39] Dostoevsky, like Flaubert, is an example of Phase 22, as Joyce may be in his personal transition from the medieval to the modern. Balanced between spirit and matter, such men tend to be obsessed with the precise working out of abstractions behind which they sense a great spiritual force. The passage quoted says that Dostoevsky's characters, as expressions of parts of his mind, are haunted by their sense that they are portions of a larger unity. Their situations are parallel to those of the characters in Joyce's novels who have intimations of the immanent and transcendent Joyce. Moreover, Dostoevsky and Joyce both divided their personalities into their works. Raskolnikov's split personality in *Crime and Punishment,* which resembles Dostoevsky's, leads to Myshkin and Rogozhin in *The Idiot,* complementary opposites who are bound together and have a mysterious sense of being connected. Similarly, Joyce's ambivalence about Stephen expands into Stephen and Bloom, who are connected as aspects of Joyce. Both writers eventually unfold themselves into five-member families that seem enormous.

As a point of entrance into the created world, the crossing of the twins also corresponds to the stage of maturity at which an individual realizes that he is responsible for himself rather than a product of his parents, and this is one way in which this change shows progress, if only toward the end of a cycle. The sleeping giant increases in self-knowledge insofar as the twins come to know each other and to fuse through the interchanges that make up the learning process of the central discourse, "THE CONVERGENCE OF THEIR CONTRAPULSIVENESS" (*FW* 286.27). For example, at one of many points at which the voices of the twins shift back and forth in a way that makes them hard to distinguish, one of them says, "I fee where you mea" (*FW* 295–296), and one meaning of this, as Margaret Solomon points out, is "I see where you are me"[40] — or "I perceive to the extent that we coincide."

When the twins fuse, they move upward on the Tree to form the awakening HCE or Finnegan or Joyce. But this is an unstable compound, disturbing to the dream selves. Dolph loses his spiritual integrity by communicating his truth. And Kev is incapable of staying aware of the uncertain nature of this truth: for him, "THE UNCER-

TAINTY" of "DIVINITY" can only be "JUSTIFIED BY OUR CERTITUDE" (*FW* 282.7-12). He is soon driven to impose his will on Shem's domain by a "sickenagiaour" (*FW* 305.3), a gesture that combines force and signification because it is the sock in the jaw that is his signature. It signifies the rationalization of the mind.

Yeats says that Phase 22 is a period of violence in the name of abstractions.[41] And the striking of Dolph by Kev is the civil war that changes the Renaissance into the Age of Reason, demoting the spiritual. The English version of this pattern is most familiar, but Joyce probably saw a similar sequence in the more recent history of Ireland. He often observed that the spirituality of the Irish was promoted by their misfortunes, and he may have felt that Irish independence would be accompanied by spiritual decline. He satirically associates Shaun with Eamon De Valera, prime minister of the Republic.[42]

On the Freudian level, what shocks Kev into asserting his dream of manhood is a confrontation with the castrated mother, a stirring of the anxiety associated with the image of woman as bereft of her organ. This pattern gains remarkableness when it is recognized as a motivation within one part of the mind. If Shaun is an attitude with a complex, Joyce's point is that if feelings are to be seen as alive, they have to be granted the complication of people. One of the main sources from which Joyce learned how parts of the mind could have their own personalities, in addition to the Kabbalah, was Morton Prince's case history of a girl with four personalities whom he called Christine Beauchamp.[43]

Prince demonstrates that a person can have subconscious selves with different experiences and memories than her primary mind, and he shows how such an arrangement works. In reading his detailed account, one grows aware of the consequences of these selves that go on living continuously and simultaneously though they may rarely reach consciousness. Most case histories of multiple personality indicate extreme pathology, but Prince depicts Christine as an intelligent, likable person who was able to function effectively most of the time. Her sudden changes are curious rather than horrible. Joyce's daughter, Lucia, was going through similar changes, and he wanted to believe that she was healthy. Though Prince is careful to state that Christine is probably very unusual, it is an easy step from following the interchanges of this case to imagining that such subordinate selves may be common, and they served to satisfy Joyce's need for images of psychic vitality.

Joyce believed that strong feelings and vital ideas tended to have their own personalities. Feelings like anger, lust, or idealism cannot exist without implying their own sets of memories, associations, structures, processes, and attitudes — sets that differ from each other radically. Such feelings also imply physiological reactions of muscles, nerves, digestion, and hormones, even if they are only potential. Thus, when I am sad, I see, feel, remember things and make associations differently than when I am happy: I take on a sad past and a sad body. If we do not recognize such contexts, we reduce feelings to crippled abstractions — like waves without seas to support them. The most magnanimous way to represent feelings is to make them persons, and Joyce experimented extensively with personifying them in the Nighttown episode of *Ulysses*.

Roberto Assagioli, in his *Psychosynthesis*, develops techniques for integrating different "sub-personalities" within the person;[44] but the major psychoanalyst to speak of subconscious selves was Carl Gustav Jung. In his 1935 Tavistock Lectures, Jung, whose archetypes often resemble people within the mind, said that complexes and the feelings attached to them tended to have their own personalities, and compared these partial selves to the figures an author projects in his work.

The lecture in which Jung said this was attended by Samuel Beckett, and it had a powerful effect on him, encouraging him to proceed with *Murphy*.[45] Beckett does not remember if he told his friend Joyce about this lecture;[46] but the year before, at the very time Joyce divided II.2 into columns, Joyce was visiting Jung in Zürich to treat Lucia. On 29 October 1934, he wrote to George Joyce that Jung had made a good impression on him (*Letters*, 3:326–327). This letter, in Italian, was sent from the Carlton Elite Hotel, whose name adorns the cover of the first manuscript to use columns. It is likely that Joyce's discussion with Jung of the schizophrenic Lucia touched on the concept of multiple personality.

Prince's fascinating observations of Christine and her interior companions, however, bring out implications about ordinary human behavior that go beyond what Jung said. For example, Prince considers that subconscious selves have ongoing lives of their own beneath the surface.[47] The happiness or fear I feel today can never be a mere replay of the happiness or fear I felt yesterday, not even if the situations that call them forth are virtually the same. Emotions have to constantly call forth new qualities of response in order to feel unprecedented and irreducible, to be authentic and alive. My feelings have to develop to match my development, moving forward in a modality of their own that I am not aware of. Their development need not parallel mine:

they may well keep pace with me by opposition or by taking off in a new direction. My happiness and fear will come to me tomorrow in new forms that I can neither predict nor prepare for. Therefore, it is necessary to see such feelings as carrying on their own continuous lives in the contexts of their own personalities, experiences, and memories — going on though I am not aware of them.

Such patterns are strongly suggested in *Ulysses,* especially in "Circe," where, in a technique related to medieval allegory, Bloom projects the cynical grandfather-insect Lipoti Virag and the idealizing Henry Flower, while Stephen projects Philip Drunk and Philip Sober (*U* 511–523). Virag, in particular, is a highly wrought figure who gives the impression of having a past and a future. Readers often think about the pasts and futures of Joyce's protagonists, indefinable though they may be. It is clear that these figures were ongoing presences in Joyce's mind. Ellmann reports a dream Joyce had in which Molly Bloom berated Bloom and himself, and he confused Bloom with himself in retelling the story (*JJ* 549).

A more immediately relevant example emerges from a remark Joyce made about "Nausicaa." When Arthur Power asked him what happened between Bloom and Gerty MacDowell, he answered, "Nothing happened between them. . . . It all took place in Bloom's imagination." This seems to mean that Gerty's monologue, with its elaborate romanticizing, is at least partly a projection of Bloom.[48] It is incredible that Bloom could project such a highly developed characterization — especially as he does not seem to be aware of Gerty's thoughts, which include facts he could not know — but this must be considered at least a possibility in Joyce's mind. After all, Bloom's typical pretentions to rationality in the last half of "Nausicaa" must speak a very different language from whatever is speaking in him when the fireworks go off, and it would make sense to have Bloom mimic Gerty at that point in order to achieve the effect of reciprocity.

Gerty, then, is for Bloom the equivalent of Issy for HCE: a lower level of discourse within the man to which he refers in order to release his desire — something like a soundtrack to be tuned in. In his notesheets for "Ithaca," Joyce wrote, "desire = hidden identity."[49] This view accords with the scarcity of nonerotic thinking in both girls. They are probably also conceived as actual characters whose thoughts coincide with male projections in the seamless way in which Joyce's narrative projections blend with the thoughts of his characters. Joyce thus shows how women are socially conditioned to fill their minds with the other ends of male fantasies.

126 The Mind as Family

To desire an object is to give it life in your mind, and this means giving it, among other things, a past and a future. And so Issy's footnotes, like the marginal comments by the brothers, have to have their own continuity as separate narrative.[50] She is the life of desire, Dolph is the life of idealism, and Kev is the life of materialism, and such lives go on living within the personality even when they are not called to the surface.

The Structure of the Letter

In the course of his analysis of Miss Beauchamp, Prince uses a number of diagrams of the relations between her different minds and mental states. These diagrams sometimes resemble the Tree of Life, and so I present here Prince's most complete structure side by side with it. I have simply given the numbers of the *sephiroth* on the Tree, not their names. Perhaps Joyce noticed the parallel between these diagrams.[51] If so, it may have helped him to translate the Tree from its more apparent role as a cosmic diagram to its more esoteric one as a psychic structure. In any case, Prince's book developed Joyce's ability to conceive of the relations between minds that form a unity. Thus Prince's was one of a number of systems that contributed to the mental structure Joyce was building, together with the *Timaeus* and *A Vision*.

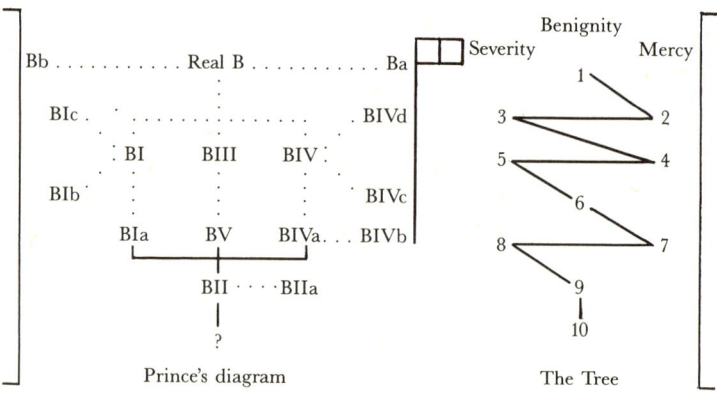

Prince's diagram   The Tree

The *Etz Haiyim*, however, is the main model for "THE MIND FACTORY, ITS GIVE AND TAKE" (*FW* 282.3) because the Tree includes a great cluster of useful images and ideas, not all of which have analogues in other systems. It is not only a mind composed of minds, but an image of the universe and its creation that is contained in the human soul. Moreover, because the adept strives to move upward on the

Tree, the structure embodies a learning process, as II.2 does. Then there is its numerology, which includes the three trinities Joyce refers to three times and the three columns with the central one balanced between the outer two.

Each *sephirah* on the Tree not only is capable of vital changes, but lives in four worlds, being an angel in three of them and a demon in the fourth.[52] A parallel between this pattern and the four ages of Vico is conceivable. Especially suggestive for Joyce, however, is the complexity of the relations between the *sephiroth*. I have shown how pregnant the sexual nature of emanation was for him. The Tree consolidated his portrayal of the mind as family by presenting a mental being that contained a relation between male and female parts on a higher level and relations between male parts on lower levels — together with a vertical relation between emanations or generations and a drive that moves from a founding principle at the top to an attracting one at the bottom, a drive that leaves equilibrium behind to cause a wide range of emanations, immortal and changeable created beings.

In fact, the relations between the *sephiroth* are so incredibly complex that Joyce in his Wakeful watches must have derived a tonic from whatever glimpses he may have attained of the Tree in action. Unlike Yeats's tinctures, emanations can move and form relations frontward, backward, or sideways in three dimensions, for they are connected by twenty-two paths that extend beyond one plane. Moreover, each of the *sephiroth* is a path as well as an entity. Waite describes for each of the thirty-two paths a unique nature that changes in different states.[53]

Finally, this system had the conceptual power Joyce needed because it represented the descent of God into the world He created. Joyce's metaphysical training enabled him to realize that a world without a cause beyond that of self-criticism could not be real. As Aquinas put it, "To make something the nature of which is simply to exist, is a contradiction in terms, for subsistent existence is noncreated existence" (Q. 7, A. 2). To give his world dynamism, Joyce had to give it a cause of its own, rather than merely a cause working against it.

The Kabbalah provided Joyce with his most sophisticated model of the procession of the artist into his work by delineating the stages by which a mind divides itself to generate the interacting parts of a cosmos. The mental structure presented in the lesson chapter is shared by Joyce and his world. Through this pattern, he depicts himself passing into his creation, and his creatures perceive the form of his presence. One of the most prominent images of this presence and of the shape of its procession into the *Wake* world is the letter.

The letter, which stands for what has been transmitted from the past, embodies the first cause of the *Wake* because it is the text on which is founded the world in which it appears. Moreover, it tends to expand to include the whole *Wake*. It is a measure of Joyce's ambition that the relation of the letter to the *Wake* seems to be the relation of the *Wake* to the world. Descriptions of the letter indicate that it reproduces the mental structure of the tenth chapter, for it expresses a group of forces working against each other: "All old Dadgerson's dodges one conning one's copying and that's what wonderland's wanderlad'll flaunt to the fair. A trancedone boyscript with tittivits by. Ahem" (*FW* 374.1-4). This version of the letter is a newspaper article exposing the secret sins of HCE in the form of Charles Lutwidge Dodgson. His story is composed by two hands working against each other, as the study period was. His Shaun hand *cons* — a word that suggests both study and falsification — what his Shem hand transcribes. His dodges and wanderings are understood to be driven by desire for Isabel as Alice, who provides the letter with tittering footnotes. References to the *Boston Transcript* always refer to the transpersonal letters Christine Beauchamp wrote to herself while she was her main alter ego, Sally, in Boston. These letters were written in trances that allowed the extremes of her personality to express themselves as separate minds. *A Vision* also is a product of automatic writing, and according to the Eleventh *Britannica,* one reason orthodox Jews were hostile to kabbalists is that the latter tended to go into trances. Trances are waking dreams, and in its dreaming state the mind is released from the strategic need to maintain unity, as it is released when it is narrating, and freed to unleash its constituents.

Margaret Solomon argues that the letter in the *Wake* stands for everything that human beings can communicate to each other.[54] As such, it is presented as a transmission from an unknown power because the source of life is lost in obscurity. As with Poe's purloined letter, its exact form can never be known. No version of the letter can be definitive, but the images of its structure that I am tracing here have the advantage of comprehending a large number of characters and functions.

I have already cited passages from the fifth chapter, which concentrates on describing the letter. There it is consistently described as a product of "a multiplicity of personalities" which the inspector strives to make "coalesce" into "one stable somebody" (*FW* 107.24-30). The content of the letter is defined as a structure of interacting parts that results from the division of a primary unity that it is useful to identify with Joyce. Mental activity always operates in the context of this familial structure, which is articulated most fully in the kabbalistic Tree. This structure is potentially present in every word, which speaks with a number of voices from different directions: "It will remember itself from every sides, with all gestures, in each our word" (*FW* 614.20-21).

The most extensive development of the multiple mind is found in III.3, the longest chapter in the *Wake,* which shows Yawn (Shaun) under inquest. Here the four old men who represent authority are shown fishing in the ocean of Yawn's mind (*FW* 477.11 ff.). The image of an ocean that contains a psychic totality harks back to the fourth chapter, in which HCE was buried under water (*FW* 76 ff.), and forward to the end of the book. With their nets, the old men draw a series of personalities from the exhausted postman or letter bearer. Though these minds are summoned forth sequentially, they all exist synchronously within him as an interacting organization, "the map of the souls' groupography" (*FW* 476.33).

The order in which these beings appear here is in a general way the reverse of the order in which the same beings appeared earlier. That is, in the lesson chapter, and in the first chapters of the *Wake,* HCE appeared first and was followed by ALP and then by the brothers. But in the section starting with Yawn, the brothers arise early and are followed by ALP and then by HCE. Kate, the washerwoman, comes early in the lesson chapter, but late in the inquest; but Issy follows her mother in both.

The reversal distinguishes the process of formation in the earlier chapters from that of dissolution in III.3. The later striving to return to unity that replaces the earlier unfolding is a step toward withdrawal from the dream. The reader is now looking up the Tree that he was earlier looking down; and the Tree itself, seen from an earthly point of view, appears in the more concrete form it assumes in Northern myth, and in Darwin's evolution (*FW* 504-505). From Shaun's place on the Tree, which is a low one because of his distance from his spiritual origin, the other members appear in a different configuration than from HCE's. Each position on the Tree has its own paths, its own patterns that shape the modality of its thought. But the entire family is present in the mind of each of its members, even in the unimaginative Shaun.

One must have other people in one's mind to be fully alive. Most of the time, they work together so smoothly as to be indistinguishable, and this may be why Shem and Shaun are often so hard to tell apart. Alternative minds may not become apparent until they fall into situations of pathological conflict. But these different agents in the mind have to diverge to work against each other productively at moments of stress, discovery, or change, precisely the moments when one is most alive. At these moments, one stops being a mere leaf or branch and becomes part of a tree. Conflict, even the conflict of love, makes one feel through tension the members to which one is attached; and through the multiplicity of dilemma's division, one partakes of a unity that reaches to the roots of one's being. Joyce went through such moments when he was actively engaged in his art or balanced between the forces in his work.

The version of the Kabbalah that Joyce presents is thoroughly personal, for the members of the *Wake* family express aspects of his mind. The tenth chapter gives us the branchings of Joyce's own preoccupations arranged to approximate the ancient Tree. In this he continues to follow the procedure Stephen presented in *Portrait,* which Eco describes as one of defining beauty by the stages of the process of one's perception.[55] In the *Wake,* Joyce makes the process of his mind the source of existence, and those stages have been cultivated to allow greater multiplicity and conflict in order to include a greater scope and depth of experience. By unfolding himself into the shape of the Tree, Joyce extends his authority, projecting his personality through many thousands of years to evoke the vast, buried psychological foundation of metaphysics in the West. At the same time, he injects into the heart of each of his verbal creatures a complex generative pattern that enacts the process of his mind.

Joyce aimed in his novels to expand the image of the mind to the greatest complexity in order to discover the powers and mysteries of God in humanity through his own person. The maximal mental structure of the Tree allowed him to project a unified theoretical construct equating four kinds of creation. The creation of the world by God, the creation of the book by the author, and the creation of humanity by itself are all understood as psychological processes through Joyce's creation of the multiple being that informed his work.

7 Conclusion
The Population of Absence

Internal Theater

Joyce was trained in childhood to see the mind as part of something larger. To defend himself against this idea, in a personal variation of the strategy of the son who takes over fatherhood, he internalized the larger totality by developing the involution of his own mind. The more multiple and indeterminate the creatures he generated, the more he could enact and include the mystery behind being. Insofar as they lived, he could constitute this mystery for them though he could not grasp it in himself.

McIntyre cites Bruno's argument that "the *final* cause which the intellect sets before itself is . . . that all possible forms may have actual existence . . ."[1] In its drive toward absolute expression, the mind creates the image of God as it creates the image of itself. Mere multiplication, however, does not enrich this image if the creatures enumerated fall into types. More critical to the fulfillment of the artist-god is the differentiation and relation of his figures. Their actions toward each other constitute his mind as the mind of the work. Because this totality increases not by repetition, but by the energy and variety of its interactions, it operates as drama, and Joyce, in his later work, continued to expand on Mallarmé's "theater of the mind."[2]

As the cast of this theater grows, it may seem to lose its credibility as a mind. But the redundancy and flexibility of the brain we use so little of for our conscious purposes suggest the reality of such possibilities. It may be that the evidence for what Jaynes calls "two persons in one head" only begins to suggest the actuality of the mind.[3] If scientists have succeeded in finding the differentiation of only a few elements of consciousness in various areas of the brain, and that has been only within the past generation, it seems likely that there are large numbers of levels of the mind with their own kinds of minds for which we lack procedures of detection. These subordinate minds may be less complex than the totality they reside in, but they may be more complex than any concept of mind we can devise.

Many psychic apparatuses have been designed to include elements in the mind that may have their own personalities, though these personalities tend to lapse into abstraction in the practice of theory. These various schemes may seem to form an unmanageable profusion, especially if one insists that there has to be a single right one. To the extent, however, that such externally defined categories overlap, they may, at least at times, take part in the same subordinate personality. The unconscious, for example, in its many definitions, may unite to some extent with the mind that dominates during sleep, the mind retained from childhood, the mind of the lower half of the body, the mind of the right lobe, and the mind of vice. If the unconscious is thought of as a person, then it is easier to see him, or perhaps her, going through these transformations by sustaining these aspects.

A mind so personified—as a dense, populous stew with a group of shifting personalities suspended in it—resembles the *Wake*. The pattern is clearer in the simpler form of the hallucinatory sequences in "Circe." These sequences, which are not remembered later by the protagonists, often seem to represent subconscious voices in the minds of Bloom and Stephen. Some of these apparitions, such as the new Bloomusalem, a huge building in the shape of a pork kidney (*U* 484), seem to express an external mind mocking the characters. But part of Bloom's mind is antagonistic to him, as his masochistic fantasies suggest, and there may be elements in his mind that could not be represented without making fun of them, which is one reason a godlike intelligence must mix in.

If everyone contains such a grouping of minds, then Joyce's desire to expand the mind to approach the multiplicity of godhead unites both kinds of realism, spiritual and factual. He may have anticipated present and future research through his sense of the danger involved in abstractly representing feelings without the implied persons behind them. He saw that by animating the parts of the mind as people, he could give them the ability to react to each other in a wide variety of extramechanical ways. Parts of the mind may love each other, hate each other, be uncertain about each other, or even dream of each other. If the organization of the mind's parts is required to be mechanical or logical,

Internal Theater 133

rather than dramatic, these parts are denied the chance to change each other and react to each other qualitatively. This requirement may impose an outside system on natural mental activity, distorting it in a grave way—as if the mind were required to be dead.

Because they are not necessarily defined by physical limitations, the personalities in the mind, like the inhabitants of the *Wake,* have powers of merging and transformation not available to physical people. Thus, the fact that the creatures of fiction occupy imaginary space tends to qualify them to represent the mind because one of the primary characteristics of the contents of the mind, according to Jaynes, is that they are projected in spatialized images.[4] It is by projecting internal space that one possesses mind.

The powers of merging and transformation that the *Wake* figures exhibit are found in language, and this may be another feature that qualifies them to inhabit the mind. I have indicated that Jaynes says that consciousness is made up of metaphors, while Lacan says that the structure of the unconscious is the structure of language. Jaynes, however, speculates that parts of the brain may communicate with each other in languages or metaphorical systems that we are not conscious of, transmitting feelings we do not have words for.[5] It may be that parts of the *Wake* communicate with each other in languages we are not conscious of. Certainly, the book strives to avoid the structure of existing languages and, despite inevitable dependence, it succeeds admirably.

Because it can project parts of the mind as people and things made of words capable of merging and transformation in imaginary space, literature is the most satisfying psychic apparatus ever conceived—though other structures are susceptible to more precise measurement because of the ways in which they simplify the mind. This psychological power has been developed in stories that suggest the tendencies of their characters to add up to single minds, and such stories tend to deal with families. All sacred stories about holy families follow this pattern: the holy family makes up the structure within which God appears in the world. And such stories, starting with that of Isis and Osiris, tend to be prominent in Joyce's late work, as do secular treatments of family unity, starting with the *Odyssey.* In the Egyptian myth, Isis reassembles the dismembered Osiris in order to conceive Horus, who revenges his father. The unity of family motivation is emphasized by this plot in that mother and son act for the dead father, and the plot of the *Odyssey* is parallel on a less supernatural level.

The literary form best suited to showing the interaction of people in a group is drama—in fact, insofar as figures in a literary work interact, it is drama—and Joyce hoped early in his career that he would be a dramatist. Stephen's esthetic theory in *Portrait* implies that the dramatic is the highest form in all the arts, including the visual ones. Joyce's preoccupation with internal subject matter led him to fiction, but his mature fiction focused increasingly on interpersonal interaction.

Joyce was familiar with plays whose characters explicitly represented parts of the mind, both archaic examples such as the medieval moralities and modern examples such as Strindberg's dream plays. In "Scylla and Charybdis," Stephen describes Shakespeare as repeating throughout his canon a plot structure based on a pattern of familial interaction (betrayal) built into his mind. And Stephen speaks of Othello and Iago as aspects of Shakespeare (*U* 212), showing an awareness that the key figures in Shakespeare's familial knot embody forces in his soul. Joyce was inclined to believe that many of the best writers expressed their minds in familial groupings. Of Ibsen, whose internal drama *When We Dead Awaken* was imitated in *Exiles,* Joyce said that he wrote "essentially the same drama over and over" and "met the four or five characters whom he uses throughout his plays before he was twenty-five" (*JJ* 266).

The most vital image of the multipersonal mind, the family as a mental unity in which its members are parts, is especially prominent in modern Irish plays, such as *Exiles,* Yeats's *Purgatory,* O'Neill's *Long Day's Journey into Night,* and Beckett's *Endgame.* Nancy Scheper-Hughes suggests that the talent of the Irish for drama may be related to the tendency of their minds to be divided by historical and cultural forces.[6]

Drama and fiction, of course, are only metaphors for the mind, but we should not forget that all descriptions of the mind are only metaphors. The discovery of chemical and electrical reactions in the brain makes it tempting to see these reactions as explaining mental content, but such explanation is superficial. After all, there are elaborate chemical and electrical reactions in the physical production of a play; and we have no sound reason to believe that the physical reactions in the brain are more intrinsically related to the content of the mind than the physical reactions in a play are to its content. It may be true, for example, that the lights tend to be brighter at the end of a comedy than at the end of a tragedy, but this leaves a lot to be explained about the plays. Those who impose systems on the mind should remember that such hypotheses are essentially fictional, for the point at which a metaphor for the mind goes wrong is the point at which it is taken literally.

Jaynes argues that consciousness is constructed in an area formerly dominated by the voice of deity. Whether or not his historical theory is valid, it is generally agreed that drama originates in religious ritual and appears first as a division in the sacred voice. This pattern has been traced through the origins of both Greek and medieval drama. To convey the word of God in human terms, it must be divided into conflict, and so the story the priest is telling takes on more than one voice of its own. The voice of God must continue to speak through sacred drama in several parts: the different actors in early drama embodied parts of the God or god who was manifested in the action they participated in.

The voice of God has often been heard most effectively in several parts, in polyphony. The indeterminate harmonies of the great religious choral works are powerful evocations of transcendence. Joyce achieves parallel and similar effects in the most intense parts of his writings, which are often uncanny. This is especially evident in the great chords of uncertainty that end all of his books.

Automysticism

The developments of realism, modernism, and postmodernism have separated the individual agents of drama and removed them from their sources by multiplying irony, randomness, interference, and space. By these methods, of which Joyce was a master, the writer gives his figures the potential for greater possibilities of life by a process of decreation, acting as the Gnostic demiurge who gives knowledge. The life that fills this potential, however, must be motivated by a drive toward recreation that represents the constructive Platonic demiurge. The text does not for long move toward or away from creation: it oscillates or breathes between them.

The historical growth of negation has never posited an alternative primary source. The old metaphysical authority is still to be discerned, however dim and disturbing it may be, behind Borges's labyrinths, Beckett's Godot, Pynchon's conspiracies, and Barthelme's Dead Father. Even works that deny the First Cause tend to derive their energy from their relation to it.

However much they may deny it, writers cannot help suspecting that they are responsible for the metaphysics of their worlds. In literature, metaphysics is always produced by personality, though this personality may be tempted to represent itself as an abstraction, projecting "the myth of the teller's impersonality."[7] The refusal of the author to get involved or to judge is often based on the belief that he can free his world by withholding himself. But his faith in that separation of the author from his work which Joyce refers to as "the Real Absence" (*FW* 536.5) may be naive idealism. While part of an author is isolated from his characters, the part that is invested in them may be greater than he realizes. By assuming his isolation to be essential or total, he loses track of the responsibility within himself for the freedom he creates. He overlooks the fact that his every withdrawal is an action that has an effect on his creation. His disappearance may operate as neglect or stringency.

The effort to eliminate metaphysics can produce an inhuman god, cutting down more possibilities for created beings than it adds. Characters in such supposedly liberated worlds are likely to end up severely bound by abstract theories. It may be that without a living being to mediate between themselves and theoretical principles, they must inevitably be deprived of life by being attached to dead models.

Joyce was an agnostic, gnawed by doubt, rather than an atheist, because he realized that to deny the existence of God, attractive though it was to him, ultimately meant to deny the possibility of a principle of meaning. The writer has to project some measure of belief in order to give solidity and activity to his characters, setting, and story.

Joyce's method of expressing belief toward and within a divided form whose unity must always remain potential may seem to bear out Derrida's claim that discourse is secondary and fleeting. Derrida, however, denies that the deferral of meaning has a goal, whereas Joyce realized that such deferral is deference — that the more meaning is put off, the more it is glorified. Derrida criticizes all existing language as stolen, *la parole soufflée*. As a fiction writer, however, Joyce uses the secondary nature of the language of his creations to constitute himself as the otherness behind speech. The stolen word, as Derrida notices, is spirit, *souffle*.[8]

No psychological gesture can resemble itself unless we assume it to be attached to a personality — and a vital personality cannot be imagined without a transcendent function. It may be that we have enough theories of the author as self-eliminating and that what is needed is knowledge of how the author operates as an active being, the kind of knowledge Joyce developed consummately on a metaphysical basis. Only in the context of such knowledge can absence be made meaningful as the absence of someone.

Presence and absence are woven through Joyce's work so that one always rests on the other,[9] just as the Joycean voice always rests on another behind it. Ellmann indicates that Joyce was preoccupied by the idea expressed by a friend's remark that "absence is the highest form of presence" and took it seriously (*JJ* 252–253). From Father Flynn in "The Sisters" to father Finnegan, the center of attention in Joyce's work is someone who has departed or has not yet arrived, the dead or the artist as a mature man.

The power of this hidden being grows as he comes to fill out Joyce's mentality more completely: the more he makes, the more he has and is. The most powerful way to expand creation as an expression of personality is to generate a free will outside your knowledge so that it can surprise you, and the way to do this is to speak to the other within yourself. This other is heard by dividing the mind, and so it is released through a process of analytic decreation. Yet the energy that adds the new life can only be creative, and it must aim at some goal beyond either of the two existing minds in conflict.

The kind of intentional self-division Joyce cultivated is suggested by Derrida's statement in "*La parole soufflée*" that schizophrenia is "the structure that opens the truth of man."[10] If Joyce was using the structure of schizophrenia as a tool, then Jung was quite accurate when he reacted to Lucia and Joyce by saying that they "were like two people going to the bottom of a river, one falling and the other diving" (*JJ* 679). Joyce was doing intentionally what Lucia, who may simply have been following her father, was doing helplessly.

What sort of metaphysics does such a divided being produce? I have given some indications already, but now I want to talk about the last and most extreme form of this metaphysics of interaction. This extreme, which may be called the goal toward which the canon moves, was recently described by White. In the flux of the *Wake,* according to White, time, space, causality, and identity disappear: everything happens before and after everything else and everything is everything else.[11]

I agree with White that such a continuum is present in the *Wake,* but I disagree with his assumption that the book has only one consistent metaphysical scheme, for all of the characters, events, and images in the book are exceptions to this scheme. I see the book as based on a contradictory personality through which several systems interact. White's continuum functions as an outer limit to the Wakean cosmos, and a void out of which the other systems emerge. White says that it will be difficult to talk about such a world unless we invent a new philosophical language. I believe that such a language exists, that Joyce knew it, and that it distinguishes the role of undifferentiated substance more accurately in many respects than White does. It is the language of infinity, eternity, and total unity that Scholasticism and other religious systems use to describe God, though Joyce adapts it to fit personal psychology.

Here are two passages that resemble the continuum White describes: both use the image of entering a body of water to represent the godhead as an eternal streaming of forms. The first occurs at the end of the *Paradiso,* when Dante gets closest to God in heaven. He sees a river of light flowing between banks of flowers:

> and from the river as it glowed and rolled
> live sparks shot forth to settle on the flowers.
> They seemed like rubies set in bands of gold;
> and then, as if the fragrance overthrew
> their senses, they dove back into the river;
> and as one dove in there, out another flew.
> (XXX.64–69)[12]

When Dante dips his head into this river, he has a vision of God as a ring of light, but I find the river itself more vivid because of its dynamism. If the river is made up of psychic substance, it seems to me a strong image of the mind of the author. The jewels that "dart in and out of it" (1. 77) seem to show personality when the fragrance overthrows "their senses." These jewels, in their oscillation, act like the images, characters, and narrators generated by the artist's imagination. Dante may not have had this in mind, but he favored diverse readings because they promoted awareness of the multivalence behind the text.

The other passage is from the ending of Hermann Hesse's *Siddhartha* (1922). As Siddhartha, an incarnation of the Buddha, is dying, his friend Govinda kisses him and has a vision:

> He no longer saw the face of his friend Siddhartha. Instead he saw other faces, many faces, a long series, a continuous stream of faces — hundreds, thousands, which all came and disappeared and yet all seemed to be there at the same time, which all continually changed and renewed themselves and which were yet all Siddhartha.[13]

As the passage goes on for two pages, Govinda sees myriads of people, animals, and objects in an infinite variety of states and relations flowing and merging. We do not know if Joyce read this, but the flux described here closely resembles the substance of the *Wake*—or rather it resembles the continuum of the *Wake* without the book's characters, scenes, or motifs. Joyce's career was a constant, growing effort to make contact with such primal matter within himself by dividing himself into inlets of Winnicott's intermediate space. It was perhaps because of the discipline of his Jesuit education that he was able to do this without being in any danger of losing control of his mind. The principle of authority inculcated in him was powerful enough so that his opposition to it provided him with an endless source of humor.

Joyce's urge to reject authority, however, did not prevent him from being quite an author. He could not be a word shaper without being a world shaper, and he could not shape his own world without shaping the larger one. Despite his improvident father, he mastered the strategies necessary to perform the miracle of becoming not only prodigiously successful in literary terms, but moderately wealthy, without compromising his extreme artistic integrity. What distinguished his beliefs from those of traditional religious writers such as Augustine and Aquinas was not so much his ceaseless questioning as the fact that his answers resided in his own personal flux rather than in external, fixed forms. Like Richard Rowan in *Exiles,* he was "an automystic" because he sought the mystery of truth in the spaces of his own inner division.

God has usually emerged from a divided mind. As Jaynes indicates, schizophrenics are commonly regarded as prophets in primitive societies.[14] If God is identified with the creative principle, then He operates through the interaction of active and passive agencies within the mind. All discourse consists of one mind creating and being created by another. Speech must be located between two different minds — even when it is interior monologue; and so interior monologue serves to bring out the extra mind within.

Intrapersonal Fiction

Fictional technique has always rested on a relation between voices, and these voices have always originated in intrapersonal contexts. Even oral storytellers have to communicate with themselves before they speak to their audiences. In the case of the writer, it is manifest that whatever voices speak in his fiction must, with rare exceptions, have spoken to each other first within his mind. Of course, convention requires that these internal voices be clothed in forms extrinsic to their origins, such as that of the storyteller speaking to his audience or the letter writer addressing his reader. The most authoritative voice of narrative, which the others tend to imitate as far as they are able, is the omniscient narrator, which is based on the model of God speaking to man. Jaynes sees this model working in the earliest epics as an externalization of a voice from within.

When an individualized narrator mediates this voice, he takes on himself control over the function of God; and when the voice is narrowed to a character (as it is for us in our lives), it emerges out of a substratum of personality in which the character's active existence is rooted. In every case at least two voices articulate each other, and advances in novelistic technique tend to involve adding on new voices and modes of voice, new levels of thought and expression to interwork.

To focus on what Joyce accomplished, we should recognize the ways in which earlier techniques externalized the sources of their voices. This separation of voices allowed the isolation of homogeneous personalities. Consider, for example, Henry James's selective omniscience, sometimes regarded as the most natural and logical of points of view. Here the author presents the thoughts of one character, and the effect is supposed to be unmediated. In fact, this technique predicates two men, one of whom has superhuman judgment and watches the other continuously. It seems especially realistic to people who project personalities by which they judge themselves, and however conditioned and abstracted by enlightenment such projection may be, it is fundamentally religious.

As a modernist, James explores divisions and undercurrents in his characters; but insofar as he is preoccupied with judging them, he is obliged to see them as unified. Joyce, on the other hand, as we have seen, began to disassemble the personal monad as early as the 1904 "A Portrait of the Artist." The interior monologue he developed enacted a discourse between one part of the mind and another, for any word articulated in the mind must follow the pattern of coming from someone and going to someone else. The social structure of speech is built into the mind, and this speech must be mutual at least insofar as all speech is shaped by the audience it aims at, so that the turning of the mind must be conversation.

Instead of James's dramatic scenes, watchers, confidants, and ghosts, Joyce moved toward a system of interior drama. This development grew out of Joyce's primary concern, from his earliest works, not with what people say to each other, but with what effects their statements to each other call forth in their minds — not with their relations to others, but with their relations to themselves.

A person cannot be conscious of the speaker and the audience in his mind at once, though both are present when he is conscious. Therefore, about half the mind must always be attached to a being it is not aware of. This assumption, which accords with the redundancy of the brain, defines the unknown part of the mind that Augustine and Jaynes see as traditionally occupied by God. The information that may be derived from the unknown part of the mind may be remarkable, but even more remarkable is the fact that this unknown aspect has its own will, its own identity. This inner authority is a being Joyce felt obliged to represent through his own person.

In portraying the mind as made up of minds, Joyce was trying to make us aware of the reality of mental life. From this perspective, the assumption of one person speaking in one voice is an illusion imposed by external considerations of practicality. It is related to the illusion that each person is an independent being, an uncreated consciousness. These items of faith are clung to so desperately in our society that they are not perceived as either religious or unreal. Such assumptions are necessary to maintain the credo that people are reasonable, which is as socially useful to us as faith was to the medieval period, and no more probable.

The most brilliant of Joyce's British modernist peers, Virginia Woolf, carried on his critique of personal identity. In *To the Lighthouse,* Lily Briscoe remarks repeatedly that what we call a person is merely a string of impressions. The protagonist of *Orlando* is described at one point (in chapter 6) as having 2,052 selves.[15] And the subject of *The Waves* is a collective mind involving seven friends. In America, Faulkner presents the Compson family and the Sutpen family as unities.

Joyce strove to systematically disintegrate the simple unity of the mind in order to reveal a more complex integration that pointed to a higher unity. He realized that this higher unity was beyond human knowledge and that the most authoritative representation of it was to be found in theology. The thought that this unity he aimed at was divine amused him, fascinated him, terrified him, and impelled him.

To break down the old construction of the mind, Joyce required a superhuman compound intelligence, a mind beyond what existed. By understanding and enlarging the possibilities of his creatures and by seeing their discrete personalities as parts of a larger being; he expanded our recognition of what the mind could be. For humanity to recognize its own individual multiplicity is for it to assume its godhead, and this was one goal Joyce sought to promote by his enactment of the multiple role. His challenge to God, at its bravest, was an effort of self-respect by which he hoped to implicate all of us and to give God a truer shape.

Appendices
Notes
Index

Appendix 1
Synchronicities in *Ulysses*

The following list of synchronicities in *Ulysses* is not complete, but it is the most complete list now available. More than half of these points of connection have been cited before by the numerous critics who refer to psychic coincidences in *Ulysses*. The term *synchronicity* was introduced in my last book because this Jungian concept extends beyond coincidence to a wide range of psychic activity. It includes all indications that the text refers to a psychic system or series of systems outside any individual mind, to a mental force in the fictional world that does not follow the realistic or empirical causality of that world. The value of Jung's idea for criticism rests on the fact that all events in a text are synchronicities: they are acausal in that they do not follow physical causes, but psychic ones.

An example of a synchronicity that is not a coincidence is the opening reference to the Mass on line 6 of the book. It is the first of a series of lines from the Mass that appear throughout the book and lead up to the Eucharist of "Ithaca." I have included only a few of the more striking references to external systems that operate causally: I could hardly cite every reference to the *Odyssey*, though they are all synchronicities. Most of the examples listed are ideas that occur to more than one mind in the book, suggesting linkage. Therefore, I usually cite each synchronicity twice, with a page and line number at which each version of the shared matter begins. Brackets indicate my own summaries of text passages. If a quote refers to another passage in *Ulysses*, the page and line of that passage are given after the quote.

"Telemachus"

3.5	—*Introibo ad altare Dei.*
3.29	Two strong shrill whistles answered through the calm.
4.21	a black panther 218.1, 586.7.
6.13	he can't wear grey trousers 57.11.

146   *Appendix 1*

6.28	As he and others see me. 376.2.
9.32	[The cloud causes horror associated with an aging female, but is replaced by warm, running sunlight.] 61.7.
10.3	Turko the terrible. 57.22.
12.38	*the one pot* 450.9.
20.1	a green stone. 55.41.
20.19	He wants that key. 57.1.
21.3	[Mass by Palestrina] 82.19.

"Nestor"

25.14	Had Pyrrhus not fallen 133.29.
25.21	—Tell us . . . / —. . . a ghoststory. 538.14.
25.33	*Lycidas* 630.15.
25.34	*Sunk though he be beneath the watery floor* 72.3.
33.38	*The harlot's cry from street to street / Shall weave old England's winding sheet.* 597.17.
34.13	Vain patience to heap and hoard. Time surely would scatter all . . . the dishonours of their flesh. [prefigures Bloom]

"Proteus"

37.2	Signatures of all things I am here to read.
37.6	By knocking his sconce against them, sure. 705.24 ff.
37.10	Shut your eyes and see. 182.5 ff.
37.11	to hear his boots crush crackling wrack and shells 90.26.
38.1	navelcord [linked to death] 112.30.
38.15	the divine substance wherein Father and Son are consubstantial?
39.1	—We thought you were someone else. 110.24.
39.33	Houses of decay 110.7.
40.17	(he is kneeling) 103.16.
42.29	Belluomo rises from the bed of his wife's lover's wife.
42.33	mouths yellowed 97.6.
43.16	The froeken . . . who rubs male nakedness in the bath 85.8.
43.22	The blue fuse burns 104.4
44.23	a silent tower entombing their blind bodies 114.29.
44.37	stoneheaps of dead builders, a warren of weasel rats 114.13.
44.40	rolls all them bloody well boulders, bones for my steppingstones 96.12, 96.36.
46.32	Out of that . . . 97.39.
47.5	[Dream] Street of harlots.
47.5	[Dream] Haroun al Raschid 540.19, 586.6.
47.7	[Dream] The melon he held against my face 734.41.
47.8	[Dream] In. Come. 370.41.
47.8	[Dream] Red carpet spread. 381.12.

48.16	His shadow lay over the rocks as he bent . . . 381.33–34.	
48.18	darkness shining in the brightness 381.34.	
48.18	delta of Cassiopeia 728.6.	
48.24	Who ever anywhere will read these written words? 381.30.	
49.5	What is that word known to all men? 77.39	
49.26	My ashplant will float away. 381.32.	
49.33	floating foampool, flower unfurling. 79.38, 86.42.	
50.7	A corpse rising saltwhite 114.37.	
50.12	titbit 68.40.	
50.15	devour a urinous offal 55.5.	
50.19	Seadeath, mildest of all deaths 114.30.	
51.5	threemaster [Trinity] . . . crosstrees 625.13.	

"Calypso"

55.4	gave to his palate a fine tang of faintly scented urine 50.15.	
55.41	green stones 20.1.	
57.1	latchkey. Not there. 20.19.	
57.11	I couldn't go in that light suit. 6.13.	
57.22	Turko the terrible 10.3.	
58.3	if they ran a tramline along the North Circular 221.2.	
61.7	[The cloud causes horror associated with an aging female, but is replaced by warm, running sunlight.] 9.32 ff.	
64.4	*Voglio e non vorrei.* 77.15, 197.5–6.	
69.13	*the laughing witch* 598.32.	
69.38	[The costumes of the hours] 138.25 ff., 576.4 ff.	

"Lotus-Eaters"

72.3	in the dead sea, floating on his back. . . . Couldn't sink if you tried . . . 25.34.	
77.15	*Voglio e non* 197.5–6.	
77.38	that other world. Please tell me what is the real meaning of that word. 49.5, 115.5, 581.75.	
79.38	a lazy pooling swirl of liquor bearing along wideleaved flowers of its froth 49.33.	
82.19	Palestrina 21.3.	
85.6	bath. . . . Nicer if a girl did it. 43.16.	
86.4	throw it away 325.31, 647.19.	
86.42	languid floating flower 49.33.	

"Hades"

88.7	[The carriage passes Stephen.]	
90.26	My boots were creaking I remember now 37.11.	
92.18	[The carriage passes Boylan.]	

148   *Appendix 1*

95.10	—Eight plums a penny! 145.23.
96.12	Rattle his bones. Over the stones 44.42-45.1.
96.35	the life of the damned. Wear the heart out of a stone [Sisyphus] 44.40-45.1.
97.6	like yellow streaks on his face 42.33.
97.39	Out of that! 46.32.
102.10	more women than men in the world. 580.23.
103.16	[Bloom] knelt his right knee upon it. 40.17.
104.4	bad gas and burn it. Out it rushes: blue 43.22.
110.7	The Irishman's house is his coffin. 39.33.
110.24	If we were all suddenly somebody else. 39.1.
112.30	His navelcord. 38.1.
114.13	rat toddled along the side of the crypt 44.37.
114.29	[burial in] Parsee tower of silence? 44.23.
114.30	Drowning they say is the pleasantest 50.19.
114.37	Saltwhite crumbling mush of corpse 50.7.
115.5	There is another world after death named hell. 49.5, 77.38, 581.15.

"Aeolus"

117.36	*Co-ome thou lost one,* 275.35.
123.18	—The ghost walks 188.10.
129.34	behind him hue and cry 193.23, 586.18.
138.25	[Groups of girls dancing in costumes of different esthetic colors] 69.38 ff.
140.15	*soultransfigured and of soultransfiguring* 465.6.
141.25	[Taylor] looked (though he was not) a dying man. 464.35.
145.23	purchase four and twenty ripe plums 95.10.
148.19	spitting the plumstones 377.7.
151.5	sucking red jujubes white. 590.20, 591.17.

"Lestrygonians"

152.38	*Hamlet, I am thy father's spirit* 188.35.
160.28	[fox hunt] 193.20.
164.42	Nature abhors a vacuum. 208.17.
165.35	The ends of the world with a Scotch accent. Tentacles: octopus. 507.11-12.
168.20	huguenots 188.21.
169.36	Look on this picture then on that. [*Hamlet* III.iv.54]
171.1	Never know whose thoughts you're chewing.
171.10	Staggering bob. 420.7.
171.12	Rawhead and bloody bones. 581.28.
177.39	—Iiiiiichaaaaaaach! [Bloom is absent] 490.7.
181.27	[on blindness—MS addition] something blacker than the dark. 37.11-18.

"Scylla and Charybdis"

185.31	the Logos who suffers in us at every moment.
187.22	—The absentminded beggar 748.29.
188.21	huguenot's 168.20.
188.35	*Hamlet, I am thy father's spirit* 152.38.
193.20	Christfox . . . hiding . . . from hue and cry. 129.34, 160.28 ff.
194.32	in the future . . . I may see myself as I sit here now but by reflection from that which then I shall be.
196.16	auk's egg 737.25.
196.42	unless their Creator endow their souls with that knowledge in the life to come.
197.5	what he would but would not 64.4.
197.13	the sea's voice . . . heard only in the heart of him who is the substance of his shadow.
202.9	Do and do. Thing done. In a rosery of Fetter Lane of Gerard, herbalist, he walks, greyedauburn. . . . One life is all. One body. . . . Afar, in a reek of lust and squalor, hands are laid on whiteness. 280.26.
203.23	Secondbest / Bed. 543.21.
208.17	nature . . . abhors perfection. 164.42.
212.31	bawd and cuckold 470.21.
213.20	always meeting ourselves. 369.25.
213.21	The playwright who wrote the folio of this world
217.33	[Dream] Street of harlots after. A creamfruit melon he held to me. In. [As Bloom appears] 370.41, 381.12, 734.41.

"Wandering Rocks"

221.2	North Circular road. It was a wonder that there was not a tramline . . . 58.3.
223.16	joybells were ringing in gay Malahide 482.27–28.
227.3	—Our father who art not in heaven 238.17, 251.38.
229.16	The disk shot down the groove, wobbled a while, ceased and ogled them: six [sixth section].
233.5	Down went Tom Rochford 598.25.
238.17	The man upstairs is dead. 227.3, 251.38.
242.36	Who has passed here before me? . . .
242.41	—*Se el yilo nebrakada femininum!* 440.2.
244.23	Hold that fellow with the bad trousers. 522.10.
249.23	Buck Mulligan slit a steaming scone in two and plastered butter over its smoking pith. 580.6.
249.26	He is going to write something in ten years.
249.32	I don't want to be imposed on. 250.12.
250.12	—*Coactus volui.* 249.32, 520.1.
251.38	My father is dead 227.3, 238.17.

"Sirens"

268.32	those tight trousers [They are talking about Bloom as he sits in the next room.] 270.33.
270.13	—Sure, you'd burst the tympanum of her ear, man 521.23.
270.33	Trousers tight as a drum on him. 268.32.
275.3	*Martha* it is. Coincidence.
276.7	Siopold!
280.26	In Gerard's rosery of Fetter lane he walks, greyed-auburn. One life is all. One body. Do. 202.9.

"Cyclops"

296.7	shaggybearded widemouthed largenosed longheaded 521.27.
301.34	Having requested a quart of buttermilk this was brought 473.19.
302.5	he requested that it should be told to his dear son Patsy that the other boot which he had been looking for was at present under the commode in the return room
311.37	[Garryowen's poetry] 352.24.
315.20	Gob, he'd have a soft hand under a hen. 388.13.
321.24	signor Brini 495.21.
325.31	*Throwaway*, says he, at twenty to one. 86.4.
335.21	—He's a bloody dark horse himself
338.4	—Expecting every moment will be his next 559.10.

"Nausicaa"

352.24	Garryowen that almost talked 311.37 ff.
354.3	[Benediction parallels Gerty: Sacrament exposed, but not eaten.]
355.33	halcyon days 548.17.
356.26	vessel of singular devotion [applies to Gerty].
356.31	saint Bernard said in his famous prayer of Mary, the most pious Virgin's intercessory power 391.26.
360.21	and a prettier, a daintier head of nutbrown tresses was never seen on a girl's shoulders 521.6.
369.25	meet what you feel 213.20.
370.6	Was that just when he, she?
370.41	[Dream] Come in. All is prepared. I dreamt. 47.8
376.2	See ourselves as others see us. 6.28.
377.7	He gets the plums and I the plumstones 148.18.
379.20	Howth settled for slumber . . . (he was old) [refers to *Wake*]
381.11	[Dream] She had red slippers on. Turkish. Wore the breeches. 47.8, 439.9–10.
381.32	Washed away 49.26 [Ashplant parallels stick].
381.32	Tide comes here a pool near her foot 49.19–35.
381.33	Bend, see my face there, dark mirror 37.30, 48.16.
381.33	breathe on it, stirs 9.27.

Synchronicities in Ulysses 151

381.33	All these rocks with lines and scars and letters. 37.2.
381.34	O, those transparent! 37.5.
381.35	What is the meaning of that other world. 49.5, 77.39.

"Oxen of the Sun"

Every point in "Oxen" is a coincidence between the action of the hospital scene, the development of the foetus, and the history of English prose style. There are few other synchronicities.

388.12	the meekest man and the kindest that ever laid husbandly hand under hen 315.20.
391.26	Bernardus saith aptly that she hath . . . an almightiness of petition 356.31.
393.17	Greater love than this, he said, no man hath that a man lay down his wife for his friend.
393.30	return, clan Milly
397.28	[Dream] of his dame Mrs Moll with red slippers on 47.8.
412.34	The black panther was himself the ghost of his own father 218.1, 586.7.
420.7	staggering bob 171.10.

"Circe"

432.10	*He flourishes his ashplant shivering the lamp image* 583.3.
440.2	Nebrakada! Feminimum. 242.41.
450.9	doing it into . . . the bucket of porter 12.38.
451.8, 10	[The names Carr and Compton refer to real people.]
464.35	hectic cheekbones of John F. Taylor 141.31.
465.6	of soultransfigured and of soultransfiguring 140.15.
470.6	he organized her. 319.4.
470.21	bawd and cuckold 212.31.
473.19	That buttermilk didn't agree with me. 301.34.
475.13	Are you looking for someone? He's inside with his friend.
480.10	John Howard Parnell . . . in a chessboard tabard 248.21.
482.27	Joybells ring in . . . gay Malahide 223.16.
490.7	Iiiiiiiiaaaaaaach! 177.39.
495.21	BRINI, PAPAL NUNCIO 321.24.
498.23	[Litany of the Daughters of Erin employs structural perspective not available to any character.]
504.4	Circe's or what am I saying Ceres' altar
505.1	What went forth to the ends of the world 727.36 ff.
507.11	*The End of the World, a two-headed octopus* . . . 165.26.
507.32	[Elijah calls everybody by name, using information no single character has.]
510.11	bicycle pump 165.29.
520.1	*Coactus volui* 250.12.

152   *Appendix 1*

521.6   *And a prettier, a daintier head of winsome curls was never seen on a whore's shoulders.* 360.21.
521.23   He burst her tympanum 270.13.
521.27   hairynostrilled, hugebearded, cabbageeared, shaggychested 296.7.
522.10   Hold that fellow with the bad breeches 244.23.
525.3   ["Winds that Blow from the South"] 156.9, 763.12.
538.14   Tell me . . . a bloody goodghoststory . . . 25.21–22.
540.19   Haroun Al Raschid 47.5.
543.20   You have made your secondbest bed 203.23.
548.17   *Halcyon Days* 355.33.
553.21   Nebrakada! 242.41.
559.10   Moment before the next 338.4.
562.6   What day were you born?/Thursday. Today.
563.6   Black Liz 315.21.
563.13   [Chiasmic coincidence involving sixteen and twenty-two years.]
567.17   *The face of William Shakespeare*
571.11   [Dream] I dreamt of a watermelon. 734.41.
571.18   It was here. Street of harlots. 47.5.
573.10   A dark horse [Bloom's Throwaway in Stephen's vision]
576.4   [The Dance of the Hours] 69.27.
579.7   [A whirl of dance mixes Stephen, Bloom, and images from "Wandering Rocks" in one paragraph. It goes from Stephen (*lacquey's bell, Conmee, hornpipe*) to Bloom (*Corny* in *coffin*) to Stephen (*Frauenzimmer*) to Bloom (*hackney jaunt Blazes blind coddoubled bicyclers*) to Stephen (*Dilly*).]
580.4   *Buck Mulligan . . . a smoking buttered split scone in his hand.* 249.23.
580.23   More women than men in the world. 102.10.
581.15   I pray for you in my other world. 77.38.
581.28   Raw head and bloody bones! 171.12.
586.6   *Haroun al Raschid* 47.5.
586.7   [Leopold in black] with step of a pard 4.21, 412.34.
590.20   [Edward VII] *He sucks a red jujube.* 151.5.
590.21   robed as a grand elect perfect and sublime mason
590.23   a plasterer's bucket 450.9.
591.17   a white jujube 151.5.
598.25   *Tom Rochford . . . leaps into the void* 233.5.
598.32   Laughing witches 69.13.
600.26   *Exit Judas. Et laqueo se suspendit.* [Refers to the 1927 suicide of Vincent Cosgrave]
608.23   Black panther vampire 586.7.

"Eumaeus"

615.42   He began to remember that this had happened, or had been mentioned as having happened, before 618.40.

Synchronicities in Ulysses 153

618.40 He had seen that nobleman somewhere or other 615.42.
623.15 You know Simon Dedalus?
625.13 The threemaster *Rosevean* 51.5.
630.15 dreaming of fresh woods and pastures new as someone somewhere sings. 25.33.
647.19 *Throwaway* . . . dark horse 86.4.
661.39 in Fetter Lane near Gerard the herbalist 280.26.

"Ithaca"

675.36 Reminiscences of coincidences, truth stranger than fiction, preindicative of the result of the Gold Cup 86.4.
677.10 jocoserious . . . massproduct
684.30 Queen's hotel 723.31.
686.20 she stated were Greek and Irish and Hebrew characters.
700.36 the appearance of a star . . . (a new luminous sun generated by the collision and amalgamation. . . . of two nonluminous exsuns)
703.23 A star precipitated . . . towards the zodiacal sign of Leo.
705.24 [Bloom hits head on sideboard.] 37.6.
715.31 a family crest and coat of arms 210.3.
723.31 Queen's Hotel 684.30.
727.36 Ever he would wander, selfcompelled 505.2.
728.5 he would somehow reappear reborn above delta in the constellation of Cassiopeia and . . . return 210.9, 213.1.
729.17 The cause of a brief sharp unforeseen heard loud lone crack 37.6
737.25 auk's egg 196.16.

"Penelope"

748.29 the absentminded beggar 187.22.
756.25 books with a Molly in them
757.10 general Ulysses Grant
758.36 see it all around you like a new world 77.40.
759.35 Don Miguel de la Flora
761.25 H M S Calypso
763.12 Winds that blow from the south 156.9, 525.3.
769.31 O Jamesy
780.2 Id have to get a nice pair of red slippers 47.8, 397.28.

Appendix 2
"What Are the Wild Waves Saying?"

Dombey and Son, a great success, was published in book form in 1848, having started as a serial in 1846. The song "What Are the Wild Waves Saying?" which depends for its impact on chapter 16 of Dickens's novel, "What the Waves Were Always Saying," was published in England, probably in the early 1850s. The lyricist, Dr. Joseph Edwards Carpenter, increased his musical activity after 1851. The career of the composer, Stephen Glover, ended in 1867. My source is Helen Kendrick Johnson, *Our Familiar Songs and Those Who Made Them* (New York: Holt, 1881), pp. 346–351. The music is melodramatic, but emotionally effective.

"What Are the Wild Waves Saying?"

Paul.
"What are the wild waves saying,
    Sister, the whole day long,
That ever amid our playing,
    I hear but their low, lone song?
Not by the seaside only,
    There it sounds wild and free;
But at night, when 'tis dark and lonely,
    In dreams it is will with me."

Florence.
"Brother! I hear no singing!
    'Tis but the rolling wave,
Ever its lone course winging
    Over some lonesome cave!
'Tis but the noise of water
    Dashing against the shore,
And the wind from some bleaker quarter
    Mingling, mingling with its roar."

Paul and Florence.
"No! It is something greater,
    That speaks to the heart alone;
The voice of the great Creator,
    Dwells in that mighty tone.["]

Paul.
"Yes! But the waves seem ever
    Singing the same sad thing,
And vain is my weak endeavor
    To guess what the surges sing!
What is the voice repeating,
    Ever by night and day?
Is it a frieindly greeting,
    Or a warning that calls away?"

Florence.
"Brother! the inland mountain,
    Hath it not voice and sound?
Speaks not the dripping fountain,
    As it bedews the ground?
E'en by the household ingle,
    Curtained and closed and warm,
Do not our voices mingle
    With those of the distant storm?"

Paul and Florence.
"Yes! But there's something greater,
    That speaks to the heart alone;
The voice of the great Creator
    Dwells in that mighty tone!"

Notes

Chapter 1

1 Julian Jaynes, *The Origin of Consciousness in the Breakdown of the Bicameral Mind* (Boston: Houghton Mifflin, 1976), pp. 48–60; Jacques Lacan, "The agency of the letter in the unconscious," in *Écrits; A Selection*, trans. Alan Sheridan (New York: Norton, 1977), pp. 146–175.
2 See Robert Richard Boyle, S.J., "Worshipper of the Word: James Joyce and the Trinity," in Edmund L. Epstein, ed., *A Starchamber Quiry: A James Joyce Centennial Volume, 1882–1982* (London: Methuen, 1982), p. 139.
3 A description of how the organizational principle of the *Wake* shifts from triple to quadruple to quintuple appears in Clive Hart, *Structure and Motif in Finnegans Wake* (London: Faber and Faber, 1962), pp. 62–77, 136.
4 Michael Maher, S. J., *Psychology,* Catholic Manuals of Philosophy, Stonyhurst Series, 2d ed. (New York: Benziger, n.d.), p. 521. This book, which came out during the nineties and eventually went through nine editions, is listed in Joyce's Trieste library in Richard Ellmann, *The Consciousness of Joyce* (New York: Oxford, 1977), p. 118. I am very grateful to Michael Patrick Gillespie for sending me a list of Joyce's markings in Maher. Gillespie's annotated catalogue of Joyce's Trieste library, which includes the suggestion that Maher was Joyce's college text, will soon be published by the Humanities Research Center.
5 The two short quotes are from "Hamlet" (1886): the longer one is from a one-paragraph companion-piece to this essay, "Hamlet and Fortinbras" (1896). Both are in *Mallarmé: Selected Prose Poems, Essays and Letters,* trans. Bradford Cook (Baltimore: Johns Hopkins University Press, 1956), pp. 59. 139. For a discussion of Mallarmé's influence, see David Hayman, *Joyce et Mallarmé,* 2 vols. (Paris: Les Lettres Modernes, 1956).
6 In *Intentions,* in *The Artist as Critic: Critical Writings of Oscar Wilde,* ed. Richard Ellmann (New York: Vintage, 1970), p. 343.
7 Jaynes, *Origin of Consciousness,* pp. 73–80, 107–22.

8 Boyle tends in a subtle way to see Joyce as Christian in the above essay and in *James Joyce's Pauline Vision: A Catholic Exposition* (Carbondale: Southern Illinois University Press, 1978). Joyce's opposition to Christianity is emphasized in J. Mitchell Morse, *The Sympathetic Alien: James Joyce and Catholicism* (New York: New York University Press, 1959). He is seen as heretic in William T. Noon, S. J., *Joyce and Aquinas* (New Haven: Yale University Press, 1957).
9 Boyle, *James Joyce's Pauline Vision,* pp. 46, 55.
10 This line does not appear in the abridged version of Lacan's forty-minute talk, "Joyce le Symptôme," in Jacques Aubert and Maria Jolas, eds., *Joyce & Paris: 1902 . . . 1920-1940 . . . 1975: Actes du Cinquième Symposium International James Joyce* (Paris: Edition du CNRS, 1979), pp. 13-17.
11 Thomas Aquinas *Summa Theologiae,* Vol. 7: *Father, Son and Holy Ghost,* ed. and trans. T. C. O'Brien (London: Blackfriars, 1976), Question 39, Article 8, p. 133.
12 Ludwig Wittgenstein, *Tractatus Logico-Philosophicus,* trans. D. F. Pears and B. F. McGuinness (London: Routledge & Kegan Paul, 1961), p. 3.
13 Hugh Kenner, "The Portrait in Perspective," in Seon Givens, ed., *James Joyce: Two Decades of Criticism* (New York: Vanguard, 1948, 1963), p. 166. An extreme but indicative statement.
14 Norris said this on a panel, "Joyce's Consubstantiality," at the Eighth International James Joyce Symposium, Dublin, June 1982.
15 Jacques Derrida, "Force and Signification," in *Writing and Difference,* trans. Alan Bass (Chicago: University of Chicago Press, 1978), p. 11.
16 Ovid, *Metamorphoses,* trans. Rolfe Humphries (Bloomington: Indiana University Press, 1955), pp. 187-188. The original sentence that includes the epigraph of *Portrait,* Book VII, ll. 188-189, reads, "*Dixit, et ignotas animum dimittit in artes / naturamque novat.*"
17 See Robert Richard Boyle, S.J., "*Finnegans Wake,* Page 185: An Explication," *James Joyce Quarterly* 4 (Fall 1966): 3-16.
18 W. K. Wimsatt, *The Verbal Icon* (Lexington: University of Kentucky Press, 1954), pp. 6-15. Joyce refers to Goethe extensively in *Ulysses* and the *Wake.* His interest in Croce appears in *JJ* 340.
19 John Paul Riquelme, *Teller and Tale in Joyce's Fiction: Oscillating Perspectives* (Baltimore: John Hopkins University Press, 1983), p. 95. Genette's theories appear in *Narrative Discourse: An Essay on Method,* trans. Jane E. Lewin (Ithaca: Cornell University Press, 1980).
20 Patrick Cruttwell, "Makers and Persons," *Hudson Review* 12 (Winter 1959-1960), 487-507.
21 Arthur Power, *Conversations with James Joyce* (New York: Harper and Row, 1974), p. 92.
22 Frank Kermode, *The Genesis of Secrecy: On the Interpretation of Narrative* (Cambridge: Harvard University Press, 1979), pp. 89, 111.

23 David Hayman, *Ulysses: The Mechanics of Meaning*, rev. ed. (Madison: University of Wisconsin Press, 1982), pp. 92-93, 124. The first edition came out in 1970.
24 Hugh Kenner, *Joyce's Voices* (Berkeley: University of California Press, 1978), pp. 67-98.
25 Hugh Kenner, *Ulysses,* Unwin Critical Library (London: George Allen and Unwin, 1980), pp. 68-69.
26 Karen Lawrence, *The Odyssey of Style in Ulysses* (Princeton: Princeton University Press, 1981), p. 178.
27 Bruce F. Kawin, *The Mind of the Novel: Reflexive Fiction and the Ineffable* (Princeton: Princeton University Press, 1982), p. 19. For Kenner, see *Ulysses*, p. 112.
28 Brook Thomas, *James Joyce's Ulysses: A Book of Many Happy Returns* (Baton Rouge: Louisiana State University Press, 1982), p. 118. Thomas's excellent book represents a current tendency to concentrate on the skeptical aspect of Joyce's work at the expense of its emotional and affirmative aspects.
29 Riquelme, *Teller and Tale in Joyce's Fiction,* pp. 56-60.
30 Punctuation being important here, I have taken this passage from *James Joyce Ulysses: The Manuscript and First Printings Compared,* ed. Clive Driver (New York: Farrar, Straus and Giroux, 1975), p. 65 of Shakespeare and Company edition. At this point the manuscript adds a comma to *U* 67 after "qualm." The version in the Shakespeare and Company and Random House, 1961 editions, without this comma, is actually more subtle.
31 Spinoza, "Second Part," *Ethic,* in *Selections,* ed. John Wild (New York: Scribner's, 1930), pp. 143-204.
32 Arnold Goldman, *The Joyce Paradox: Form and Freedom in His Fiction* (London: Routledge & Kegan Paul, 1966), pp. 95, 97.
33 Marilyn French, *The Book as World: James Joyce's Ulysses* (Cambridge: Harvard University Press, 1976), pp. 24-25, 267.
34 Elliott B. Gose, *The Transformation Process in Joyce's Ulysses* (Toronto: University of Toronto Press, 1980), pp. 13-40.
35 John Gordon, *James Joyce's Metamorphoses* (Dublin: Gill and Macmillan, 1981), p. 47.
36 Jackson I. Cope, *Joyce's Cities: Archaeologies of the Soul* (Baltimore: Johns Hopkins University Press, 1981), pp. 54-60.
37 Riquelme, *Teller and Tale in Joyce's Fiction,* p. 17.
38 Umberto Eco, *The Aesthetics of Chaosmos: The Middle Ages of James Joyce,* trans. Ellen Esrock, University of Tulsa Monograph Series, no. 18 (Tulsa: University of Tulsa, 1982), pp. 2-3. This work, originally published in Italian in 1962, presents an extensive description of how dependent Joyce was on medieval ideas throughout his career, though Eco's main emphasis is ultimately on the chaotic side.
39 Colin MacCabe, *James Joyce and the Revolution of the Word* (London: Macmillan, 1979), pp. 127 ff., 143.

40 Thomas Aquinas, *Summa Theologiae,* Vol. 1: *The Existence of God,* Part One: Questions 1–13, ed. Thomas Gilby (Garden City: Doubleday Image, 1969), Question 9, Article 2, and Question 8, Article 1, pp. 140, 128. Future references to questions and articles in this volume will appear in parentheses and be preceded by Q. and A.

41 Freud speaks of a series of supernatural beliefs that are built up in childhood and remain capable of being called forth by disorienting perceptions in "The 'Uncanny,' " in *The Standard Edition of the Complete Psychological Works of Sigmund Freud,* ed. James Strachey et al. (London: Hogarth Press, 1953–1974), 17:219–252.

42 Dante Alighieri, *The Paradiso,* trans. John Ciardi (New York: New American Library, 1970), p. 217.

43 See Hans Jonas, *The Gnostic Religion: The Message of the Alien God and the Beginnings of Christianity,* 2d ed. (Boston: Beacon, 1963), pp. 78, 133, 195–196. Jonas presents several points of interest to Joyceans. He quotes Simon Magus, the first major prophet of Gnosticism, as saying, "I am God . . ." (p. 104). This suggests an answer to the question Stephen considers when he is attracted to the priesthood, ". . . what was the sin of Simon Magus . . ." (*P* 159).

44 The summary is by David Farrell Krell, and appears in Martin Heidegger, *Basic Writings,* ed. Krell (New York: Harper and Row, 1977), pp. 145–146.

Chapter 2

1 Augustine, *Confessions,* V.8, trans. R. S. Pine-Coffin (Harmondsworth: Penguin, 1961). I will use this edition for English, unless I note otherwise, and for Latin, *St. Augustine's Confessions, With an English Translation by William Watts, 1631,* 2 vols., ed. W. H. D. Rouse, Loeb Classics (London: Heinemann, 1912). Roman numerals are books, Arabic ones, chapters.

2 ". . . learning these facts, which do not reach our minds as images by means of the senses but are recognized by us in our minds, without images, as they actually are, is simply a process of thought by which we gather together things which, although they are muddled and confused, are already contained in the memory" (X.11).

3 Morse, *Sympathetic Alien,* esp. chaps. 2 and 8.

4 Power, *Conversations with James Joyce,* p. 89.

5 Lacan, "The Freudian thing," in *Écrits,* p. 128. By appropriating the innate values of the church to promote his own personality, Stephen contradicts some of Lacan's ideas.

6 Morse, *Sympathetic Alien,* pp. 129–130, develops this theme.

7 Herbert Gorman, *James Joyce* (New York: Rinehart, 1939, 1948), p. 48.

8 Jacques Mercanton, "The Hours of James Joyce," in William Potts, ed., *Portraits of the Artist in Exile: Recollections of James Joyce by Europeans* (Seattle: University of Washington Press, 1979), pp. 222, 229.

9 William Barrett, Forward, in Robert E. Meagher, *An Introduction to Augustine* (New York: New York University Press, 1978), p. xiii.
10 Wilhelm Stekel, *Sadism and Masochism: The Pyschology of Hatred and Cruelty*, trans. Louise Brink (New York: Liveright, 1929, 1953), is the classic statement of the idea that sadism and masochism are parts of one complex and that one rarely occurs in an individual without the other. Compare the images of being penetrated in *Confessions*, VI.6 or VII.8, with *P* 115, 126.
11 Darcy O'Brien, *The Conscience of James Joyce* (Princeton: Princeton University Press, 1968), describes how Joyce's view of the world continued to be influenced by Catholic attitudes.
12 Mark Schechner, *Joyce in Nighttown: A Psychoanalytic Inquiry into Ulysses* (Berkeley: University of California Press, 1974), pp. 83-85, 140-147.
13 This is Watts's translation, more accurate here. The inner *lux* is female, Joyce's daughter's name.
14 Lacan, "Freudian thing," p. 141.
15 Ibid., p. 118.
16 This paragraph was influenced by an unpublished paper, "Susceptible of Change," which Elliott B. Gose read at the Eighth International James Joyce Symposium in Dublin on June 15, 1982.
17 See my "Structure and Meaning in Joyce's Exiles," *James Joyce Quarterly* 6 (Fall 1968): 29-53, which is substantially reprinted in *Joyce between Freud and Jung* (Port Washington, New York: Kennikat, 1980), pp. 94-122.
18 Gordon, *James Joyce's Metamorphoses*, pp. 5-47.
19 Ellmann indicates that this story comes to him at third hand.
20 *A Cathechism of Christian Doctrine*, rev. ed. (London: Catholic Truth Society, 1971), Questions 29-30, p. 7. This point is not in the Maynooth Catechism, which Joyce used.
21 Augustine, *The Trinity*, trans. Stephen McKenna, The Fathers of the Church (Washington; D.C.: Catholic University of America Press, 1963), pp. 310-312, 506-507. This work was written from about 400 to 415.
22 Riquelme, *Teller and Tale in Joyce's Fiction*, p. 150.
23 Morse, *Sympathetic Alien*, pp. 129-138.
24 Donald Barthelme, *The Dead Father* (New York: Farrar, Straus and Giroux, 1975), p. 116.
25 Augustine's first work, *Beauty and Proportion*, is described in *Confessions*, IV 14 ff. John K. Ryan, in the introduction to his edition of the *Confessions* (Garden City: Doubleday Image, 1960), pp. 21-22, states that Augustine was a Neoplatonist for a time and that Plotinus (who died in 270 A.D.) presents the Divinity as a triad that is unified. In fact, the three-part nature of Plotinus's godhead corresponds to that of his triple soul. Of course, Augustine did not invent the Trinity, which St. Athanasius installed as doctrine at the Council of Nicaea in 325; but in developing the theory of this image, he drew on concepts of multiple godhood that came from Neo-

platonism to influence not only Christianity, but Gnosticism and Kabbalism, to which I will return.

The most detailed treatment in English of Augustine's use of Neoplatonism is the work of Robert J. O'Connell, S. J., of which the most relevant example is *Art and the Christian Intelligence in St. Augustine* (Cambridge: Harvard University Press, 1978). O'Connell argues here that instead of deriving Christian principles from Plotinus, Augustine was inspired by Christian truths involved in Neoplatonism, truths that led to his conversion to Christianity. Like all typological arguments, this one, of which Augustine would approve, depends on the retroactive discovery of coincidence.

26 My italics. The Linati schema appears in Richard Ellmann, *Ulysses on the Liffey* (New York: Oxford, 1972), between pp. 188 and 189.
27 William Barclay, *The Men, the Meaning, and the Message of the New Testament Books* (Philadelphia: Westminster, 1976), p. 23. Carl Gustav Jung refers to "St. John's gospel, a work that is, very obviously, of Gnostic inspiration" in his "A Psychological Approach to the Dogma of the Trinity," in *Psychology and Religion: West and East,* The Collected Works of C. G. Jung, Vol. 11, trans. R. F. C. Hull, ed. Sir Herbert Read et al. (Princeton: Bollingen, 1958), p. 117.
28 Weldon Thornton, *Allusions in Ulysses: An Annotated List* (Chapel Hill: University of North Carolina Press, 1968), pp. 212-213.
29 Robert M. Adams, *Afterjoyce: Studies in Fiction after Ulysses* (New York: Oxford, 1977), p. 3.
30 Thomas Pynchon, *V.* (New York: Bantam, 1964), p. 305.
31 For primary-process thought, the disorganized flux of mental content below the level of consciousness, see Sigmund Freud, *The Interpretation of Dreams,* Standard Edition, 5:599-611.
32 Jacques Derrida, "Coming into One's Own," in Geoffrey H. Hartman, ed., *Psychoanalysis and the Question of the Text: Selected Papers from the English Institute, 1976–1977* (Baltimore: Johns Hopkins University Press, 1978), p. 135.

Chapter 3

1 Riquelme, *Teller and Tale in Joyce's Fiction,* p. 133.
2 Gorman, *James Joyce,* p. 98; cf. *SH* 171.
3 This accords with Coleridge's definition of primary imagination as "a repetition in the finite mind of the eternal act of creation in the infinite I AM" in chapter 13 of *Biographia Literaria.*
4 The most complete selection of Joyce's Aristotle notes is Richard F. Peterson, "More Aristotelian Grist for the Joycean Mill," *James Joyce Quarterly* 17 (1980): 213-216.
5 Gose, *Transformation Process in Joyce's Ulysses,* pp. 12 ff.
6 J. Lewis McIntyre, *Giordana Bruno* (London: Macmillan, 1903), p. 122.
7 Ibid., p. 338.

8 *Aristotle's Metaphysics,* trans. Hippocrates G. Apostle (Bloomington: Indiana University Press, 1966), Book A (I), chapter 3, and Book B (III) chapter 2, pp. 16, 41. All references to this book will be by the page numbers of the Berlin Edition, edited by Bekker, which appear in the margin of virtually all English editions of Aristotle. The Bekker page numbers of the passages cited here are 983b and 996b.
9 Power, *Conversations with James Joyce,* p. 54.
10 Noon, *Joyce and Aquinas,* p. 135.
11 Boyle, *James Joyce's Pauline Vision,* pp. viii ff., 22 ff.
12 Derrida, "Force and Signification," pp. 26-29.
13 David A. White, *The Grand Continuum: Reflections on Joyce and Metaphysics* (Pittsburgh: University of Pittsburgh Press, 1983), pp. 48-53.
14 *Jerusalem,* in *The Poetry and Prose of William Blake,* ed. David V. Erdman (Garden City: Doubleday, 1970), Plate 27, p. 170. "Marybone" is spelled "Marylebone" in *Poems of William Blake,* ed. W. B. Yeats, Muses' Library (London: Routledge, [June 1905]), p. 221. Ellmann, *Consciousness of Joyce,* p. 102, lists this book in Joyce's Trieste library.
15 *A First-Draft Version of Finnegans Wake* ed. David Hayman (Austin: University of Texas Press, 1963), p. 48.
16 Margot Norris, *The Decentered Universe of Finnegans Wake: A Structuralist Analysis* (Baltimore: Johns Hopkins University Press, 1976).
17 MacCabe, *James Joyce and the Revolution of the Word,* pp. 29-35; Gordon, *James Joyce's Metamorphoses,* pp. 13-27.
18 Giordano Bruno, *Cause, Principle and Unity,* trans. Jack Lindsay (New York: International Publishers, 1964), p. 149.
19 Power, *Conversations with James Joyce,* p. 74.
20 Heidegger, "The Origin of the Work of Art," in *Basic Writings,* pp. 153-154. I disagree with the thesis of this paper.
21 Bruno, *Cause, Principle and Unity,* pp. 26, 102 ff.
22 Kenner, *Joyce's Voices,* p. 69.
23 Lacan, "The subversion of the subject and the dialectic of desire in the Freudian unconscious," *Écrits,* p. 299.

Moreover, Lacan's insistence that the signifier is barred from the signified should not be taken to preclude a theological perspective. In the essay that announces this barrier, "The agency of the letter in the unconscious or reason since Freud," Lacan states, "One cannot go further along this line of thought than to demonstrate that no signification can be sustained other than by reference to another signification." This sentence is attached to the following endnote: "10. Cf. the *De Magistro* of St. Augustine, especially the chapter '*De significatione locutionis*' which I analysed in my seminar of 23 June, 1954." *Écrits,* pp. 150, 176n. This reminds us that the idea of a signified that can never be reached by its signifier is precisely the idea of theology.

Chapter 4

1 Mercanton, "Hours of James Joyce," p. 209, cited in Gose, *Transformation Process in Joyce's Ulysses,* p. 61.
2 Jonas, *Gnostic Religion,* pp. 190–193.
3 McIntyre, *Giordano Bruno,* p. 157.
4 Etienne Gilson, *Being and Some Philosophers,* 2d ed. (Toronto: Pontifical Institute of Mediaeval Studies, 1952), p. 11. For my purpose I am isolating a simple point from Gilson's complex argument.
5 Mercanton, "Hours of James Joyce," pp. 209. 223.
6 Gorman, *James Joyce,* p. 98.
7 Bruno, *Cause, Principle and Unity,* p. 150.
8 The term *uni-fication* was suggested to me by Father Boyle.
9 Riquelme, *Teller and Tale in Joyce's Fiction,* p. 79.
10 Power, *Conversations with James Joyce,* p. 89.
11 See Don Gifford and Robert J. Seidman, *Notes for Joyce: An Annotation of James Joyce's Ulysses* (New York: Dutton, 1974), p. 83.
12 Kenner, *Ulysses,* p. 70.
13 Kermode, *Genesis of Secrecy,* p. 143.
14 D. W. Winnicott, *Playing and Reality* (Harmondsworth: Penguin, 1974), pp. 3–15, 62–66, 122–127.
15 The examples cited are respectively my *Joyce between Freud and Jung,* pp. 29 ff.; Norris, *Decentered Universe of Finnegans Wake,* pp. 130 ff.; Suzette A. Henke, *Joyce's Moraculous Sindbook: A Study of Ulysses* (Columbus: Ohio State University Press, 1978), p. 46; MacCabe, *James Joyce and the Revolution of the Word,* pp. 127 ff.
16 Jung, "Synchronicity: An Acausal Connecting Principle," in *The Structure and Dynamics of the Psyche, The Collected Works of C. G. Jung,* Vol. 8, (Princeton: Bollingen, 1960), pp. 486–495. Joyce's awareness of psychic phenomena in *Ulysses* is indicated by Stuart Gilbert, *James Joyce's Ulysses* (1930; rpt. New York: Vintage, 1955), pp. 26, 57, 344. My *Joyce Between Freud and Jung,* pp. 168–182, explains synchronicities in detail, citing some of the important critical treatments of Joyce's use of coincidence. See also Appendix 1, p. 145–153.
17 Jung, "On Psychic Energy," in *Structure and Dynamics of the Psyche,* pp. 23–25.
18 Henke, *Joyce's Moraculous Sindbook,"* pp. 48–50.
19 Robert Kellogg, "Scylla and Charybdis," in Clive Hart and David Hayman, eds., *James Joyce's Ulysses: Critical Essays* (Berkeley: University of California Press, 1974), p. 168.
20 For the dual consubstantiality of Christ, see Bernard Lonergan, *The Way to Nicea: The Dialectical Development of Trinitarian Theology,* trans. Conn O'Donovan (Philadelphia: Westminster, 1976), p. 92.
21 See Jean-Michel Rabate, "A Clown's Inquest into Paternity: Fathers, Dead

or Alive, in *Ulysses* and *Finnegans Wake,*" in Robert Con Davis, ed. *The Fictional Father: Lacanian Readings of the Text* (Amherst: University of Massachusetts Press, 1981), pp. 73-114.

22 This probably refers to Thomas Aquinas, *Summa Theologiae*, Vol. 9: *Angels*, ed. and trans. Kenelm Foster (London: Blackfriars, 1967), Q. 50, A. 3, p. 19. In dealing with the question of how angels can be more than one if they are perfect, Aquinas here defends a statement (in italics) by Dionysius the Areopagite: "*Many are the blissful hosts of the supernal intelligences, far exceeding the . . . limits of matter.* We can argue to this from what we know of God's principle purpose in creating anything at all, which was to represent his own perfection; whence it follows that the more perfect is the nature of the things to be created, the more abundantly does God exercise his creative power to produce them. And as in the corporeal world such abundance is reckoned in terms of spatial magnitude, so in the spiritual world it can be reckoned in terms of number."

23 Wolfgang Iser, *The Implied Reader: Patterns of Communication in Prose Fiction from Bunyan to Beckett* (Baltimore: Johns Hopkins University Press, 1974), pp. 179-195.

24 Ibid., p. 222.

25 S. L. Goldberg, *The Classical Temper: A Study of James Joyce's Ulysses* (London: Chatto and Windus, 1961), pp. 284-285.

26 In a letter to Harriet Shaw Weaver of 6 August 1919, Joyce insisted that his techniques were necessary "for me" to render the subject: ". . . in the compass of one day to compress all these wanderings and clothe them in the form of this day is for me only possible by such variation which, I beg you to believe, is not capricious" (*Letters*, 1: 129).

27 Gose, *Transformation Process in Joyce's Ulysses,* pp. 25 ff.

28 A line Joyce added rather sloppily to the manuscript of *Ulysses* has yet to appear in a printed text. Line 27 of *U* 181 should read "Weight or size of it, something blacker than the dark. Wonder would . . ." See *James Joyce Ulysses: A Facsimile of the Manuscript*, ed. Clive Driver (New York: Farrar, Straus and Giroux, 1975), 1: 172-173.

29 Derrida, "*La parole soufflée,*" in *Writing and Difference*, p. 176.

30 James Joyce, *Exiles* (New York: Viking, 1951), p. 114.

31 Jorge Luis Borges, "Everything and Nothing," in *Dreamtigers*, trans. Mildred Boyer (New York: Dutton, 1970), pp. 46-47. The original title of this book is *El Hacedor*, "The Maker," as in *el Supremo Hacedor*.

Chapter 5

1 Freud, *Civilization and Its Discontents, Standard Edition,* 21: 64-74. Joyce recognizes that the status of an unborn infant is that of a deity in "Oxen": "Before born babe bliss had. Within womb won he worship" (*U* 384).

2 Jakob Boehme, *The Signature of All Things and Other Writings* (Cambridge, Eng.: James Clarke, 1969), p. 11.

3 Hayman, *Ulysses,* pp. 88–89.
4 Boyle, "Worshipper of the Word," p. 132.
5 A. Walton Litz, *The Art of James Joyce: Method and Design in Ulysses and Finnegans Wake* (New York: Oxford, 1964), pp. 132–140.
6 *James Joyce Ulysses: The Manuscript and First Printings Compared,* ed. Driver, p. 3 of Shakespeare and Company edition.
7 Helen Kendrick Johnson, *Our Familiar Songs and Those Who Made Them* (New York: Holt, 1881), p. 146. See Appendix 2, below.
8 James Joyce, *Collected Poems* (New York: Viking, 1957), p. 43.
9 Charles Dickens, *Dombey and Son,* ed. Alan Horsman (London: Oxford, 1974), pp. 224–225. Two analogues of the image of death as a river are discussed in my final chapter.
10 Karen Lawrence, "'Aeolus': Interruption and Inventory," *James Joyce Quarterly* 17 (Summer 1980): 395–396.
11 Thomas Flanagan describes Dublin as "a Protestant city" in *The Year of the French* (New York: Holt, Rinehart and Winston, 1979), p. 453.
12 Lacan, "The function and field of speech and language in psychoanalysis," in *Écrits,* p. 104.
13 Thomas, *James Joyce's Ulysses,* p. 70; Vladimir Nabokov, *Lectures on Literature,* ed. Fredson Bowers (New York: Harcourt Brace Jovanovich, 1980), pp. 316–320.
14 *Joyce's Notes and Early Drafts for Ulysses: Selections from the Buffalo Collection,* ed. Phillip F. Herring (Charlottesville: University Press of Virginia, 1977), pp. 8, 27.
15 *Joyce's Ulysses Notesheets in the British Museum,* ed. Phillip F. Herring (Charlottesville: University Press of Virgina, 1972), p. 405.
16 *James Joyce Ulysses: The Manuscript and First Printings Compared,* ed. Driver, p. 188 of Shakespeare and Company edition.
17 Gifford and Seidman, *Notes for Joyce,* p. 45.
18 Cheryl T. Herr, "Theosophy, Guilt, and 'That Word Known to All Men' in Joyce's *Ulysses,*" *James Joyce Quarterly* 18 (Fall 1980): 49.
19 I got this idea from an outstanding student, Stephane Duckett.
20 Robert Adams Day, "How Stephen Wrote His Vampire Poem," *James Joyce Quarterly* 17 (Winter 1980): 187.
21 David Hayman, "Stephen on the Rocks," *James Joyce Quarterly* 15 (Fall 1977): 5–17. Another indication of parallels between "Proteus" and "Nausicaa" may be seen in the illustrations Frank Budgen did for the two episodes, which are reproduced in Budgen, *James Joyce and the Making of Ulysses* (Bloomington: Indiana University Press, 1960), opposite pp. 16 and 208. In each of these an arch reaches down from the sky to connect the protagonist with other objects on the beach. Joyce may have approved these drawings.
22 Kenner, *Ulysses,* p. 57.
23 Riquelme, *Teller and Tale in Joyce's Fiction,* pp. 10–25.
24 *Joyce's Ulysses Notesheets,* p. 203.

25 Robert Martin Adams, *James Joyce: Common Sense and Beyond* (New York: Random House, 1966), p. 165.
26 Gordon, *James Joyce's Metamorphoses,* p. 81.
27 Augustine, *Trinity,* p. 15.
28 Roland McHugh, *Annotations to Finnegans Wake* (Baltimore: Johns Hopkins University Press, 1980), p. 57. As this book has the same pagination as the *Wake,* further references to McHugh's *Annotations* will not require notes.
29 Eugene Jolas, "My Friend James Joyce," in *James Joyce: Two Decades of Criticism,* p. 13.
30 Jennifer Schiffer Levine, "Originality and Repetition in *Finnegans Wake,*" *PMLA* 94 (1979): 113.
31 Edmund Leach, *Claude Lévi-Strauss,* Modern Masters (New York: Viking, 1970), pp. 59–60.
32 Jorge Luis Borges, "Pascal's Sphere," in *Other Inquisitions: 1937–1952* (New York: Washington Square Press, 1966), pp. 5–8.
33 See Fritz Senn, "Dublin Theaters," in Clive Hart and Fritz Senn, eds., *A Wake Digest* (Sydney: Sydney University Press, 1968), p. 23.

Chapter 6

1 In the "Epilogue" of *Crime and Punishment* and in the story "The Dream of a Ridiculous Man."
2 Cope, *Joyce's Cities,* pp. 62–102.
3 Helena Petrovna Blavatsky, *Isis Unveiled,* 2 vols. (London: Theosophical Publishing Society, 1877), will hereafter be cited by volume and page number. Hart, *Structure and Motif in Finnegans Wake,* pp. 44, 49, 63, 103, 142–143.
4 Giambattista Vico, *The New Science of Giambattista Vico,* trans. Thomas Goddard Bergin and Max Harold Fisch, rev. ed. (Ithaca: Cornell University Press, 1968), par. 520, p. 179.
5 Joseph Campbell and Henry Morton Robinson, *A Skeleton Key to Finnegans Wake* (New York: Harcourt, Brace, 1944), pp. 26, 196n.
6 James S. Atherton, *The Books at the Wake* (New York: Viking, 1960), pp. 12 ff., cites several critics who feel that Joyce is the dreamer and cites evidence for this view. It is supported by Bernard Benstock, *Joyce-again's Wake: An Analysis of Finnegans Wake* (Seattle: University of Washington Press, 1965), pp. 118 ff.; and by Adams, *James Joyce: Common Sense and Beyond,* p. 165, and Boyle, *James Joyce's Pauline Vision,* p. 57. The idea is developed at length in Gordon, *James Joyce's Metamorphoses,* pp. 151–178.
7 Arthur Edward Waite, *The Doctrine and Literature of the Kabalah* (London: Theosophical Publishing Society, 1902), p. 25. Cope (*Joyce's Cities*), in his first note on p. 136, shows that Joyce probably read this book.
8 William Butler Yeats, *A Vision,* rev. ed. (1938; rpt. New York: Macmillan, 1961), p. 12. The *Wake* refers to this late edition.
9 The manuscript on which Joyce introduced the columns, MS 47478, 161–178, is labeled by him "Hotel Elite, Zurich." David Hayman reports

that Joyce visited here from September 1934 to January 1935. *Finnegans Wake, Book II, Chapter 2: A Facsimile of Drafts, Typescripts and Proofs,* 2 vols., ed. Hayman and Danis Rose, *Joyce Archive,* nos. 52, 53 (New York: Garland, 1978), 1: xvi, 29, 53-79; 2: 274-280. A continuous version of the earliest drafts of this section appears as a single discourse in Hayman's *First-Draft Version of Finnegans Wake,* pp. 142-167.
10 See David Hayman, "'Scribbledehobbles' and How They Grew: A Turning Point in the Development of a Chapter," in Jack P. Dalton and Clive Hart, eds., *Twelve and a Tilly: Essays on the Occasion of the 25th Anniversary of Finnegans Wake* (Evanston: Northwestern University Press, 1965), pp. 107-118.
11 Edmund L. Epstein argues that during his solo passage, Shaun is immersed in ALP and transformed, in "James Joyce and the Body," in *Starchamber Quiry,* p. 98. Maybe, but the passage remains a passive interruption of the main action, a period during which the consequences of that action sink in.
12 In William York Tindall, *A Reader's Guide to Finnegans Wake* (New York: Farrar, Straus and Giroux, 1969), p. 178.
13 Freud, "The Antithetical Meaning of Primal Words," *Standard Edition,* 11: 153-162.
14 See Three Initiates, *The Kybalion: A Study of the Hermetic Philosophy of Ancient Egypt and Greece* (Chicago: Yogi Publication Society, 1912), pp. 32-35. Frances A. Yates, *Giordano Bruno and the Hermetic Tradition* (New York: Vintage, 1969), pp. 350-351, argues that Bruno saw his theories as a return to Egyptian religion. For the alchemy of right and left, see C. G. Jung, *The Psychology of the Transference,* in *The Practice of Psychotherapy, Collected Works,* 16: 211-218. For Joyce's use of alchemy, see Barbara DiBernard, *Alchemy and Finnegans Wake* (Albany: State University of New York Press, 1980).
15 Jonas, *Gnostic Religion,* pp. 179 ff.
16 Robert Waelder, "The Principle of Multiple Function: Observations on Over-Determination," *Psychoanalytic Quarterly* 5 (1936): 45-62.
17 White, *Grand Continuum,* pp. 171-182. For Husserl, see Jean-Paul Sartre, "The Transcendence of the Ego," in *Phenomenology: The Philosophy of Edmund Husserl and Its Interpretation,* ed. Joseph J. Kockelmans (Garden City: Doubleday Anchor, 1967), pp. 324-338 (an excerpt from a book of the same title by Sartre). For the attempt to integrate phenomenology into psychoanalysis, see *Being-in-the-World: Selected Papers of Ludwig Binswanger,* trans. Jacob Needleman (New York: Harper Torchbooks, 1967), Lacan uses phenomenological insights in his analysis of the Imaginary, but he dislikes existentialism.
18 McIntyre, *Giordano Bruno,* p. 130. Joyce probably also read this anticipation of the thesis of Freud's *Moses and Monotheism* in its original context in an Italian text of Bruno's *The Expulsion of the Triumphant Beast,* trans. Arthur D. Imerti (New Brunswick: Rutgers University Press, 1964), p. 240.
19 Christian David Ginsburg and Stanley Arthur Cook's article on Kabba-

lah in the Eleventh Edition of the *Encyclopaedia Britannica* is regarded as Joyce's likeliest source on the subject by Atherton, *Books at the Wake,* p. 47.
20 Edward Albertson, *Understanding the Kabbalah* (Los Angeles: Sherbourne, 1973), p. 40.
21 Campbell and Robinson, *Skeleton Key to Finnegans Wake,* pp. 171, 193-195.
22 *Joyce Archive: Finnegans Wake, Book II, Chapter 2,* 1: 77, 2: 278.
23 Heinz Kohut, *The Analysis of the Self: A Systematic Approach to the Psychoanalytic Treatment of Narcissistic Personality Disorders* (New York: International Universities Press, 1971), pp. 37-47.
24 Campbell and Robinson, *Skeleton Key to Finnegans Wake,* p. 164.
25 *Zohar,* III.290, quoted by Ginsburg and Cook, *Encyclopaedia Britannica,* S.V. "Kabbalah." The *Idra Zuta,* the section from which this passage is taken, is omitted from the English edition. See *The Zohar,* trans. Harry Sperling and Maurice Simon (London: Soncino, 1934), 5: 379, 398. Future references to the *Zohar* will be by volume and page numbers of the standard Hebrew edition, which appear in all English editions.
26 Three Initiates, *Kybalion,* p. 40.
27 Gershom Scholem, "Kabbalah and Myth," in *On the Kabbalah and Its Symbolism,* trans. Ralph Manheim (New York: Schocken, 1965), p. 104.
28 Lacan, "The signification of the phallus," in *Écrits,* p. 281.
29 See my *Joyce between Freud and Jung,* p. 39.
30 Waite, *Doctrine and Literature of the Kabalah,* p. 49.
31 Hart, *Structure and Motif in Finnegans Wake,* p. 44.
32 Riquelme, *Teller and Tale in Joyce's Fiction,* p. 50.
33 Derrida, "Freud and the Scene of Writing," in *Writing and Difference,* pp. 201-206.
34 Albertson, *Understanding the Kabbalah,* p. 34.
35 Riquelme, *Teller and Tale in Joyce's Fiction,* pp. 16-17, 81-82, 218. The first major treatment of chiasmus in Joyce was Evert Sprinchorn, "A Portrait of the Artist as Achilles," in John E. Unterecker, ed., *Approaches to the Twentieth Century Novel* (New York: Thomas Y. Crowell, 1965), pp. 22-27.
36 Plato, *Timaeus,* ed. H. D. P. Lee (Baltimore: Penguin, 1965), p. 63.
37 Hart, *Structure and Motif in Finnegans Wake,* pp. 131-132.
38 Yeats, *Vision,* p. 159. The factors in this interchange appear in a parody of Yeats on *FW* 300.20-24. Compare *Vison,* p. 158.
39 Ibid., pp. 160-161.
40 Margaret Solomon, *Eternal Geomater: The Sexual Universe of Finnegans Wake* (Carbondale: Southern Illinois University Press, 1969), pp. 107-108.
41 Yeats, *Vision,* p. 161.
42 John Garvin, *James Joyce's Disunited Kingdom and the Irish Dimension* (Dublin: Gill and Macmillan, 1976), pp. 136-151.
43 Morton Prince, *The Dissociation of a Personality* (1905, 1908; rpt. New York: Longmans, Green, 1930), was first described as a source in Adaline Gla-

sheen, "*Finnegans Wake* and the Girls from Boston, Mass.," *Hudson Review* 7 (1954): 89–96.
44 Roberto Assagioli, *Psychosynthesis: A Manual of Principles and Techniques*, Esalen Book (New York: Viking, 1971).
45 C. G. Jung, *Analytic Psychology: Its Theory and Practice*, The Tavistock Lectures (New York: Pantheon, 1968), pp. 79–82; Deirdre Bair, *Samuel Beckett: A Biography* (New York: Harcourt Brace Jovanovich, 1978), pp. 208–210.
46 Note from Beckett, October 1982.
47 Prince, *Dissociation of a Personality*, pp. 3, 58, 73, 123.
48 Power, *Conversations with James Joyce*, p. 6. Gordon, *James Joyce's Metamorphoses*, pp. 75 ff., develops the idea of Gerty as a projection.
49 *Joyce's Ulysses Notesheets*, p. 420.
50 Levine, "Originality and Repetition in *Finnegans Wake*," p. 111, describes the footnotes as "another discourse," and Shari Benstock, "At the Margin of Discourse: Footnotes in the Fictional Text," *PMLA* 98 (March 1983): 211–220, describes them as a narrative.
51 The diagram of Christine is from Prince, *Dissociation of a Personality*, p. 465. The Tree is a composite of Waite's frontispiece and plate IX of S. Liddell MacGregor Mathers, *The Kabbalah Unveiled* (1888; rpt. London: Routledge & Kegan Paul, 1975), opposite p. 51. Adaline Glasheen, *Third Census of Finnegans Wake* (Berkeley: University of California Press, 1977), p. 189, lists eight possible references to Mathers in the *Wake*. When the central column refers to "gramma's grammar," Shem gives another good name for the whole chapter, "Allma Mathers" (*FW* 268.17).

Lacan presents a diagram similar to these two in "Subversion of the subject and the dialectic of desire in the Freudian unconscious," p. 315, which argues that Freud has subverted the traditional idea of the unified subject by conceiving of the mind as a dialectic of interacting forces. Lacan's diagram involves ten points and sixteen paths between them, four of which are curved. Moreover, this essay describes subjectivity, or primary-process thought, as a linguistic structure of sliding signifiers. Therefore the Lacanian Joyce studies of Norris and MacCabe are deeply justified. For in this perspective the creatures of the *Wake*, with Joyce acting as their Other (the Lacanian version of God), not only resemble, but actually *are*, Lacanian personalities.
52 *Encyclopaedia Britannica*, 11th ed. S.V. "Kabalah."
53 Waite, *Doctrine and Literature of the Kabbalah*, pp. 65–71.
54 Solomon, *Eternal Geomater*, pp. 65–68.
55 Eco, *Aesthetics of Chaosmos*, p. 20.

Chapter 7

1 McIntyre, *Giordano Bruno*, p. 158.
2 Mallarmé, *Selected Prose Poems, Essays and Letters*, p. 58.

3 Jaynes, *Origin of Consciousness,* p. 114.
4 Ibid., pp. 55, 59 ff.
5 Ibid., p. 105.
6 Nancy Scheper-Hughes, *Saints, Scholars, and Schizophrenics: Mental Illness in Rural Ireland* (Berkeley: University of California Press, 1979), p. 82.
7 Riquelme, *Teller and Tale in Joyce's Fiction,* p. 131.
8 Derrida, *"Parole soufflée,"* p. 179.
9 Rosemarie Battaglia, who is finishing a dissertation on the subject, described the relation between presence and absence in Joyce's work in a paper she gave at Temple University late in 1982.
10 Derrida, *"Parole soufflée,"* p. 177.
11 White, *Grand Continuum,* pp. 149–58.
12 Dante, *Paradiso,* p. 329.
13 Hermann Hesse, *Siddhartha,* trans. Hilda Rosner (New York: New Directions, 1957), p. 151.
14 Jaynes, *Origin of Consciousness,* pp. 338 ff., 405–406.
15 Virginia Woolf, *Orlando* (New York: Signet, 1960), p. 201.

Index

Adam Kadmon, 105
Adams, Robert Martin, 41, 97
Age of Reason, 12, 16, 123
Ain-Soph. *See* Kabbalah
ALP, 89, 102, 115-16. *See also Finnegans Wake.*
Alpha and Omega, 90, 95, 97
Aquinas, St. Thomas: on beauty, 11; on God's activity, 23; on God's unity, 36; on causality, 50; on excellence, 57; on the heavenly host, 74, 164n22; on God as ocean, 102; creation exceeds existence, 127
Aristotle: definition of mind, 3, 21; entelechy, 10, 24, 27, 54, 61, 68; and Bruno, 44-47; *Poetics,* 45; *Metaphysics,* 45-50, 54; godhead through mind, 46, 55-57, 83; prime mover, 55, 57; art, 56; definition of soul, 64; artistic unity, 73
Arius, 103
Arnold, Matthew, 48
Art: as division, 11; as sacrifice, 12; as godlike creation, 14-15, 38-39, 45; as expression, 16, 28, 30; power beyond individual, 24; unconscious parenthood, 39; all art aspires to intrapersonal drama, 131-34, 139
Artist: as presence, 10, 89; as character, 24
Assagioli, Roberto, 124

Augustine, St.: source, 27; name, 28; *Confessions,* 29-31, 38-40; dependence on God, 31; assumed divinity, 32; psychology of *The Trinity,* 37; God as artist, 38-39, 160n25; on interpretation, 39-40, 67; God in unconscious, 42, 140, 141; psychic structure in *Confessions,* 92; unknowability of Trinity, 98; God as creativity, 107; on learning, 116; on signification, 162n23

Barclay, William, 41
Barrett, William, 32
Barthelme, Donald, 39, 135
Beardsley, Monroe C., 16
"Beauchamp, Christine," 123-24, 126, 128
Beckett, Samuel: as prime mover in *The Unnamable,* 57; and Jung, 124, 169n46; *Murphy,* 124; *Endgame,* 134; *Waiting for Godot,* 135
Bible: myth and realism, 17; St. Paul, 31, 98; interpretation, 39-41; Genesis, Book of, 39-40, 86-87, 95; John, Gospel of, 41, 161n27; power of obscurity, 67; time perspective, 76; Alpha and Omega, 95, 97
Blake, William: *The Marriage of Heaven and Hell,* 20, 25-26, 118; God as human creation, 20, 30, 60; reason as contractile, 25-26; *Jerusalem,* 51, 105;

Blake, William (*continued*)
    Joyce on, 86; Albion myth, 105, 106; inlets of soul, 118
Blavatsky, Helena Petrovna (*Isis Unveiled*), 94, 104, 105, 108, 111, 114
Bloom, Leopold: meant to unite with Stephen, 5, 73; love for Molly, 11; faith in phenomena, 12, 80, 121; depth of realism, 64–65; shares thoughts with Stephen, 73, 78, 91–95; descent to nothing, 91; fear of unknown, 96
Bloom, Milly, 11, 96
Bloom, Molly, 5, 66, 115, 125, 156*n2*
Boehme, Jakob, 84
Borges, Jorge Luis, 81, 101, 135
Boyle, Robert Richard, S. J., 5, 9, 20, 86, 157*n8*, 163*n8*
Brain lobe theory, 8, 52, 110
Bruno, Giordano: double-aspect theory, 3, 21; union with God, 14, 30; personality, 16; God in matter, 20; coinciding contraries, 21; and Aristotle, 44–47; unity and opposition, 53–54, 62; on Kabbalah, 111; on goal of intellect, 131
Budgen, Frank, 165*n21*
Byron, Lord (George Gordon), 16

Campbell, Joseph, 105–6, 112, 114
Canon, unity of Joyce's, 62–63
Catechism, 37, 90, 160*n20*
Cervantes, Miguel de, 38
Chamber Music, 4, 88
Christ, Jesus: reality in Gospels, 17; obscurity, 41; division, 67; dual consubstantiality, 70; presence in communion, 74; shadow in Stephen, 78; incomprehensible, 100–101
Clarke, Arthur C., 100
Clery, Emma (E. C.), 115
Clifford, Martha, 92, 93
Coleridge, Samuel Taylor, 161*n3*
Confessions. *See* Augustine
Confucius, 98
Conroy, Gabriel, 94
Cook, Stanley Arthur, 112, 114, 115, 116, 167–68*n19*

Cope, Jackson I., 20, 104
Croce, Benedetto, 16, 157*n18*
Cruttwell, Patrick, 16

Daedalus: *in* Ovid, 14–15
D'Annunzio, Gabriele, 20
Dante Alighieri (*Paradiso*): God exceeds creation, 23; God beyond perception, 54; in beach scene, 86; river of light, 138
D'Arcy, Bartell, 6
Day, Robert Adams, 165*n20*
Deasy, Mr., 15
Deconstruction: dependent on construction, 13; of language, 22; fits God's view, 25, 49, 83; analytic, 44–45; spiritual technique, 75, 101
Dedalus, Stephen: meant to unite with Bloom, 5; on Shakespeare, 7, 87; theory of artist, 9, 10, 11, 39; attachment to God, 13, 14, 78; looks forward to Joyce, 16, 69, 86–87; opposition to God, 90; on terror, 90–91, 96; desire to build human mind, 104; and Thoth, 110; desire as anxiety in, 115. *See also* Bloom, Leopold
Deism, 12
Demiurge: defined, 59–61; internal, 64; speaks for things, 70; two kinds, 135
Derrida, Jacques: on God, 14, 83; on autobiography, 42; attack on metaphysics, 48; on stolen voice, 79, 136; *Glas,* 113; mental trace, 119; difference, 136; on schizophrenia, 137. *See also* Deconstruction
Dervin, Daniel A., 3
de Valera, Eamon, 123
Dickens, Charles (*Dombey and Son*), 88–89
Dionysius the Areopagite, 78, 164*n22*
Dodgson, Charles Lutwidge (Lewis Carroll), 128
Dostoevsky, Fyodor, 103, 122
Double-aspect theory: defined, 3; embodied by Bloom and Stephen, 5; in narrated monologue, 19; controversy in Maher, 21; and language, 22; in *Ulysses,* 42; in Bruno and Spinoza,

46–47; in Joyce's world, 55; interface of text, 59; HCE and ALP, 117
Dream as godlike, 50, 104, 106
Dubliners: mind restricted in, 4–5; conflict in "A Painful Case," 5; "The Dead," 5, 6, 94; entrapment in, 25; division in narration, 53; as extension of *Ulysses*, 62; flawed god in, 71–72; "The Sisters," 71–72, 137; "An Encounter," 71–72
Dumas, Alexandre (père), 41

Eco, Umberto, 22, 130
Écrits. *See* Lacan
"Elijah" (Alexander J. Dowie), 80
Ellmann, Richard, 33, 35, 37, 136
Essence precedes existence, 13
Everyman, 31
Exiles: connects people, 5; realistic, 6; love in, 11, 36; silent center of canon, 63; automystic, 139

Faulkner, William, 141
Feelings as personalities, 74, 123–25
Finn, 97, 101, 102, 106, 122
Finnegans Wake: expansive scope, 4; mental world, 5, 103; flow, 25; multiple voices, 51–52; paraphrases *Portrait*, 87; Alpha and Omega motif, 95; refers to *Ulysses*, 95; importance of author in, 97–102; II.2 (study period), 104, 107–10, 113–23, 124–25; the letter, 104, 126–30; Joyce as the dreamer, 106. *See also* ALP; HCE; Kabbalah
Flanagan, Thomas, 165$n11$
Flaubert, Gustav, 80, 122
French, Marilyn, 20
Freud, Sigmund: concept of mind, 3–4, 110–11; on the uncanny, 23, 159$n41$; goal of analysis, 31; primary process, 42, 50, 69, 97, 110, 161$n31$; God as oceanic feeling, 84; on jokes, 96; totem sons, 102; antithetical words, 110; unconscious, 116; castrated mother, 123

Gance, Abel, 113
Genesis. *See* Bible

Genette, Gérard, 16
Gifford, Don, 88, 94
Gilbert, Stuart, 104
Gilson, Etienne, 60
Ginsburg, Christian David, 112, 114, 115, 116, 167–68$n19$
Gnostics, 24–25, 60, 110, 161$n27$
God: mind containing minds, 7–8, 74; divided image, 11, 12, 36, 135; love, 12, 81; of deism, 12; active in life, 13, 22–23, 100; source of realism, 17; point of view, 25, 31, 77; artistic, 38–39, 41, 107; faulty, 71–72, 80–82; as parent, 72; Borges's version, 81; indifferent, 83; oceanic flux, 84, 86, 87, 95, 102, 137–38; terror, 91, 96; Alpha and Omega, 95, 97; scientific view, 100; foetus, 164$n1$
Goethe, Johann Wolfgang von, 14, 16, 80, 157$n18$
Goldberg, S. L., 76
Goldman, Arnold, 19
Gordon, John, 20, 36, 53, 97
Gorman, Herbert, 31
Gose, Elliott B., 20, 46, 59, 70, 78, 160$n16$

Haines, 79
Hamlet. *See* Shakespeare
Hardy, Thomas, 48
Hart, Clive, 104, 117, 121, 156$n3$
Hauptmann, Gerhart, 39
Hayman, David, 17–18, 84–85, 95, 166–67$n9$
HCE: as fallible god, 82; sum of Shem and Shaun, 97, 100; generates others, 108, 129; as substratum, 116–17; trapped in matter, 119; as Dodgson, 128
Heidegger, Martin, 26
Henke, Suzette, 69–70
Herbert, George, 101
Hermetic science, 110, 114
Herr, Cheryl T., 94
Herring, Phillip F., 91
Hesse, Hermann, 138
Highet, Gilbert, 109
Husserl, Edmund, 111

174 Index

Ibsen, Henrik, 39, 134
Identity, 53-55, 61
Intentional fallacy, 15-16
Isabel (Issy), 89, 108, 109, 114, 125-26, 128
Iser, Wolfgang, 75, 76

James, Henry, 140
Jaynes, Julian: mind made of metaphors, 4; bicameral theory, 7-8, 113, 131; voices of gods, 29; mind spatialized, 133; schizophrenics as prophets, 139
Jesus. *See* Christ
John, Gospel of. *See* Bible
John of Damascus, 102
Jolas, Eugene, 99, 106
Joyce, James: expanding concept of mind, 4-7, 9, 13, 44; as a god, 8-15, 19, 23, 25-26, 30, 32, 42-43, 78, 83; self-division, 9, 10, 11, 15, 22, 36, 82; manifestation in text, 15, 45, 64-65, 66, 69, 79, 89-90; presiding intelligence, 17, 20; fusion with characters, 19, 65, 77-78, 92, 94; pride and irony linked, 20-21; as inscape, 25-26, 40; skepticism, 25, 29; inward movement of canon, 26; belief in self expression, 28, 30, 74, 119; joy in work, 31-32; faith in change, 35; original sin, 36-37; vitality vs. understanding, 39; concept of identity, 49, 61, 82; against objectivity, 55; self as world, 55, 119; expressed by discordance, 58, 66, 100; unification of canon, 62-63; latitude of interpretation, 66, 67, 99; union of Stephen and Bloom in Joyce, 73, 74, 76, 90-98, 122; person made of people, 74, 100; feelings as personalities, 74, 123-24; as anti-matter, 96-97, 98; encompasses his universe, 97, 101; images of procession, 102; desire as hidden identity, 125. *See also* individual characters and works
Joyce, Lucia, 124, 137, 160*n13*
Joyce, Nora, 10, 33-35
Joyce, Stanislaus, 7

Jung, Carl Gustav: concept of God, 57; on synchronicities, 68, 92, 145, 163*n16*; personalities of feelings, 124; on Joyce, 137; on the Gospel of John, 161*n27*

Kabbalah: Tree of Life, 104, 108, 112-13, 118, 120, 126-27; *Zohar,* 104, 114, 117, 120; Adam Kadmon, 105; connection with other systems, 108, 111; Ain-Soph, 112, 114-16; *sephiroth,* 112, 115-17, 127; emanation, 112, 113, 116-17, 127; place of manifestation, 115, 117; makroprosopos, 119; Joyce's personal version, 130. *See also* Tree of Life
Kaempffer, Dr. Gertrude, 36
Kate, 129
Kawin, Bruce F., 18
Kenner, Hugh, 13, 18, 58, 65
Kermode, Frank, 17, 22, 67
Kohut, Heinz, 114

Lacan, Jacques (*Écrits*): mind as language, 4, 169*n51*; on Joyce, 9; translates Freud, 31; on Other, 34, 169*n51*; truth in unconscious, 35; subjectivity, 58; fatherhood as name, 73; on signification, 75, 162*n23*; on symbols, 90; sexuality through threat, 114
Lawrence, Karen, 18, 63, 89
Lem, Stanislaw, xii
Lévi-Strauss, Claude, 68, 99
Lidwell, George, 88
Linati schema, 65, 73, 84, 91
Lonergan, Bernard, 70, 163*n20*
Longinus, *On the Sublime,* 16
Love: as division, 11; as sacrifice, 12; as self-development, 34-35; as "word known to all men," 93-94; desire, 120
Lubbock, Percy, 12

MacCabe, Colin, 22, 53, 75
MacDowell, Gerty, 93, 95, 125
McHugh, Roland, 98, 112, 115, 121
McIntyre, J. Lewis, *Giordano Bruno,* 46-47, 60, 131
Maher, Michael, 6, 21

Mallarmé, Stéphane, 6, 131
Man in the macintosh, The, 91
The Marriage of Heaven and Hell. See Blake
Mathers, S. L. MacGregor, 169*n51*
Mercanton, Jacques, 32, 59, 61
Milton, John, 82
Mind: Aristotle's definition, 3, 21; double-aspect theory, 3, 5, 19, 21, 42, 46-47, 55, 117; Freud's concept of, 3-4, 42, 50, 69, 110-11, 116; Jung's concept of, 3-4, 69, 124; God's, 4, 7-8, 11, 36, 74; Jaynes's concept of, 4, 7-8, 113, 131, 133; made of metaphors, 4, 8, 41, 133; multipersonal, 4-6, 26, 27, 82, 103-35; Lacan's theory of, 4, 34, 58, 169*n51*; Joyce's expanded, 4-7, 9, 13, 44; mechanical, 22, 111, 133; self-antagonistic, 132. *See also* Double-aspect theory; Kabbalah; Multiple mind; and individuals named above
Morse, J. Mitchell, 29, 38-39
Mozart, Wolfgang A., 78
Mulligan, Buck, 79, 88
Multiple mind: Joyce's concept of, 4-6; inclusive, 26, 82; conclusion of Joyce's work, 27; as *Wake* family, 103-30; demonstrated by Prince, 123-25; Jung on, 124; as internal theater, 131-35

Nabokov, Vladimir, 91
Narrative methods: separation of author from work, 16-17; narrated monologue, 19; interruption as manifestation, 44-45; polyphonic narrative, 54; transformations of narrator, 70; divine perspectives, 77; signature and synchronicity, 84-85
Neptune, 88
Nietzsche, Friedrich, 20, 42, 57
Noon, William T., S. J., 48
Norris, Margot, 13, 49, 53

O'Connell, Robert J., S. J., 161*n25*
O'Neill, Eugene, 134
Origen, 103
Ovid, 14-15

Patrick, St., 121
Paul, St. *See* Bible
Plato: causality, 47, 48; demiurge, 60; *Timaeus,* 60, 108, 121
Poe, Edgar Allan, 128
Polyphony, 24, 40, 52-53, 108-10, 135
"A Portrait of the Artist" (1904), 14, 61, 140
A Portrait of the Artist as a Young Man: esthetic theory, 10, 11, 39; self-immersion, 12; prefigures *Finnegans Wake,* 14, 87; circular form, 25; on inconceivability of eternity, 60; prefigures *Ulysses,* 86-87, 88; contact with sea, 86-87; on terror, 90-91; desire as anxiety in, 115. *See also* Dedalus
Poststructuralists, 24, 44-45
Power, Arthur, 30
Primal Matter: double-aspect, 21; in Augustine, 39-40; in *Ulysses,* 40, 42; and Freud's primary process, 42, 50, 69; as will, 42, 61; as conclusion, 66; shared by author and character, 78; as sea, 88; at the end of "Nausicaa," 97; in *Siddhartha,* 138
Prince, Morton, 123-24, 126
Procession, 22, 23, 27, 102, 127
Pynchon, Thomas, 38, 41, 135
Pythagoras, 111

Rabelais, 16
Reader's role, 14, 68, 87, 99, 106-7
Reality: naturalistic and mythic, 16-17, 132; as mental interaction, 26; Scholastic, 17, 45, 65, 77; as difference, 83; subsidence of God, 99
Riquelme, John Paul: on Stephen as author, 16; narrated monologue, 19; comic divinity, 21; oscillation, 24; identification of teller, character, and reader, 63; alpha and omega, 95; navel, 118; chiasmus, 121; myth of impersonality, 135
Robinson, Henry Morton, 105-6, 112, 114
Rowan, Richard, 36, 139. *See Exiles*

Schema 95. *See* Linati
Scholasticism: reality, 17, 45, 65, 77;

176 Index

Scholasticism (*continued*)
  larger mind, 23, 77; complexity, 48–49; causal view, 69; language of totality, 137–38. *See* Aquinas; Aristotle; Augustine
Scholem, Gershom, 114
Scott, Sir Walter, 48
Seidman, Robert J., 88, 94
Shakespeare, William: *Hamlet* as theater of the mind, 6; art as sacrifice, 12; Vice in *Twelfth Night,* 24; magnitude of creation, 41; animated Aristotle's causality, 49; Borges's version, 81; in the heart of *Hamlet,* 87; Hamlet on infidelity, 90; *Othello,* 134
Shaun, 15, 51–52, 121, 126, 129. *See* Shem and Shaun
Shechner, Mark, 33
Shem, 15, 24–25, 51–52, 126
Shem and Shaun: difficulty of distinguishing, 51–52; union of, 97; impossibility of revolt, 100; right and left columns, 108, 110, 112; psychic forces, 110; interchange of, 120–23
Signatures, 84–86, 91, 101
Signifier and signified, 75
Simon Magus, 159*n43*
Singer, Isaac Bashevis, 96
Skepticism. *See* Uncertainty
Solaris, xii
Solomon, Margaret, 122, 128
Spinoza, Baruch, 3, 19, 21, 46–47
Stephen Hero, 13, 16, 62, 86
Sterne, Laurence, 16
Swinburne, Algernon Charles, 88
Swift, Jonathan, 16, 113
Synchronicities: defined, 68; in Stephen and Bloom, 73, 91–95; distinguished from signatures, 85–86; listed, 145–53; sources on, 163*n16*

Tarkovsky, Andrei, xii
Tennyson, Alfred, Lord, 45
Thomas, Brooke, 19, 91, 99
Thoth, 110
Timaeus. See Plato
Tree of Life (Kabbalah): defined, 104; both universe and mind, 108; divided into columns, 112; *sephiroth,* 115–17; columns reversed, 120; diagrammed, 126; range of functions, 126–27; different views of, 129. *See* Kabbalah
Trinity, 11, 32, 37, 103
Tristan, 121

Ulysses: development of multiple personality, 5; double-aspect in, 5, 77; breakdown of boundaries, 6, 91–95, 97; theater of the mind, 6; self-division in, 12; "Ithaca's" skeptical style, 13; presiding intelligence, 17; "Circe" as fantasy of its creator, 19; "Oxen of the Sun" beyond human intelligence, 20; peripatetic, 25; dual perspective, 52; polyphony in "Sirens," 52–53, 88, 90; "Scylla and Charybdis" defines artist, 69–73, 87, 89, 90; "Ithaca" as eucharist of Joyce, 74; birth in "Oxen of the Sun," 75–77, 89, 90, 95; divine perspectives, 77, 89–90; "Wandering Rocks," 77, 78–79, 90; theme of imposition, 77–80; hell in, 79; Wonderworker as god, 80; "Circe and Ithaca" as revelation, 80; "Telemachus" parallel to *Portrait,* 86–87; "Aeolus," 89; "Lestrygonians," 89–90; "Cyclops," 90; "Circe's" subconscious voices, 90, 132; "Eumaeus," 90; "Penelope," 90; dread in "Proteus," 90; diaphane, 91, 93; the unknown in "Hades," 91; "Hades" links to "Proteus," 91–92; "Nausicaa" links to "Proteus," 93–95; "word known to all men," 93–94; fear in "Ithaca," 96; black hole, 97; lapse into unconscious, 97; cosmos of "Ithaca" contained in Joyce, 101; "Nausicaa" as projection, 125. *See also* individual characters
Ulysses manuscript, 93, 158*n30*
Ulysses notesheets, 92, 95, 125
Uncertainty: creative power of, 25, 38, 40; as conclusion, 66, 135; lifegiving, 67; modern approach to spirituality, 74–75; human state, 102; as feminine attraction, 116; truth Shaun resists, 122–23
Unity, 47, 53–54, 61–62

Index

Vice (clown), 24
Vico, Giambattista, 105
Virag, Lipoti, 125

Waelder, Robert, 110-11
Waite, A. E., 108, 112, 115
"Water Parted from the Sea" (song), 102
"What are the Wild Waves Saying?" (song), 88-89, 154-55
White, David A., 50, 111, 137-38
Wilde, Oscar, 6-7
Wimsatt, W. K., 16

Winnicott, D. W., 67, 72, 118, 138
Wittgenstein, Ludwig, 13
Woolf, Virginia, 141
Writing, scene of, 23, 115, 117-18

Xenophones of Colophon, 101

Yeats, William Butler: personality, 16; *A Vision,* 108, 121-22, 123, 127; "Purgatory," 134

Zohar. *See* Kabbalah

COMPOSED BY METRICOMP, GRUNDY CENTER, IOWA
MANUFACTURED BY CUSHING MALLOY, INC., ANN ARBOR, MICHIGAN
TEXT AND DISPLAY LINES ARE SET IN BASKERVILLE

Library of Congress Cataloging in Publication Data
Brivic, Sheldon, 1943–
Joyce the creator.
Includes index.
1. Joyce, James, 1882–1941 — Technique. 2. Joyce,
James, 1882–1941 — Religion and ethics. 3. Creation
(Literary, artistic, etc.) 4. Creation in literature.
5. God in literature. I. Title.
PR6019.O9Z526317 1985   823'.912   84-40492
ISBN 0-299-10080-4

LIBRARY OF DAVIDSON COLLEGE